Modal and Tonal
Counterpoint

Modal and Tonal
Counterpoint

From Josquin to Stravinsky

HAROLD OWEN

School of Music, University of Oregon

SCHIRMER BOOKS
An Imprint of Simon & Schuster Macmillan
NEW YORK

Prentice Hall International
LONDON • MEXICO CITY • NEW DELHI • SINGAPORE • SYDNEY • TORONTO

Schirmer Books
An Imprint of Simon & Schuster Macmillan
1633 Broadway
New York, N.Y. 10019-6785

Library of Congress Cataloging-in-Publication Data

Owen, Harold.
    Modal and tonal counterpoint: from Josquin to Stravinsky/Harold
Owen.
      p.   cm.
    Discography: p.
    Includes bibliographical references and index.
    ISBN 0-02-872145-4
    1. Counterpoint.   2. Counterpoint–History.   I. Title.
MT55.O97 1992
781.2'86'09–dc20
                                        91-4775
                                          CIP
                                         MN

The paper used in this publication meets the minimum requirements
of American National Standard for Information Sciences—Perma-
nence of Paper for Printed Library Materials. ANSI Z39.48-1984 ⊗™

Printed in the United States of America

printing number
    4 5 6 7 8 9 10

Contents

PART THREE

Counterpoint in the Early Baroque (1600–1700)

PART FOUR

Counterpoint in the Late Baroque (1700–1750)

Preface

Counterpoint was born in the Middle Ages and is still very much alive today. Every era has produced masterpieces of polyphony, and yet the study of counterpoint for most students has been limited traditionally to two courses: one devoted to the style of Palestrina, and the other to the style of Bach. While this approach allows for some depth, it denies the student a comprehensive study of the development of counterpoint throughout history. The great polyphonic masterworks of the seventeenth century by Monteverdi, Schütz, and Purcell are usually ignored in modal and tonal counterpoint classes, as are the nineteenth–century contrapuntal masterpieces by Beethoven, Mendelssohn, and Brahms. The study of twentieth–century counterpoint is usually available only to graduate students. This book attempts to present the development of contrapuntal technique from the sixteenth century through the first half of the twentieth century in a historical and stylistic framework. Although it is best suited to a year-long course, it can also function for separate courses devoted to sixteenth- and eighteenth–century styles. Students beginning their study with eighteenth–century style can jump to Chapter 15 after reading Chapters 1 and 2, which are devoted to introductory concepts. Chapter 15 is designed as a review for continuing students and a starting point for new students.

Another unique feature of this book is its "discovery" approach. Complete musical examples are presented at the beginning of each chapter together with questions for discussion. A lively discussion will lead the students to the "discovery" of the concepts. The observations which follow clarify and amplify these concepts. I have found that students gain a better grasp of principles, and consequently have a better attitude toward the study of counterpoint using this approach than they do when presented with the traditional sets of rules, often out of musical context.

Finally, the book serves as anthology, text, and workbook combined. Complete musical examples are presented in all but a few instances. The text, in the form of observations, is brief, allowing for amplification by the instructor. The exercises are varied in length and difficulty. Those marked with an asterisk are advanced problems suitable for students in composition and graduates in other major musical fields.

A quasi-species approach has been used in the early chapters to lay a solid foundation in the use of consonance and dissonance, but the species have been "expanded" rhythmically to allow for more musical results. At the end of each chapter is a list of scores and sources for further study intended for those students who are interested in exploring the subject matter in more depth. Students unfamiliar with the modes or interpretation of figured bass symbols will find the appendices helpful.

A survey of contrapuntal practice spanning 450 years cannot treat all polyphonic music in the same depth. Renaissance and Baroque styles, especially the music of J. S. Bach, have been given greater attention, and the section dealing with twentieth–century counterpoint is limited both by space and classroom time. The instructor is encouraged to introduce additional examples whenever possible, and to use a portion of each class period for listening to and performing the examples.

Before undertaking this study, students should have completed core studies in theory (harmony and musicianship). They should have a working knowledge of the principles of four-part voice leading, triad and seventh chord inversions, spacing and doubling, and identification by Roman numerals.

To the students: There is no better way to learn the art and craft of counterpoint than by hearing, performing, and analyzing great polyphonic music, and then trying to write music in the same style. This is the method used by the greatest composers throughout history, and it is the approach used in this text. Whenever possible, perform the examples yourself or with other students. Many of the examples used in this book are available on recordings. Let the music speak to you before you try to analyze it. The discussion questions should help you discover the principles of counterpoint. You may be tempted simply to find all the answers in the observations without trying to arrive at them yourself, but you will not have the same grasp of the subject and feeling of accomplishment which comes from personal discovery and class discussion.

The aim of the exercises is to create good music, not just correct solutions. Sing and play through your work as you write and after you have finished writing. As you listen to your music, ask yourself, "Would Lasso (Purcell, Bach, Bartók) do this?" "Is the alto part as good a melody as the soprano?" If you are confused on some technical point, don't look in a textbook. Go to the music itself—the answers are all there.

Harold Owen
Eugene, Oregon, 1991

PART ONE

Introductory Concepts

The Nature of Polyphonic Music

Terms and General Concepts

Polyphonic music has been with us since the Middle Ages, and is an important part of the music of our own century, yet the term polyphony is not easy to define. A literal translation of "polyphony" is "many sounds," but a good definition must reach far beyond this simple description. Musicians will agree that polyphony is a kind of musical texture, but that is only the beginning.

Consider the short setting of "Amen"* shown in Ex. 1-1. If possible, sing or play it in class.

EX. 1-1

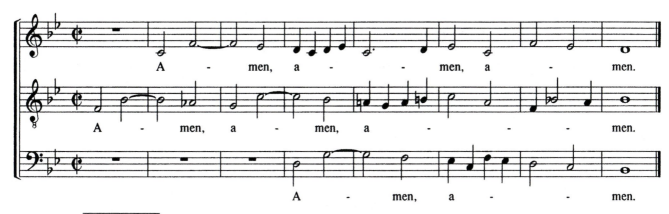

*Examples throughout this book that are not identified by title and composer have been composed by the author.

This is obviously an example of polyphony, but why? Before we can attempt to study counterpoint, we need to consider some basic terms and the concepts they represent. The following questions may be used as the basis for a class discussion, after which you should try to formulate your own workable definitions for each of the terms.

Questions for Discussion

1. What is polyphony? How many parts does it involve? Can there be as many as forty? As few as two, or even one? What do the parts share and how do they maintain independence?
2. What is counterpoint? Is it a texture? Is it a technique? Is it the name of a formal study? Is it part of the music being considered? What does it have to do with polyphony?
3. What is homophony? How does it differ from polyphony? How would you compare the texture of a Bach chorale such as "Jesu, meine Freude" with that of a hymn like "Amazing Grace"?
4. What is simultaneity? Is it polyphonic? Is it contrapuntal?
5. What creates unity in a piece of contrapuntal music?
6. What creates diversity in a piece of contrapuntal music?
7. What is imitation? What is a canon? What is a round?
8. "A round is a special type of canon; a canon is a special type of imitation; imitation is a special type of counterpoint." Is this a true statement? What are its implications?

Observations

Polyphony and Counterpoint

Your definition of the word *polyphony* should include several ingredients: (a) music in which there are at least two distinguishable parts of roughly equal importance; (b) the parts maintain a melodic identity; (c) they maintain independence of motion both of pitch and rhythm; (d) they share the same metric and harmonic context; (e) they often share motivic ideas; and (f) they complement one another, creating a unified whole.

The word *counterpoint* comes from the Latin phrase "punctum contra punctum" meaning "note against note." Musicians use the word in several ways. It is the name of a formal study—the technique of polyphonic composition. "The counterpoint" can also refer to a strand of the musical texture in a piece. Counterpoint can be synonymous with polyphony, since contrapuntal music is polyphonic, and vice versa.

Homophony and Simultaneity

Although a hymn like "Amazing Grace" usually appears in a setting with four parts, there is little melodic identity in the alto, tenor, and bass parts, and there is little, if any, independence of rhythmic motion. The tune in the soprano part is of chief importance. This is a clear example of *homophony*.

Imagine this scenario: You are standing in the hall outside two practice rooms with their doors open. In one, a soprano is practicing scales. In the other, a saxophonist is playing jazz. What you are hearing would be an example of *simultaneity*. It could be considered as a special type of "textural polyphony," but would not be thought of as counterpoint. Composers in our own century such as Charles Ives have used this kind of texture effectively.

Imitation; Canon; Round

When the parts in a piece of polyphonic music share melodic ideas, they are said to be in *imitation*. If the imitation is exact and continues through the whole piece, the piece is called a *canon*. A portion of a piece is described as *canonic* if the imitation persists throughout the section. In describing points of imitation there are two crucial measurements to consider: (a) the distance between leader and follower in *time;* and (b) the *interval* distance between the first note of the leader and that of the follower. Sixteenth–century canons often use interval distances of a perfect fourth or fifth as well as octave and unison. A *puzzle canon* is one where the composer gives only the *dux,* or leading voice, and it is up to the performer to discover the correct time and interval distance for the *comes,* or following voice (or voices when the canon is for three or more parts). Several puzzle canons have been included in the exercises.

A *round* is a familiar type of canon where the time distance is the length of a complete phrase and the interval distance is a unison (or an octave when men and women sing together). Rounds are cyclic: as each voice reaches the end, it begins again. A round is normally sung as many times through as there are voice parts.

Examples

Apply your definitions to each of the excerpts in Ex. 1-2. Which of them are unquestionably polyphonic? Which are unquestionably homophonic? Which display a hybrid texture? Do any qualify as canons? Which are imitative? (Note: these examples are identified in Appendix A.)

EX. 1-2a

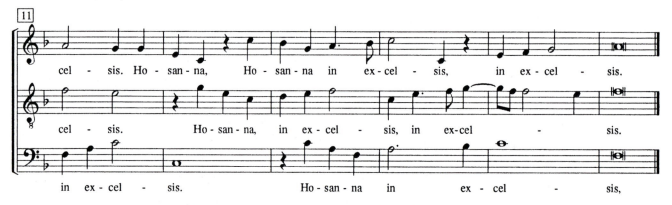

Blessed is he who comes in the name of the Lord. Hosanna in the highest.

EX. 1-2b

EX. 1-2c For copyright information see Appendix A, p. 353.

EX. 1-2d

Gloria unto thee be sung with tongues of men and angels, with harps and cymbals.

Through the twelve pearls of the gates of thy city we come with the archangel unto thy throne.

EX. 1-2e

EX. 1-2f For copyright information see Appendix A, p. 353.

EX. 1-2g

O how soft the spring winds through the meadow! O how beautiful when love finds love!

Exercises

EXERCISE 1-1. Compare your definitions for polyphony, homophony, simultaneity, counter-point, imitation, canon, and round with those given in standard music dictionaries (see "Readings" at the end of the chapter) and the Glossary.

EXERCISE 1-2. List several compositions which you would consider to be: (a) purely polyphonic; (b) purely homophonic; (c) hybrid in texture.

EXERCISE 1-3. Find an example of polyphony in three or four parts which displays virtually no imitation.

*EXERCISE 1-4. Find an example of (a) a four-part canon where each part begins on a different pitch; and (b) a double canon (where two different parts are "answered" in canon by the other two parts).

*EXERCISE 1-5. Find a piece of polyphonic music scored for a solo stringed instrument.

*EXERCISE 1-6. Classify Ex. 1-2 a through g as to: (a) style period; and (b) approximate date of composition. Identify as many as you can by title and composer.

Sources for Further Study

NOTE: The sources listed at the end of each chapter include only the last name of the author and occasionally the title. Consult the Bibliography for complete details.

Scores:

Anthologies such as the following contain music of a variety of textures, genres, and historical periods.

Berry and Chudacoff: *Eighteenth-Century Imitative Counterpoint: Music for Analysis*

Brandt: *The Comprehensive Study of Music;* four volumes

Burkhart: *Anthology for Musical Analysis*

Hardy and Fish: *Music Literature;* two volumes

Harvard Anthology of Music; two volumes

Palisca: *Norton Anthology of Western Music;* two volumes

Turek: *Analytical Anthology of Music*

Wennerstrom: *Anthology of Musical Structure and Style*

Wennerstrom: *Anthology of Twentieth-Century Music*

---

*Exercises marked by an asterisk are advanced problems suitable for students in composition and graduates in other major musical fields.

Readings:

Music dictionaries and encyclopedias such as the following should be consulted for their definitions of the terms polyphony, counterpoint, homophony, simultaneity, imitation, canon, and round:

The New College Encyclopedia of Music
The New Grove Concise Encyclopedia of Music
The New Grove Dictionary of Music and Musicians
The New Harvard Dictionary of Music

CHAPTER

2

Polyphony and Style

A Comparison of Examples From the Fourteenth to the Twentieth Centuries

In spite of the evolution of style through the ages, contrapuntal technique has changed very little since the fourteenth century. In this chapter we will examine some technical differences that exist among contrapuntal pieces from the fourteenth century to the twentieth century.

Examine these five examples of two-part counterpoint (Ex. 2-1a-e), then discuss them in class using the questions below as a guide.

EX. 2-1a Ballata: "Angelica biltà" by Francesco Landini (1325–1397)

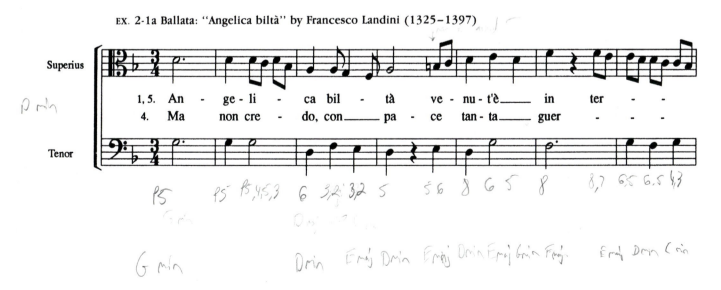

Angelic beauty has come down to earth. Hence let him who loves beauty, virtue, pleasant deeds, and elegance come to see her who is pure grace. He will receive these gifts from her, as do I in my soul, but I doubt that he will have, in peace, such war.

EX. 2-1b Benedictus from *Missa ad imitationem moduli l ager* by Orlando di Lasso (1532–1594)

Blessed is he who comes in the name of the Lord.

EX. 2-1c Invention No. 4 in D Minor, by J. S. Bach (1685–1750)

EX. 2-1d Opening of the Fugue from *Prelude, Chorale, and Fugue* by César Franck (1822–1890)

EX. 2-1e *Chromatic Invention* from *Mikrokosmos,* Book III, by Béla Bartók (1881–1945).
Copyright © 1940 by Hawkes & Son (London) Ltd.; Copyright Renewed. Reprinted by
permission of Boosey & Hawkes, Inc.

Questions for Discussion

1. Are all of the examples polyphonic? Do they all fit the definition of polyphony you developed in the last chapter? What qualities do all of the examples have in common (besides being in two parts)?

2. How would you describe the melodies? How much of the melodic motion in each example is stepwise (conjunct) compared to leapwise (disjunct)? Is the melody diatonic or chromatic, modal, tonal, or vague in tonal focus? How do the examples compare in melodic range and tessitura?

3. How do they compare as to rhythm and pulse? Does the rhythm impart a strong sense of regular pulse or meter? What is the range of different time values? Is the rhythmic motion between parts mostly in the ratio of 1:1, 2:1, more than 2:1?

4. How do the parts move with respect to one another? They sometimes move in parallel, sometimes in the same direction, sometimes in opposite directions, and sometimes one part moves when the other is stationary. How would you rank the frequency of each kind of motion: parallel, similar, contrary, and oblique?

5. What are the favored intervals in each example? How often are perfect unisons, perfect fifths, perfect octaves, major and minor thirds, and major and minor sixths formed between the parts? These are traditionally considered consonances or concords. How often do you encounter seconds, sevenths, perfect fourths, tritones, and any other augmented or diminished intervals? These are considered dissonances or discords. Which intervals appear most frequently? Estimate the ratio of consonances to dissonances for each example.

6. What intervals appear when two notes begin at the same time? When two notes are sounded together, the interval has a stronger impact than an interval resulting from one part moving while the other is stationary. How do the examples compare in terms of these "strong intervals"?

7. How do the examples differ from one another? The responses to Questions 1 through 6 should provide clues to answer this important question.

Observations

Texture; Melodic Characteristics; Tonality

A good definition of the words "polyphony," "polyphonic," and "contrapuntal" should apply successfully to all of the examples. They all have the proper ingredients: melodic parts maintain independence of motion with respect to one another both in pitch and rhythm; they share the same tonal and metrical context; and they complement each other.

The examples exhibit more diversity in their melodic characteristics than in their rhythmic aspects. Conjunct motion prevails, but consecutive half steps and leaps of a tritone only appear in the last two. The earlier examples are diatonic, while the later ones are more chromatic. Despite the *musica ficta* (tones traditionally altered in performance, but not indicated by the composer), the Landini and Lasso examples exhibit modal tendencies. The Bach example is strongly tonal. Tonality in the Franck example is strong only at cadence points; the pervasive chromaticism tends to obscure the tonality between cadences. The Bartók example has no single distinguishable tonal center at all.

Rhythm and Metric Pulse; Types of Motion

All of the examples seem to distribute the rhythmic motion between the parts, and none has a wide range of time values. A strong feeling of metric pulse occurs only in Ex. 2-1c and 2-1d. The unequal phrase lengths and overlapping tend to "obscure" the barlines in Ex. 2-1e. Examples 2-1 c-e exhibit rhythmic motion in the ratio of 2:1 and 1:1 more consistently than do the other examples, which display a wider variety of ratios.

Oblique motion far exceeds contrary, similar, and parallel motion in all of the examples. This is true of all polyphony since the twelfth century.

⋈ Intervals; Consonance and Dissonance

Consonance and dissonance have been of chief concern to composers and theorists since the beginning of polyphonic music. Both are essential in all kinds of music. It is unfortunate that early theorists have described consonances in terms of "purity," "pleasantness," "perfection," and other positive attributes while characterizing dissonance as "impure," "discordant," and "unpleasant." It is perhaps more useful for us to consider intervals on a continuum from the unison, representing the highest degree of consonance, to the minor second and tritone, representing the highest degrees of dissonance. The "perfect consonances" could be described as "passive," "stable," or "lacking in tension" while the stronger dissonances are "active," "less stable," and "higher in tension." To some ears the minor seventh and the perfect fourth seem consonant, whereas to other ears these intervals seem dissonant. For our purposes, however, it is necessary to classify intervals in the traditional way: consonances are perfect unison, perfect octave, perfect fifth, major third, minor third, major sixth, minor sixth, and their compound equivalents (perfect twelfth, major tenth, minor tenth, major thirteenth, minor thirteenth, etc.); dissonances are major seventh, minor seventh, major second, minor second, tritone, all augmented or diminished intervals, and their compound equivalents; the perfect fourth is usually considered a dissonance in two-part music.

You will have found that thirds and sixths are the favored intervals in all the examples but the last. Octaves, fifths, and unisons are also high on the list for the first three examples. The ratio of consonance to dissonance in the Landini and Lasso examples is quite large. The ratio is smaller for the Bach and Franck examples, and is reversed in the Bartók.

When two notes begin together in Ex. 2-1b, consonant intervals are used consistently. This is true in Ex. 2-1a but to a slightly lesser degree, and the perfect fifth is used more frequently. In Ex. 2-1c, consonances appear when two notes begin together much of the time, but on several occasions the faster moving part creates a dissonance with an accented passing tone. In the Franck example, many of the "strong intervals" are dissonances caused by appoggiaturas, accented passing tones, and implied diminished seventh harmonies. In the Bartók example, the melodic movement is so strong that the intervals between the parts may be any interval at all (with the possible exception of the unison and octave).

Distinguishing Characteristics

The five examples seem to differ most in their treatment of consonance and dissonance and in the role of tonality and harmony. In the fourteenth, fifteenth, and sixteenth centuries consonances outnumber dissonances by a ratio of about 3:1, and the harmony is a result of the voice leading. In the Baroque era the harmony began to dictate the voice leading, which could now partake of more dissonance. By the end of the Romantic era, chromatic harmony had begun to obscure tonality, and the counterpoint became increasingly free in the use of stronger dissonances. By the 1920s dissonance had become "emancipated" in the hands of Bartók, Stravinsky, and Schoenberg and their contemporaries. Voice leading was no longer bound by the strictures of tonal harmony.

Exercises

EXERCISE 2-1. Find an example of a sixteenth century two-part motet and analyze it in order to determine the approximate ratio of consonance to dissonance. Do the same for a two-part contrapuntal piece from the eighteenth century. Briefly discuss your findings.

EXERCISE 2-2. Explain how Ex. 1-2g is constructed. What kind of piece is it?

EXERCISE 2-3. Make a diagram of the Chromatic Invention by Bartók (Ex. 2-1e) showing how imitation is used.

EXERCISE 2-4. Table 2-1 is intended to be a rough generalization. Fill in missing information. (You may wish to expand and refine it as you move through the later chapters.)

TABLE 2-1

CONSONANCE VS. DISSONANCE IN POLYPHONIC MUSIC

Era	Major composers	c:d ratio	Dissonance types
Late Middle Ages (c. 1300–1450)	Machaut Landini Ciconia Dunstable Jacapo da Bologna		
Renaissance (c. 1450–1600)	Josquin des Prez Lasso Palestrina Byrd Victoria	about 4:1	passing tone neighbor tone suspension nota cambiata double neighbor
Baroque (c. 1600–1750)	Monteverdi Schütz Purcell Vivaldi Bach Handel		
Classical			
Romantic			
Twentieth Century			

Sources for Further Study

Scores:

> Hardy and Fish: *Music Literature: A Workbook for Analysis,* Vol. II: *Polyphony*

Readings:

> Crocker: The book traces the development of musical style from Gregorian Chant to the middle of the twentieth century. Information on the fifteenth century is contained in Chapters 5 and 6; sixteenth century in Chapters 6 and 7; seventeenth century in Chapters 8 and 9; eighteenth century in Chapters 10, 11, and 12; nineteenth century in Chapters 13, 14, and 15; and twentieth century in Chapter 16.

PART TWO

Counterpoint in the Late Renaissance (1500–1600)

CHAPTER

3

Two-Part Counterpoint

Basic Principles of Sixteenth–Century Style

S Study the short motet by Lasso shown in Ex. 3-1. It is an excellent example of sixteenth–century contrapuntal style.

EX. 3-1 "Oculus non vidit" from *Cantiones duarum vocum* by Orlando di Lasso (1532–1594)

Eye hath not seen, nor ear heard, neither have entered into the heart of man,
The things which God hath prepared for them that love Him.

Questions for Discussion

Melodic Considerations

1. What is the proportion of conjunct to disjunct motion?
2. What observations can you make about the location of the longest notes? Of the shortest notes?

[handwritten margin notes: unison cadence, 7→1, 2→1; 3, 4, 5; beginning or end of points, bar, points, 3rds; mostly step, range is about 6th, leading tones, repeated rhythms, steps]

3. How can you tell when a part has reached a cadence?

4. What intervals are used for leaps? Which of these appear most frequently? Which are used only occasionally? What intervals are not used at all in melodic motion?

5. Where in the melodic line do you find leaps? What usually happens before and after large leaps?

6. What observations can you make about consecutive leaps in one direction? Consecutive notes of the same pitch?

7. How would you describe the melodic contour? How would you describe the melodic range, tessitura, shape, and distribution of highest and lowest notes?

8. What observations can you make about the chromatically altered notes (*musica ficta*)?

9. What gives the melody unity and cohesiveness?

10. What gives the melody variety or diversity?

Harmonic Considerations

1. What pitch seems to be the *tonic* (the pitch that seems to act as the principal tonal focus)? At the end? At the beginning? At cadence points elsewhere?

2. Can you associate a scale with this piece? What results when you assemble all the different pitches (except those which are chromatically altered) and arrange them in ascending order beginning with the last note?

3. Where and when do the consonances appear? Composers in the Renaissance considered the consonant intervals to be the perfect prime, perfect fifth, and perfect octave, the major and minor thirds and sixths, and their compound equivalents (perfect twelfth, major and minor tenths, major and minor thirteenths, etc.).

4. Where and when do the dissonances appear? Renaissance composers considered any intervals other than those listed in Question 3 to be dissonant intervals (all seconds, fourths, sevenths, and their compound equivalents; all augmented or diminished intervals).

5. What is the approximate ratio of consonance to dissonance?

6. What types of dissonances are used? In your theory classes you learned to recognize passing tones, neighbor tones (or auxiliary tones), double neighbor tones, escape tones (or échappées), anticipations, appoggiaturas (or leaning tones), suspensions, and perhaps others (see Ex. 15-4). Which of these do you find in the Lasso motet?

7. Which intervals are used in parallel motion?

8. What succession of intervals do you find at cadence points?

Temporal Considerations

1. How is the feeling of meter perceived by the listener? What clues are there in the music to indicate a metrical framework?

2. How is the rhythmic interest divided between the parts? How do the parts maintain their rhythmic independence? How do they complement each other?

3. What is the range of time values? Make a chart of the different time values used from the longest to the shortest. Indicate the number of instances for each. What implications can you draw from the chart?

Observations

Melodic Considerations

Melodic motion in the motet by Lasso is basically stepwise. Conjunct motion exceeds disjunct motion by a ratio of about 3:1. This is quite normal for music of the late sixteenth century. Both parts exhibit roughly the same proportion of steps to leaps.

The longest notes are used at the beginnings and ends of phrases and at important turning points in the melody. Stressed syllables of the text are given longer time values. The shortest notes come in the middle of phrases, especially just before cadences. Cadences generally occur at the end of each text phrase and are marked by the resolution of a leading tone in one part while the other descends to form an octave or unison with the first part. The leading tone in a cadence is nearly always the resolution of a suspension. This is the most common cadential formula in the sixteenth century.

Any good melody has points of tension and points of rest. Leaps, especially those which move upward, can be used to build tension. In general, the larger the leap, the less frequently it is encountered. In our example, the largest leap is that of the ascending minor sixth. Although this example does not have any octave leaps, they are relatively common in sixteenth–century melodic writing. Leaps of ninths, major sixths, sevenths, tritones, and other augmented or diminished intervals are extremely rare. Leaps may occur anywhere in a phrase, but they are usually associated with turning points. When large leaps are used, they are normally approached and left by step in the opposite direction of the leap.

Two or more consecutive leaps in one direction are rare. When they do occur, they outline a consonant harmony, usually a major or minor triad. We perceive leaps harmonically—that is, we "collect in memory" the tones involved in disjunct motion, hearing them as if they were a chord. Two perfect fourths in succession (such as D-G-C) would be perceived by the Renaissance listener as a discord. In Ex. 3-1 a single pitch is occasionally repeated. In sacred music of this period a single pitch may be used as many as three times in succession.

Lasso makes modest demands upon his singers in this motet. The range of the soprano part is only an octave. That of the alto is just a minor tenth. Each phrase moves the tessitura slightly up or down for the sake of variety (and expression of the text). The shapes of the phrases are varied: some falling, some rising, some with many changes in direction. The highest points and lowest points usually occur but once in a phrase.

The melodic style is very consistent. There are no extreme contrasts or sudden strong accents. There is a gentle ebb and flow of movement. Unity is achieved through the use of repetition, sequence, and variation of a few motives. Diversity is achieved through varying lengths of phrases, changes in the interval and temporal distance between leader and follower in points of imitation, the feeling of modulation at some of the internal cadences, and other subtle factors too numerous to mention here.

Harmonic Considerations

Modality

In tonal music, the "tonic" is the irrefutable "center of tonal gravity." In modal music, however, the "finalis" of the mode does not necessarily carry the same "gravitational force." Modal music, nevertheless, exhibits the establishment of "tonal focus," especially at cadence points. We will use the word "tonic" in this sense for our discussion. At the beginning of the piece the tonic seems to be A, but at the end it is definitely D. There are cadences on A, E, and even a slight feeling of C in mm. 16–18. If we arrange the tones (excluding those bearing accidentals) into a scale with D as its tonic, we have a D-Dorian scale. If you are unfamiliar with the ecclesiastical modes, consult Appendix B.

At the beginning of the sixteenth century the modes recognized by theorists included the Dorian, Phrygian, Lydian, and Mixolydian. By the middle of the sixteenth century the Ionian and Aeolian were added. Throughout the Renaissance the modes were subjected to various alterations. In the Lydian mode, B♭ was often used, effectively changing it to Ionian, our present major. When B♭ is used in the Dorian, it is converted to Aeolian.

Musica Ficta

Certain alterations were used during the Renaissance which were not always noted in the music. These are called musica ficta (meaning "false music") and are used:

- a) to create leading tones—C♯-D, F♯-G, G♯-A—in cadences.
- b) to avoid the tritone—F-B♭ and occasionally B♭-E♭.
- c) when the melody moves from A to B and back to A—the B is usually flatted—especially in the Dorian and Lydian modes. This condition is referred to as "una nota supra la": when there is a note above "la" one should use "fa" or B♭, instead of "mi" or B♮.)

In the examples we have indicated these alterations with an accidental above the notes in question. By the end of the sixteenth century composers tended to use alterations for the sake of color as well. Eventually all of these alterations were noted.

Consonance and Dissonance

Consonant intervals appear when two tones begin simultaneously. They appear on the strongest metrical positions except where one part is suspended across the downbeat. Dissonances appear on weak beats or between beats, except in the case of suspensions. The approximate ratio of consonance to dissonance in Ex. 3-1 is 4:1 (13:3 to be more exact).

The types of dissonance used are passing tones, neighbor tones, and suspensions. There is an accented passing tone in m. 29, but it is on the weakest beat of the measure. Intervals used in parallel motion are limited to thirds, sixths, and tenths.

Cadences are most often immediately preceded by a suspension in one of the parts. The parts move by step in contrary motion to a perfect octave or unison at cadences with the resulting succession of intervals of sixth-to-octave or third-to-unison.

Temporal Considerations

When we hear Renaissance choral polyphony, the impression of meter is not very strong. The location of consonance and dissonance, however, is regulated by the metrical framework, and this gives us clues as to the location of the strong and weak beats. Cadences also delineate strong beats. Rhythmic motion is evenly divided between the parts. Most of the time, when one of them rests, the other moves. This continuity of rhythmic motion keeps the pulse "alive." Both parts rest simultaneously only at the end or at major cadences. Both parts may move together on occasion for the sake of variety.

The rhythm is created from a small number of time values with only a few of the very longest and the very shortest in evidence. In Ex. 3-1, half notes and quarter notes account for a major proportion of the rhythm.

Exercises

EXERCISE 3-1. Find another example of a late Renaissance two-part motet and apply the questions at the beginning of this chapter to it.

EXERCISE 3-2. Create some short melodies in an approximation of the style of Ex. 3-1 using D–Dorian, E–Phrygian, and G–Mixolydian modes.

*EXERCISE 3-3. Apply the questions at the beginning of this chapter to a two-part vocal piece by Machaut. How do your answers differ from those for Question 1?

Sources for Further Study

Scores:

Dart, Thurston [Ed.]: Vol. 4, Duos, from *Invitation to Madrigals.* New York, Galaxy Music Corporation, n.d.

Glareanus: "Bicinia" from *Dodecachordon,* 1547

Josquin: Several Mass sections are in two parts, especially the Pleni sunt coeli, Benedictus, and Agnus Dei II from *Missa Pange Lingua,* and *Missa Mater Patris;* the Pleni sunt coeli from *Missa Ad Fugam* and *Missa Hercules dux Ferariae;* and the Agnus Dei II from *Missa De Beata Virgine.*

Lasso: *Cantiones duarum vocum; Cantiones sine textu; Novae aliquot*

Palestrina: Short two-part passages appear in his motets and Masses at the beginnings of imitative points. Some examples may be found in the opening of motets *Tu es pastor ovium, Hic est vere martyr,* and *Exaudi domine;* Mass movements Crucifixus from *Missa ut re mi fa sol la* and *Missa Sanctorum meritio;* and the Kyrie I from *Missa Jesu Nostra Redemptio* and *Missa Spem in Alium.*

Phalèse [Ed.]: *Bicinia, siva cantiones suavissimae duarum vocum,* 1590

Zarlino: *Le institutioni harmoniche,* 1558, includes several two-part examples.

Readings:

Crocker: pp. 182–222
Gauldin—16th c.: pp. 1–75
Jeppesen: pp. 8–30
Merritt: pp. 3–119
Roberts and Fischer: pp. 1–9
Salzer/Schachter: pp. 3–11
Smith: pp. 11–39

Two-Part Counterpoint

First and Second Species Counterpoint

Gradus ad Parnassum, published in 1725 by Johann Fux, introduced a system for the study of counterpoint which has proven to be a very useful pedagogical approach. In his work, Fux defines five *species* of counterpoint as follows: In *first species,* a note-against-note counterpoint is set to a cantus firmus consisting of whole notes. In *second species,* two notes of equal value are set against the given voice, and in *third species,* the counterpoint contains four notes to one in the cantus firmus. *Fourth species* is devoted to the setting of suspensions against a given string of whole notes, and *fifth species* is a judicial mixture of first through fourth species, still set against a cantus firmus of whole notes. We will refer to this as *strict* species counterpoint.

While the strict use of species is a helpful teaching tool, it tends to produce rather rigid, unmusical results. We will also employ an *expanded* species approach, which allows for more rhythmic freedom and can result in music which is closer to our models.

First Species

Example 4-1 shows first species in strict counterpoint. Expanded first species is shown in Ex. 4-2. In the first of these examples you will notice that for every note of the cantus firmus there is a note in the counterpoint. In the second example, rests and note repetitions are allowed, and the two parts may engage in rhythmic imitation. Nevertheless, each pitch in one part encounters but a single pitch in the other part, maintaining a 1:1 ratio of pitch change.

EX. 4-1 **Strict first species counterpoint**

3,6,5,8 (handwritten)

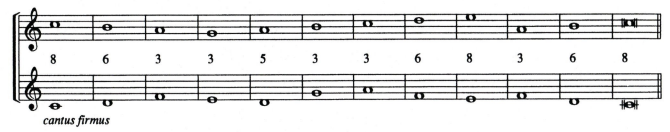

8   6   3   3   5   3   3   6   8   3   6   8

cantus firmus

EX. 4-2 **Expanded first species counterpoint**

8 – 3   – –   8 – – 3 – 6 – 3   6   6   – –   8

Questions for Discussion

1. Examine the intervals formed between the parts in Ex. 4-1 and Ex. 4-2. Examine also the intervals between the parts in Ex. 3-1 when they move note-against-note. How would you describe the nature of the intervals?

   3 (handwritten)

2. Which of these intervals appear most often?

   6, 3 (handwritten)

3. Which intervals are used when there is parallel motion?

   5ths,8ths (they are not produced independently) (handwritten)

4. Which intervals do *not* occur when there is parallel motion? Can you give a logical reason for this?

   Step, Some 3rds, leaps of repetition, lots of repetition (handwritten)

5. In what ways do the melodies in Ex. 4-1 and Ex. 4-2 exhibit the qualities of sixteenth-century melodic writing discussed in Chapter 3?

6. Can you summarize the procedures for writing a good first species counterpoint in sixteenth-century style?

   8,3,5,6 ; when moving in parallel motion don't use 8ths or 5ths, (handwritten)

Observations   *keep mostly step motion* (handwritten)

In all cases when the parts move in the same rhythm—note against note—the only intervals that occur are the consonances. Of these, the major and minor thirds and sixths are by far the most frequently used. When there is parallel motion, the only intervals used are thirds or sixths (and their compound equivalents, tenths and thirteenths).

There are no instances of perfect intervals in parallel motion. One reason for this is the fact that the perfect prime, octave, and fifth are the lowest members of the overtone series. When two parts move in parallel in unisons, fifths, or octaves, they cease to be heard as distinct parts and meld into one another, thereby destroying their independence. Remember that one of the cardinal principles of good counterpoint is maintaining independence of the parts.

Except for the rhythmic constraints imposed by first species, melodic writing adheres to the principles we discussed in the last chapter. Contrary motion is used at the cadences.

Procedures for Writing a First Species Counterpoint to a Cantus Firmus

The discoveries you have made thus far can be summarized by the following guidelines which you can use as you do the exercises:

a) Begin with the interval of a perfect octave, unison, or perfect fifth.

b) Make sure that each new note makes a consonance with the cantus firmus.

c) Use mostly stepwise motion with a few leaps for variety (use only thirds, perfect fourths, perfect fifths, ascending minor sixths, and perfect octaves). Large leaps should be preceded and succeeded by step in the opposite direction of the leap. Use consecutive leaps in one direction sparingly, and when you do, make sure they form a major or minor triad.

d) Use mostly contrary motion against the cantus firmus with some parallel motion in thirds or sixths for variety. Consecutive thirds or sixths sound well, but more than three in a row tends to destroy the independence of the parts. Make sure that you do not allow your counterpoint to move in parallel perfect intervals with the cantus firmus.

e) End with a perfect octave or unison; make sure you reach your last note by step in contrary motion with the cantus firmus. Use a sharp on the seventh degree in the cadence if the finalis is D, G, or A.

Exercises

These exercises are in first species. Write the size of each interval formed between the parts. NOTE: Reduce compound intervals to their simple equivalents (twelfths will be called fifths, tenths will be called thirds, etc).

EXERCISE 4-1 Write strict note-against-note counterpoints to each cantus firmus.

EXERCISE 4-2 Complete this canon at the octave.

EXERCISE 4-3 Complete the upper part in expanded first species.

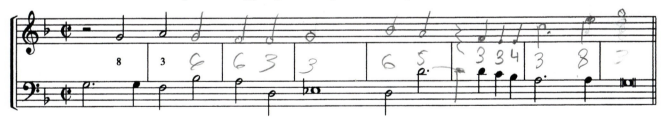

*EXERCISE 4-4 Write an imitative counterpoint to the given melody.

*EXERCISE 4-5 Compose a short example of two-part counterpoint in expanded first species.

Second Species

When there are two notes in one part against one in the other, we have counterpoint in second species. In our discussion it will be convenient to designate the note that begins at the same time as the longer note in the other part as "the first note." We will let "the second note" refer to the note which moves while the other part sustains.

EX. 4-3 Strict second species counterpoint

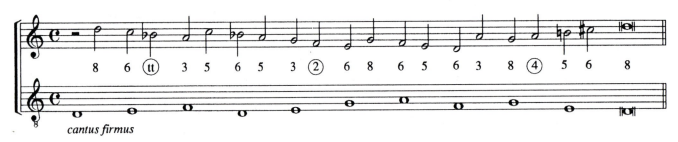

EX. 4-4 Expanded second species counterpoint

Example 4-3 is a short example of strict second species counterpoint. In Ex. 4-4, an example of extended second species, there are still just two pitches in one part against one in the other. The rests enliven the rhythm but do not change the pitch ratio. The motion is distributed between the parts, allowing for some imitation.

Questions for Discussion

Examine Ex. 4-3 and Ex. 4-4, and all the cases where there are two notes against one in Ex. 3-1.

1. What intervals are used with the first note?
2. What intervals are used with the second note?
3. What intervals are used when there is a leap from the first to the second note?
4. What intervals are used when there is a leap from the second note to the note following?
5. Where and how are dissonances used in second species?
6. Discuss the melodies in Ex. 4-3 and Ex. 4-4 in the light of your definition of good sixteenth–century melodic writing.
7. What guidelines would you give for writing a good second species counterpoint?

Observations

As we have previously observed, when two notes begin at the same time, consonant intervals are used. In second species, the first note always makes a consonance, but the second note may make either a consonance or a dissonance. If there is a leap from the first to the second note or from the second note to the one following, the second note must make a consonance with the other part. Consequently, dissonances may occur only when preceded and followed by step. The only kinds of dissonances that fit this description are *passing tones* and *neighbor tones* (upper or lower auxiliaries). You will note that passing tones are encountered far more often than neighbor tones in second species. Except for the rhythmic limits which it imposes, second species adheres to the qualities of sixteenth–century melodic writing discussed earlier.

Procedures for Writing a Second Species Counterpoint to a Cantus Firmus

a) Your first note should make a perfect octave, unison, or perfect fifth with the cantus firmus. This note may begin with the first note of the cantus firmus or may be preceded by a rest.

b) Write two notes in your counterpoint to each succeeding note of the cantus firmus but the last. Make sure that the first note makes a consonance.

c) The second note may make either a consonance or a dissonance. You may leap by third, fourth, fifth, minor sixth, or octave to or from a consonance, but make sure that movement to and from a dissonance is by step. This allows you to use some passing tones and an occasional neighbor tone.

d) Oblique motion occurs as you move from the first note to the second against each note of the cantus firmus. Use mostly contrary motion with some parallel motion for variety as you approach each new note of the cantus firmus.

e) Check your counterpoint to see that there are no parallel unisons, fifths, or octaves. Avoid unisons or octaves on successive strong beats. Perfect fifths on successive strong beats can be used if there is a third or sixth intervening. Be careful to avoid creating the interval of a tritone between two successive turning points in your melody.

f) Treat the cadence as you did in first species.

g) Strive for a smooth melodic shape. Try to use your highest and lowest notes just once each. Try to avoid using the same few pitches for an extended part of your melody.

Exercises

These exercises deal mainly with second species, but some first species will also be used. Indicate intervals as in the last set of exercises, and circle those which are dissonant.

EXERCISE 4-6 Write a strict first species counterpoint above the cantus firmus.

EXERCISE 4-7 Write a strict second species counterpoint below the cantus firmus.

EXERCISE 4-8 Complete the canon.

*EXERCISE 4-9 This is a puzzle canon. Try to find the right time and interval distance which will produce good first and second species counterpoint. [Hint: The *comes* (or "following voice") does not begin on E.]

*EXERCISE 4-10 Use only whole notes and half notes in your counterpoint. (The melody is based on a pavane from Arbeau's *Orchésographie*, 1589.)

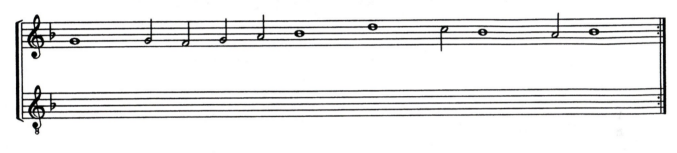

*EXERCISE 4-11 Compose a short example of two-part counterpoint in expanded second species.

Sources for Further Study

Scores:

See the list of scores at the end of Chapter 3.

Readings:

Fux: pp. 27–49
Gauldin—16th c.: pp. 26–31; 33–35; 42–43; 48–49; 278–281
Jeppesen: pp. 109–119
Merritt: pp. 123–134
Morley: pp. 139–157; 209–215
Roberts and Fischer: 11–23
Salzer/Schacter: pp. 12–55

CHAPTER

5

Two-Part Counterpoint: Third, Fourth, and Fifth Species

Example 5-1 is a fine example of third, fourth, and fifth species. Study it carefully before considering the discussion questions.

EX. 5-1 Excerpt from "Fantasia il doloroso" by Thomas Morley (1557–1602)

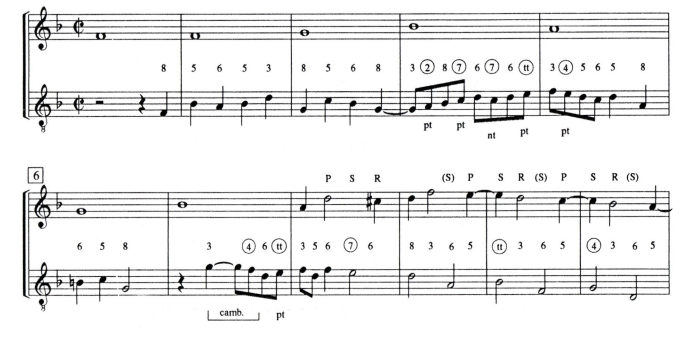

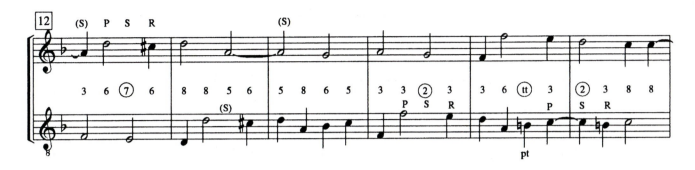

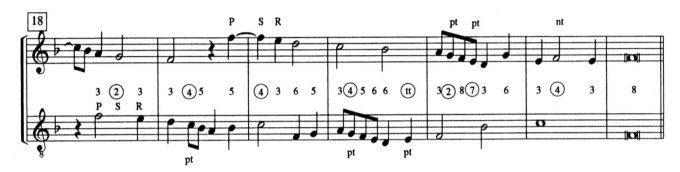

Questions for Discussion

Third Species

You will note in Ex. 5-1 that in places where there are three or more notes against one, the intervals formed between the parts have been indicated by size, those which are dissonances have been circled. These are examples of third species counterpoint. The following questions refer to these portions of the example.

1. What generalizations can you make about the location of the consonances?
2. Where are the dissonant intervals located?
3. What intervals are associated with disjunct motion?
4. What types of dissonances are used?

Fourth Species

The following questions concern the places in Ex. 5-1 marked "S" and "(S)."

1. What do we call the figures indicated by "P-S-R"?
2. What type of intervals are used at the places marked "P" and "R"?
3. What intervals occur most often at the notes marked "R"? What intervals are not to be found at these notes?
4. Where is the "R" pitch located with respect to the "S" pitch?
5. Where in the measure do the pitches marked "S" occur?
6. How does the length of "P" compare to that of "S" for each occurrence?
7. What is the difference between notes marked "(S)" and those marked "S"?

Observations

Third Species

Whenever you find three or more notes against one in the other part you have third species counterpoint. In strict third species counterpoint there are four notes to each note of the cantus firmus with the exception of the first, where the counterpoint may begin with a rest as in Ex. 5-2.

EX. 5-2 Strict third species counterpoint

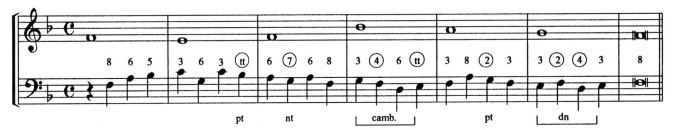

In Ex. 5-3 showing expanded third species counterpoint, the moving part contains at least three pitches to the sustained pitch in the other part.

EX. 5-3 Expanded third species counterpoint

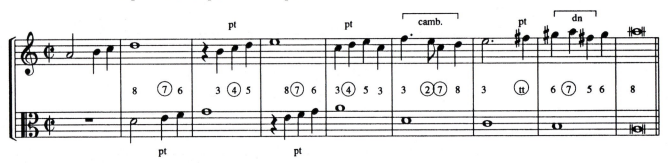

In these examples and in the parts of Ex. 5-1 which are third species counterpoint, the first note of the faster moving part always makes a consonance with the longer note in the other part, even after a rest. Any of the notes which come before the next note in the slower moving part may make consonances or dissonances. Dissonances are approached and left by step with the exceptions discussed below.

The Nota Cambiata

In Ex. 5-1, m. 7, the F in the lower part makes a fourth, followed by a leap of a third to D, which makes a sixth. The melodic figure (G-F-D-E) is called a *nota cambiata* or "changing note." Other examples of this figure appear in Ex. 5-2, m. 4, and in the upper part of Ex. 5-3, m. 6. The figure typically consists of four notes: the first is followed by a step down to the second; the third note is a third below the second, and the last note is a step above the third. The second note is usually the only one making a dissonance with the other part, but the third or fourth may make a dissonance when the interval sequence is 5-4-2-3, 3-2-7-8 (as in Ex. 5-3, m. 6), or 3-4-6-tt (as in Ex. 5-2, m. 4).

The Double Neighbor

Another figure, the *double neighbor,* although somewhat rare in sixteenth–century motet writing, is encountered in third species counterpoint. Examples of this figure appear in Ex. 5-2, m. 6, and in Ex. 5-3, m. 7. The figure is more common in highly ornamented music for keyboard or lute and is also found in ensemble dances.

Guidelines for Writing a Third Species Counterpoint to a Cantus Firmus

    a) Except for the larger number of tones in the counterpoint and the added dissonance types which can be used, the procedures are the same as those for second species.

    b) All dissonances should be approached and left by step except for the nota cambiata and the double neighbor figures.

    c) Check the first notes of each group to make sure they do not make octaves or unisons with consecutive notes of the cantus firmus.

    d) Try writing a first species counterpoint, then converting it to third species by adding tones. This process is referred to as making *divisions* or *diminutions.*

Fourth Species

Fourth species is devoted to the use of suspensions and syncopations. When a note is held across a strong beat resulting in a dissonance, we call it a *suspension* (indicated by "S"). When the result is a consonance, we will refer to it as a *syncopation* (indicated by "(S)"). Pure fourth species counterpoint is a chain of suspensions and syncopations against a cantus firmus. Examples 5-4 and 5-5 show several ways in which suspensions are used in Renaissance polyphony.

EX. 5-4 Strict fourth species counterpoint

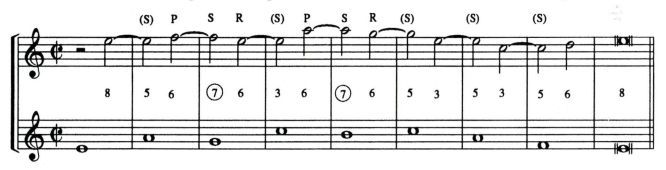

EX. 5-5 Expanded fourth species counterpoint

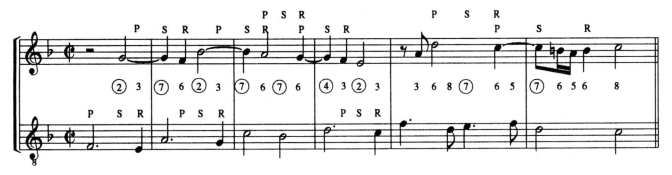

The notes involved in the suspension and its resolution are indicated by "P-S-R" standing for preparation, suspension proper, and resolution. Each part of a suspension has its own set of conditions:

The preparation ("P")

    a) is a consonance;

    b) may occur on a strong or weak beat;

    c) is equal to or longer in duration than the suspension proper.

The suspension proper ("S")

    a) is a dissonance (but not a second when "S" is the upper voice, or a seventh when "S" is the lower voice),

    b) occurs on a strong beat (in duple meter, suspensions may be used on the downbeat when "S" is a half note in duration, and on beats one or three when "S" is a quarter note in duration; in triple meter, suspensions usually occur only on the down beat),

    c) is equal to or shorter in duration than the preparation.

The resolution ("R")

    a) is an imperfect consonance (a third or sixth, but not a unison, and very rarely an octave or perfect fifth);

    b) is a step below the suspension proper.

When suspensions occur in the upper part, the interval sequence ("S" to "R") is most often 7-6 or 4-3. Although 6-5 behaves like a suspension, there is no dissonance involved, so we will call it a syncopation. When suspensions occur in the lower part, the interval sequence is most often 2-3; 4-5 is rarely used, and 5-6 will be called a syncopation. Note that 2-1 and 7-8 interval sequences are avoided, and 9-8 is only rarely encountered in two-part counterpoint.

Fifth Species

Fifth species counterpoint makes use of a combination of first through fourth species. It is sometimes called "florid counterpoint." Example 5-6 shows fifth species counterpoint set to a cantus firmus.

EX. 5-6 Fifth species counterpoint

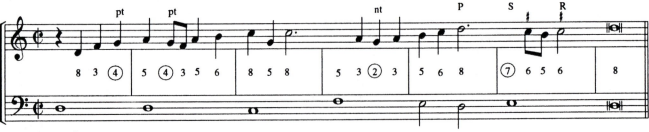

cantus firmus

Guidelines for Writing a Fifth Species Counterpoint to a Cantus Firmus

Since fifth species is a mixture of first through fourth species, the guidelines discussed earlier will continue to be useful. The following additional points should be considered:

- a) Try to vary the rhythm against each note of the cantus firmus. Begin your counterpoint with longer values, then allow it to gain momentum through the use of shorter values.
- b) Use some suspensions (or syncopations), especially at the cadences.
- c) Some shorter time values (such as eighth notes in 4/4) may be used.
- d) Embellishments before the resolution of suspensions such as the following may be used (see Ex. 5-7):
  - 1) anticipated resolution
  - 2) lower neighbor figure
  - 3) leap of a third to lower neighbor of the resolution
  - 4) leap of a perfect fifth to a consonant interval
  - 5) cadential division (in instrumental music)

EX. 5-7 Embellished resolution of suspensions

Writing Canons and Points of Imitation

When you write a canon or a point of imitation, it is important to work on the leader and the follower together. The following steps will prove helpful:

- a) Compose only as much of the dux as the distance in time between it and the comes.
- b) Transcribe this opening immediately into the comes at the desired interval distance.
- c) Write a suitable counterpoint in the dux to the notes just entered in the comes.
- d) Transcribe this new counterpoint into the comes.
- e) Repeat step c and continue in the same manner until you reach the cadence of your canon or until you wish to end your point of imitation.

This process is shown in Ex. 5-8.

EX. 5-8 Steps in writing canonic imitation

Exercises

These exercises focus on third species. Some use a mixture of first, second, and third species. Indicate all intervals, circle the dissonant ones, and label the dissonant notes using these abbreviations: pt (passing tone), nt (neighbor tone), camb (cambiata), dn (double neighbor).

EXERCISE 5-1 Continue the upper part with quarter notes. Move the cantus firmus to the upper voice and write a new counterpoint below it.

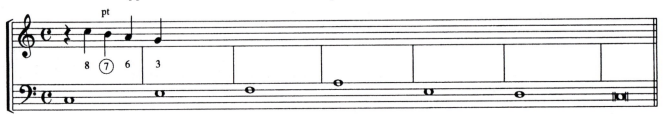

EXERCISE 5-2 Continue the lower part with three or more notes to one in the cantus firmus.

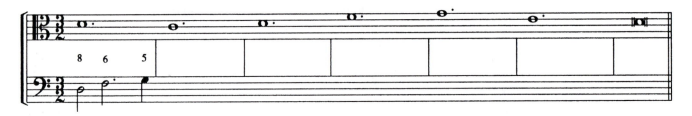

EXERCISE 5-3 Solve this puzzle canon. [Hint: in subdiapente]

*EXERCISE 5-4 Write a bass for this branle. Use first, second, and third species.

These exercises focus on fourth species. Indicate intervals as before. Indicate preparations ("P"), suspensions ("S"), and resolutions ("R"). If a suspended note makes a consonance, indicate it with "(S)".

EXERCISE 5-5 Continue to the end in strict fourth species.

EXERCISE 5-6 Use a mixture of second and fourth species.

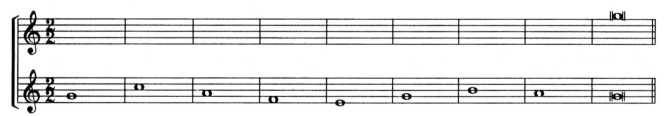

EXERCISE 5-7 Complete this fourth species canon. Appropriate use of musica ficta is advised.

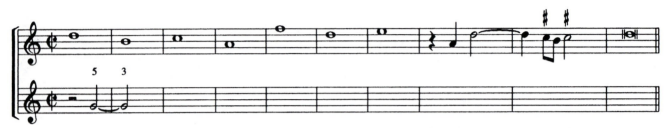

*EXERCISE 5-8 Use third and fourth species. Include at least one suspension.

*EXERCISE 5-9 Solve this puzzle canon. There will be suspensions.

These exercises are in fifth species.

EXERCISE 5-10 Try to include some each of first through fourth species. (Note that the *alla breve* meter may be used for 4/2 as well as for 2/2 in Renaissance music.

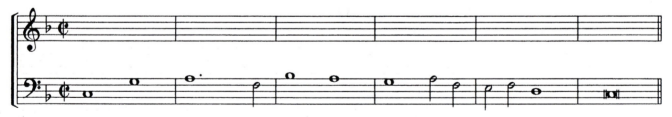

EXERCISE **5-11** Take note of the clef of the cantus firmus and align your counterpoint
carefully.

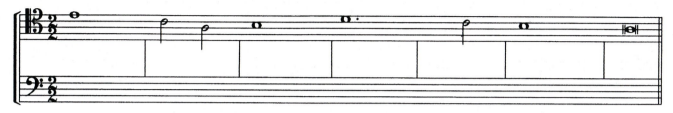

EXERCISE **5-12** Complete this canon for soprano and alto recorders. Notice the clef for the
soprano recorder.

*EXERCISE **5-13** Complete this canon for two lutes (or guitars). Cadence on E.

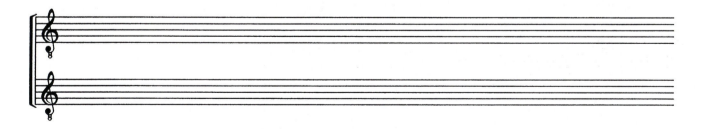

Sources for Further Study

Scores:

See the list of scores at the end of Chapter 3.

Readings:

Fux: pp. 50-67
Gauldin—16th c.: pp. 31–33; 36–41; 44–47; 50–53; 281–286
Jeppesen: pp. 119–174
Merritt: pp. 135–143
Morley: pp. 158–172; 216–220
Roberts and Fischer: 24–38
Salzer/Schacter: pp. 56–116; 127–143
Smith: pp. 57–70

CHAPTER

6

Two-Part Motets

Setting of Text; Formal Considerations

When setting text to music, composers have been guided by the basic principle that stresses in the text should be matched by stresses in the music. We will examine Ex. 6-1 and others used previously to illustrate this principle. We will also discuss how short motets are formally organized.

EX. 6-1 *Pleni sunt coeli* from *Missa L'homme armé* by Josquin des Prez (1440–1521)

Heaven and earth are full [of thy glory]

Questions for Discussion

Refer to Ex. 6-1, and also Ex. 2-1b and Ex. 3-1 as you consider these questions.

Setting of Text

1. How do composers make musical stresses? How do they use meter and rhythm to create stressed notes? How do they use melodic motion to make some notes more prominent or more important than others?

2. How can you tell from the music which syllables of the text phrases "Pleni sunt coeli et terra" (Ex. 6-1) and "Oculus non vidit" (Ex. 3-1) are stressed?

3. How is the music affected when a word or a phrase is repeated? What is the difference between a setting which repeats words or phrases of words and one which uses long strings of notes for each syllable but no word repetitions?

4. How is text used for the shortest time values in these examples?

5. How is the music affected by the ratio of notes to syllables? How is it affected when there are more syllables than notes? When there are about the same number of notes as syllables? When there are more notes than syllables?

6. Is there any word painting in the examples?

Formal Considerations

1. What is the relationship between cadence and text setting?

2. When a phrase of words is repeated, what happens in the music?

3. In Ex. 2-1b, a point of imitation is taken for the words "in nomine"

beginning with the last quarter note, m. 7. In m. 11 the same motives are used. How has the relationship of the voice parts changed?

4. What gives the music unity and diversity? Where is imitation to be found? Where is it abandoned? Are there sequences? How do these techniques affect the setting of the text?

5. How do the interior cadences differ from the final cadence?

6. How do Josquin and Lasso keep the music from coming to a stop whenever there is a cadence?

Observations

Setting of Text

Composers give stress to notes according to their rhythmic and melodic position: (a) longer notes carry more weight than shorter ones, especially when they begin on weak beats or after rests; (b) notes on down beats are usually more stressed than others unless the accent has been shifted (as in Ex. 6-1, m. 5); (c) notes which are followed by rests gain strength from the cadence which they close; (d) stresses occur on the notes at melodic turning points, especially the highest notes in a phrase; (e) a note may become stressed when followed or preceded by a leap; (f) a note gains strength by being repeated; and (g) syncopation and suspension add stress—a sustained note on a weak beat is stressed. The text phrases below will have stresses as indicated by the upper case when spoken:

> PLE-ni sunt COE-li et TER-ra
>
> O-cu-lus non VI-dit

In Ex. 6-1, "PLE" first occurs on a down beat and is given a longer time value. The next appearance is after a rest and becomes a syncopation. "COE" begins with a longer note on a weak beat and is given three notes. "TER" is given a long string of notes. When a single syllable is sung to many notes in succession, we call it a *melisma.* "Oculus non vidit" (Ex. 3-1) is treated in much the same way: the stressed syllables are given longer notes, occur on the downbeat or after rests, or are set with several notes in succession.

Repeating a word or phrase of words adds even more emphasis. Composers before Josquin were usually content to use long melismas for a text of few syllables. As the sixteenth century progressed, however, composers tended to repeat phrases of words for a greater dramatic effect.

The Liturgy of the Church provided composers with texts of varying length. In the Mass, for example, the Kyrie, Sanctus, Benedictus, and Agnus Dei have few words, while the Gloria has many, and the Credo has by far the most. Melismatic music is usually found in the sections with few words. The Gloria may have some melisma, but in shorter masses the text is syllabic—that is, one note per syllable. The text of the Credo is often syllabic, except in very long masses. Sometimes there are many more syllables than notes, as in the case of the chanting of psalms to plainsong. In such cases, the bulk of the text is carried on "reciting tones." We do not normally encounter this in polyphonic music except those works which use psalm tones as cantus firmi.

You will note that the shortest time values in our examples are always part of a melisma. In Ex. 3-1, this is true for all quarter notes and eighth notes. All eighth notes in Ex. 6-1 are also involved in melismatic passages. In "Oculus non vidit," which has been transcribed in 4/2 meter, half notes and larger notes may carry a syllable which is not part of a melisma. In "Pleni sunt coeli," transcribed in 4/4, quarter notes and larger notes may carry a syllable.

Composers in the sixteenth century usually suited the mood of the music to the text. This was done by subtle manipulation of the ratio of dissonance to consonance, by choice of mode, meter, and tessitura. Individual word painting is not common, but some striking examples can be found. Lasso gives us a rising sequence on the word "ascendit" in Ex. 3-1. Music dealing with pain and suffering often employs more suspensions than music dealing with praise and joy. In secular music, however, word painting is quite common, especially in Italian and English madrigals.

Formal Considerations

In two-part motet-style pieces such as Ex. 2-1b and Ex. 3-1, the end of each phrase of the text is marked by a cadence. Each new phrase of text begins with a new point of imitation. When a phrase of words is repeated, it will often be set with the same motives. The repetition, however, may be at another pitch level, or the parts may be interchanged.

Invertible or Double Counterpoint

In Ex. 2-1b, the first time we encounter the words "in nomine" we have a passage where the upper voice imitates the lower voice at the distance of a half–measure and a perfect fifth higher. When "in nomine" comes again in m. 11, the point of imitation now begins with the upper voice, and the lower voice now is in canon at the distance of an octave. This is an example of *double* or *invertible* counterpoint. Another example can be seen in Josquin's setting of "Pleni sunt coeli": Compare mm. 5–6 with mm. 7–8 and 9–10 of Ex. 6-1. The position of the parts has been interchanged. Invertible counterpoint involves two parts which can be successfully interchanged so that the lower becomes the upper and vice versa.

In double or invertible counterpoint at the octave, the type most commonly found, when the lower part is moved up an octave or when the upper part is moved down an octave all of the intervals are inverted. Most consonances remain consonant, unisons become octaves, thirds become sixths. The dissonant intervals remain dissonant, seconds (or ninths) become sevenths, sevenths become seconds (or ninths), tritones remain tritones. The problem is that consonant perfect fifths become dissonant perfect fourths. This must be taken into account when you write double counterpoint at the octave.

Cases of double counterpoint at the twelfth are rather common as well. Here the unisons become twelfths, fifths become octaves, and octaves become fifths. Thirds become tenths and vice versa, fourths become ninths and vice versa. The problem area is the sixths, which become sevenths. However, 2-3 suspensions become 4-3 suspensions, a definite advantage.

Double counterpoint at the tenth is somewhat rare. Unisons become tenths and vice versa, thirds become octaves and vice versa, seconds and sevenths produce dissonances. The problem area is sixths, which become fifths. Any parallel sixths in the original will become parallel fifths in the inverted version. Ex. 6-2 illustrates double counterpoint at the octave, twelfth, and tenth.

EX. 6-2 Double counterpoint

a) at the octave

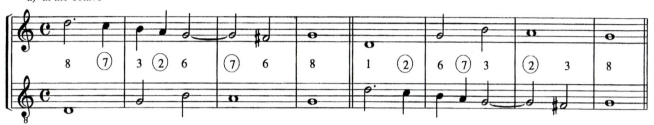

b) at the twelfth

c) at the tenth

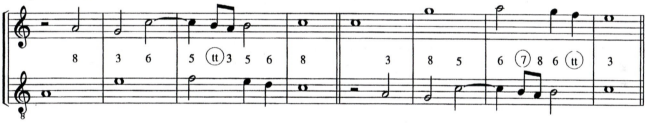

Unity and Diversity

Formal unity is achieved through imitation, sequence, and motivic development. The use of new ideas for new phrases of text provides diversity. The flow of the music is punctuated—but not interrupted—by the interior cadences. One voice is allowed to sustain (on a longer note), while the other takes up the next motive. Sometimes one voice provides the close of the cadence for both parts, allowing the other voice to have a rest. These two cases are demonstrated in Ex. 6-3.

EX. 6-3 Two types of interior cadences

a) One voice sustains while the other moves   b) One voice provides the close for both parts.

The final cadence provides a full stop. The type of cadence used for the ending would be inappropriate in the middle of a motet, unless it is used to end a section (such as the "Christe eleison" in the Kyrie of a Mass).

Exercises

EXERCISE 6-1. Set one (or more) of the following texts to the music below:
a) DE-o GRA-ti-as   (Thanks be to God)
b) Lau-DA-te DO-mi-num   (Praise the Lord)
c) Ho-SAN-na in ex-CEL-sis   (Hosanna in the highest)

level of investment may be several times the level reported in these accounts. This is a particularly important point, since debt critics hold that government expenditures absorb funds that would otherwise finance capital investment. For this reason, it is suggested that the government's investment spending be separated from its debt bill.

Some ideas for sorting out U.S. government consumption and investment expenditures include revising national accounts, making adjustments for state and local government budgets, and valuing such federal capital assets as universal rights and oil rights. Undoubtedly, such adjustments would reduce the level of existing U.S. debt. In essence, the point is to differentiate those expenditures that are strictly "consumption" from those that are "investment" when attempts are made to reduce debt. Such a separation ultimately will be a political decision resting with politicians and the electorate.[6] As we have noted, the importance of debt and deficits to a country depends on the circumstances it may find itself in.

THE ISSUE OF STABILIZATION POLICIES

This inability to forecast accurately has serious implications for stabilization policies. Together with variability of leads and lags in such policies, erroneous forecasts have pushed some policymakers to reject short-run stabilization policies altogether in favor of a policy of rules.

Finding a strong empirical relationship between several measures of money and economic activity suggests that monetary policy can play a singularly important role in stabilization policy. Indeed, failure to recognize these relationships can have serious consequences for economic activity. These relationships to economic activity, moreover, appear more certain than fiscal actions.

Furthermore, the evidence provided in a number of Federal Reserve Bank of St. Louis Studies is consistent with other evidence that suggests that the money stock is an important indicator of the total thrust of stabilization actions, both monetary and fiscal. In the first instance, changes in the money stock reflect principally discretionary actions of the Federal Reserve System as it uses open market operations, discount rate changes, and reserve requirements. Secondly, the money stock reflects the joint action of the Treasury and Federal Reserve System

in financing newly created go
in the final analysis, on decis
debt by Federal Reserve actior
in its balances at Reserve bank:
financed by monetary expansio
base and the money supply.

Many economists argue tha
results only if expenditures a
the United States, the Federal
the government. Its open mark
serve to provide funds in the
and private individuals borrow

Moreover, it is not easy to
policy—a result, in part, of tl
tools are used. A part of these f
can be redirected very quickly
more or less automatically in
the economy is expanding. S
compensation, welfare program
States, the progressive nature o

Some insight into how diffic
of fiscal policy in either directi
the programs in the United Stat
approval must be in a form tha
administration. Bills are somet
floor of Congress in ways that

Much the same is true in t
intervene to make either raisin;
process. The political give-and-
optimal tax system.

Transfer payments, although
to the same sort of forces that
temptation to embellish a prop
become accustomed to the paym
atives will not be anxious to se
stimulus passes. Discretionary c
one-way stabilization tools at be

J. de Larosiere, director of the
forcefully in March 1982 that

countries ov
flation. Rat
Keynes, fisc
in many cou
and other b
future fiscal
forecasts ab
inflation we
expanded d
in the 1970
commitmer

Readily a
public exp
countries, t
(GDP) ros
years. For
more pron
Great Brita
more than
1970s. For
Ireland, Lu
the increa:
points. In
expenditur
de Larosie
main facto

A MONE

How sh
discussed
in 1951.[10]
that pushe

Friedm
appropria
to wage-
measures
surplus w
degree of

In his view, a balanced budget would require tighter money to prevent inflation and a budget deficit with still tighter money. It is possible that budget deficits may get so large that they will simply overwhelm monetary policy. In fact, it may be impossible to design monetary policy that will prevent inflation.

Consequently, there may not be a single best mix of monetary and fiscal policy and degree of inflation. A good mix would be, Friedman thinks, a roughly balanced budget—balanced over the business cycle—together with whatever associated monetary policy would prevent inflation. Friedman argues that no policy very far from this combination is likely to be appropriate.

In 1951 Friedman argued that while high interest rates curb investment expenditures, they also curb consumer expenditures, including spending on nondurable and durable goods. One reason is that high interest rates make saving more attractive. They also reduce the capital value of existing streams of wealth and thus reduce the ration of wealth to income. In effect, high interest rates increase the desire of people to add to their wealth.

High interest rates, in 1951, 1982, or 1989, are not popular with many people for a variety of reasons. These reasons, however, are insufficient to overrule the monetary policy requisite to bring inflation under control.

Interest rates remained high in 1982, an important watershed in the world's debt problem, at least in part because financial markets did not believe that inflation was under control. It could be, as pessimists argue, that financial markets believed that record U.S. budget deficits had slipped into Friedman's worst-case scenario when they became so large that they ultimately overwhelmed monetary policy.

President Reagan's economic program during his first term was originally thought to be what the financial markets had ordered. This assumption proved to be a bit premature. The debate was over interest rates and deficits. The key issue, according to some observers, was that long-term interest rates in 1982 had embodied in them the expectation of deficits three and four years out. Financial markets feared that deficits would either stifle a recovery or rekindle inflation later. In sum, the conventional wisdom on Wall Street was that uncertainty over the record-breaking deficits, then in excess of the $100 billion Reagan proposed, was a major reason, if not the only one, as to why interest rates were high. Lenders were demanding a high premium for their money because they did not know what economic conditions would prevail when they were paid back.

Moreover, there was a widely shared feeling in the American financial community that the Reagan administration was not paying attention to their views. The Reagan administration's argument that neither the Federal Reserve nor the government could do anything about the persistence of high interest rates was less than reassuring to the financial community. This pessimistic view was written into expectations by investors and thus into high interest rates.

There is a considerable distance between the political and the financial worlds. One explanation for the gulf of misunderstanding between these two worlds is mutual suspicion. Wall Street looks upon the U.S. federal government as a bloated monster loosed upon the land by vote-starved politicians. Washington, on the other hand, tends to think of Wall Street as a tiny cell of conspirators secretly manipulating the markets of America to exploit Main Street.

In fact, deficits do matter. The U.S. economy can tolerate deficits less readily than can most other countries, according to some accounts, because it is a comparatively low-saving economy. In recent years in Japan, for example, personal saving, as a percentage of disposable personal income, was four times as large as in the United States. In the Federal Republic of Germany, it was about three times as large. In most countries, the business sector is a net borrower, and one must look at personal savings as the main source for surplus funds. In short, countries that save a lot, such as Germany, Italy, and Japan, experience less difficulty in financing a given level of deficit expressed as a share of GDP than do countries with lower rates of saving, such as the United States.

Although it is still a relatively low percentage of the gross national product (GNP), the U.S. fiscal deficit accounts for a large share of available surplus funds and is of the same magnitude as total net outlays for new plant and equipment. When extra budgetary borrowing on behalf of other agencies occurs, the borrowing requirements of the federal government leave little surplus saving available to the private sector for borrowing. Unless the projected levels of fiscal deficits can be reduced, only a very large expansion in private saving will prevent serious crowding out and "high" rates of interest.

Moreover, if it is correct, as reported in the National Bureau of Economic Research (NBER) study for the United States, that there is a relatively fixed relationship between the total debt, both private and public, and the GNP, the increase in public debt will imply a crowding out of private debt, with obvious implications for capital formation. For example, in the United States, total debt averaged about 140 percent of the GNP for several decades. In the 1960s, curiously, when the ratio of public debt to GNP in the United States was declining, the economy was growing at a lively pace, while in the 1970s, when that ratio was either stationary or increasing, the rate of growth slowed down.

In essence, high fiscal deficits accompanied by tight monetary policies measured in rate of growth of the money supply may not generate inflation but will nevertheless raise interest rates to bring about a reduction in private productive activities. This reduction itself will magnify the size of the deficit through its built-in negative effects on revenues and positive effects on public expenditures. The Federal Republic of Germany, Japan, and the United States are important examples of countries that have pursued tight monetary policies in the face of sizable fiscal deficits.

Suppose now that fiscal deficits are accompanied by an accommodating monetary policy. If the economy's productive capacities are fully utilized, the increase in aggregate demand will bring about increases in prices and wages. In the short run, the increase in the money supply may bring about a decline in nominal interest rates caused by the liquidity effect. Consumption will rise at the expense of saving as inflationary psychology prompts people to anticipate purchases. The demand for financial assets will fall, while that for real assets will rise, leading to a process of disintermediation in the capital market. Imports will expand, leading to a deterioration in the balance of payments. If exchange rates are fixed, there will be a loss in net foreign reserves that will tend to reduce the initial acceleration in money supply growth. If exchange rates are flexible, the rate will depreciate, adding further to the domestic inflation rate. In short, high budgetary deficits accompanied by an accommodating monetary policy tend to aggravate inflation.

As an alternative to borrowing from the central bank or the private sector, governments can and do borrow abroad. For industrial countries where domestic capital markets are well integrated with those abroad, the process is direct, if not always simple. Indeed, the evidence indicates that the practice of foreign borrowing to finance budget deficits has become prevalent since the mid-1970s, along with the rapid expansion of the international financial markets, as both industrial and developing countries have incurred significantly larger deficits. In fact, during the latter part of the 1970s, estimates place foreign deficit finance at about one-sixth of an industrial country's budget deficits and one-third of those of a developing country. If borrowing by public enterprises could be accounted for, these percentages would no doubt be much higher.

Moreover, the recent pool of international saving provided by OPEC countries unable to fully absorb their saving internally has become smaller. Although still sufficient to accommodate requirements of the smaller developing countries, the pool is inadequate to meet U.S. needs and those of other industrial countries over the next several years. No doubt, high interest rates in the United States will attract many of these funds and will thus contribute to financing the U.S. deficit. This will tend to aggravate the capital needs situation in other countries, which thereby face much stronger competition and higher interest rates. The implications are indeed ominous for developing countries. Deficits of large countries do have implications for the rest of the world.

Given the present and persistent size of fiscal deficits in many countries, authorities are severely restricted in their ability to use fiscal policy in a countercyclical fashion. To regain their freedom, countries are best advised to pursue policies that reduce budget deficits. This will enhance the chances that the negative effects of restrictive monetary policy will be removed, and countries will be able to enjoy growth without inflation. Under the circumstances, perseverance and political courage are required in dealing with the fiscal problem.

NOTES

1. The various views are well represented in the professional literature. See Robert. J. Barro, "Are Government Bonds Net Wealth?" *Journal of Political Economy* (November-December 1974), pp. 1095–1117; Robert J. Barro, "Neoclassical Approach to Fiscal Policy," in *Modern Business Cycle Theory*, Robert J. Barro, ed. (Cambridge, Mass.: Harvard University Press, 1989); James M. Buchman and Richard E. Wagner, *Democracy in Deficit* (New York: Academic Press, 1977); Robert Eisner, *How Real Is the Federal Deficit?* (New York: Free Press, 1986); Martin S. Feldstein, "Social Security, Induced Retirement, and Aggregate Capital Accumulation," *Journal of Political Economy* (September-October 1974), pp. 905–26. See also Richard Vedder, Lowell Gallaway, and Christopher Frenze, "Federal Tax Increases and Budget Deficit, 1947–86: Some Empirical Evidence," Joint Economic Committee Minority Staff Paper, 1987.

2. See Edward M. Gramlich, "Budget Deficits and National Savings: Are Politicians Exogenous?" *Journal of Economic Perspectives* (Spring 1989), pp. 23–35.

3. Robert Eisner, "Budget Deficits: Rhetoric and Reality," *Journal of Economic Perspectives* (Spring 1989), pp. 73–93.

4. Robert J. Barro, "The Ricardian Approach to Budget Deficits," *Journal of Economic Perspectives* (Spring 1989), pp. 54–57.

5. See Milton Friedman, "Why the Twin Deficits are a Blessing," *Wall Street Journal* (December 14, 1988), p. A14.

6. See Gramlich, "Budget Deficits and National Savings," pp. 23–35.

7. For an evaluation of fiscal activities on the local level, see Bernard F. Sliger, Ansel M. Sharp, and Robert L. Sandmeyer, "Local Government Revenues: An Overview" in *Management Policies in Local Government Finance*, J. R. Aronson and Eli Schwarts, eds. (Washington: International City Management Association, 1975), pp. 42–62.

8. J. de Larosiere, "Coexistence of Fiscal Deficits, High Tax Burdens Is Consequence of Pressures for Public Spending," *Survey* (March 22, 1982), p. 82.

9. Larosiere, "Fiscal Deficits, High Tax Burdens," p. 82.

10. See Milton Friedman, ed., *Essays in Positive Economics* (Chicago: University of Chicago Press, 1953); Herbert Stein, *Fiscal Revolution in America* (Chicago: University of Chicago Press, 1969).

5   Economic Nationalism

THE ISSUE OF NATIONALISM

Economic nationalism is an important issue in both developed creditor countries and developing debtor countries. It can be an important
constraint to the extension of cooperation theory as a framework for
dealing with the problem of world debt. It is thus useful to consider
the essence of nationalism itself.[1]

The word *nationalism* is derived from *nation* which itself has roots
in the Latin *natio*, signifying birth. It has been taken to mean a social
grouping with or without ties of blood. In the Middle Ages, the term
natio villae was used to designate a kinship in the village. Later in this
period, students at the University of Paris were divided into "nations"
according to the places of birth. Later, the term *nation* was applied
to the population of a country without regard for racial unity. By
the late eighteenth century, *nation* came to be used abstractly and
interchangeably with *country*.

Currently, scholars distinguish the nation from a race, a state, or a
language. In particular, the emphasis is placed on a common political
sentiment. The political term *nation* is used by some scholars to
designate a people that "has attained to state organization." Hans

Kohn, for example, places the emphasis on the "political doctrine of sovereignty" as the principal characteristic of modern nations.[2] In effect, the contemporary connotation of "nation" is political.

The concept of nationalism is even less precise.[3] It can be taken to mean the historical process by which nationalities become political units or modern national states constructed out of tribes and empires. It can be taken to mean the theory, principle, or ideal implicit in the actual historical process. It can be taken to mean the activity of a political party, thereby combining the historical process and political theory. It can be taken to mean a condition of the mind among the members constituting the nationality, sharing commitment to the ideal of one's own national state and the mission of the national state. It is, as Hans Kohn suggests, "first and foremost a state of mind and act of consciousness."

Some scholars argue that the concept of nationalism is best understood by the social psychologist. It is defined by some as the "self-consciousness" of a nation and by others as an "intolerant and aggressive instinct." Still others describe nationalism as a way of manifesting national spirit—history, traditions, language—and, in its abstract form, as an idea controlling the life and actions of a nation.

The essence of nationalism, on which many scholars agree, is that it reflects social mobilization whereby the commitment of an individual is transferred from the local to the national level.[4] The individual becomes aware that personal interests go beyond the local community to the national level. In effect, the individual turns from the local level to a national community for economic status, political loyalty, social dependence, cultural form, and psychological drive. Though it may differ from country to country in details of emphasis and time, this sort of social mobilization is the essence of nationalism.

In terms of economic policy, nationalism typically involves an ideological preference for a number of goals. These include as much self-sufficiency as possible, public ownership, public enterprise in key economic sectors, and intensive regulation and control of private and domestic-foreign enterprise. In general, discrimination in favor of nationals is carried on as a matter of policy. This discrimination, however, is not uniform in nationals. There is a bias in favor of the ruling elite and the bureaucracy. To be sure, this may also be an investment in the creation and maintenance of a class deemed necessary to the construction and perpetuation of a viable national state for the common good.

There may also be reasons other than economic nationalism why some governments pursue the above policies. For instance, socialists are not necessarily nationalists, yet may prefer a collective economy for ideological reasons. Governments may also see external economies to be realized in pursuing protective trade measures on behalf of the industries of their nationals. The consequences, unfortunately, may be the same as those resulting from the pursuit of parochial nationalist policies. This chapter focuses on economic nationalism and the implications of such policies for the extension of cooperation theory to relations between debtor and creditor countries.

PROSPECTS FOR NATIONALISM

What are the prospects for nationalism? Nationalism can be viewed as a historical movement that has within it the seeds of its own destruction. The nation-state, as well as the nationalism that provides the glue to hold it together, is undergoing change, thanks to a growing world economic, political, social, and technological interdependence. Thus, it may be that nationalism per se has outgrown its usefulness to the nation-state. Thanks to the initiative of their leadership, emerging nations have copied and attempted to make their own an antiquated and obsolete Euro-American model for nation building.[5] Although its surface manifestations continue to exist, the fundamental forces, conditions, and circumstances that made nationalism a powerful force for nation building in the past no longer exist in their previous form and strength. Those who wrap themselves up in the skirts of nationalism are living in the dangerous past.

The growing world interdependence has undermined the authority of the nation-state. Thus, the nation-state can no longer guarantee its nationals protection against the threat of external aggression with the same assurance that it did for centuries. This was the nation-state's primary role. Nationalism is simply ineffective as a political concept when no government, large or small, can protect itself against nuclear attack.

Domestic and foreign policies of nation-states can no longer be as sharply separated as in former years. These policies more often than not tend to merge and become dependent upon each other. There is an increased sense of international awareness in such problems as monetary policy, economics, pollution, control of disease, air travel, traffic in drugs, and related areas. At best, national efforts alone yield limited results. National problems tend to yield more and more to international solutions.

In effect, the reality that is working its way in the world as the capacity for mutual destruction has increased since World War II is that nations are becoming less interested in settling their disputes by force of arms and a little more interested in cooperating in limited fields because it is in their interests to do so. To be sure, scholars have known for generations, even centuries, that nations must cooperate in many fields to avoid damage to their own people. Scattered evidence suggests that governments are gradually adjusting to this view. In the process, nationalism is being undermined by a new internationalism or transnationalism or, better still, cosmopolitanism.

Nevertheless, this process of decay evident in nationalism is a very slow one. Nationalism continues to show vigor. The sense of national identity remains important. In confrontation with such other "isms" as capitalism, socialism, fascism, and communism, nationalism thus far is demonstrably more resilient as a historical movement. In fact, many of the "isms" only make it when identified with nationalism. Each nation, no matter what its size, is jealous of its sovereignty and does not intend to sacrifice even a small portion of its independence for the promised advantages of international cooperation. For such nations, nationalism of the Euro-American model is essential to assure what they regard as freedom of decision and action. They prefer self-government with all its dangers to servitude in tranquillity. They prefer to be governed by their own kind rather than by foreign administrators, no matter how efficient. Nationalism remains the mainspring of mass action. The mental gymnastics required to justify nationalism in an interdependent world is all too evident.[6]

A COSMOPOLITAN ALTERNATIVE

The problem in so many countries lies in economies that have not fulfilled the hopes of their citizens. During the first quarter-century after World War II, decolonization created new nations and new hopes. Membership in the UN rose from 51 to 158. The former colonies graduated in an era when both Western and Eastern economies were enjoying what seemed to be an endless growth cycle. The momentum of rebuilding war-shattered economies carried the former Axis and Allied powers into an unusual era of growth and hope by citizens. The banquet for new leaders of new nations offered a rich menu of choices.

They could join the American or West European economic spheres—trade, aid, loans, educational opportunities. Or they could sample the Soviet promise, the more Spartan wave of the future. Later they could choose the heretical Chinese version of Marxist aid—perhaps a Tansam railway—if they suspected Moscow's brand of "being just another version of white imperialism." Or they could listen for a higher bid from Nationalist China (Taiwan), perhaps ingenious agricultural aid that produced not one, not two, but three rice crops a year.

Such nonaligned countries as Guinea, Indonesia, Ghana, Egypt, and Yugoslavia experimented with the Soviet-brand product, then rejected it. India alternately considered a post-Stalinist model, then a Galbraithean interventionist model. Yugoslavia developed its own unique market-oriented work/management model.

In a few Third World nations, rising economies helped to satisfy rising expectations. But there was only the wild rise and fall of world commodity prices, or showplace bid project East or West that never seemed to launch the local society into self-sustaining growth. They never reached the so-called take-off stage.

With disappointment came coups. This served to increase the desire by the elites or establishments in many countries to attempt to insulate themselves from external influences and the dangers of votes, electoral or parliamentary, that might express dissatisfaction with the course of economic affairs. Attempts to aid free trade and internal democracy in a number of these countries—sometimes by helping exiled leaders committed to popular rule, sometimes by withholding aid, downgrading diplomatic recognition, or speaking out against offenders—have seldom worked. In fact, because of skillful propaganda, the unrest and protest in many of these nations have turned into anti-Americanism on occasion. The Soviet Union has not done much better in registering success in its dealings with these countries.

What then are the answers, if any? It is not very useful to avoid putting forward one's views. This study argues that policies promoting economic nationalism as a means to promote development have miscarried. These policies have not been able to solve the problems of development in emerging nations. They have, as expected, served well to cultivate and promote the interest and prosperity of the elite and the bureaucracy in many countries. To be sure, each country has its own particular problems and economic structure toward which its economic policy is directed. Consequently, among nations, there are important differences in economic policy. This study makes a point of recognizing these differences while at the same time stressing similarities.

More cosmopolitan and international economic policies beckon that emphasize the entrepreneurial, competitive, market-oriented incentive systems practiced in economically successful nation-states. Indeed, many of the leaders of emerging nations, whether democratic, authoritarian, or totalitarian, received their education abroad. Most are well aware of the implications of the progress of the world's developed nations. Modernization to them does mean the necessity of learning more about the results of the developed world's technical efficiency.

As students, these leaders were observant. They saw how appeals to tradition solidified national sentiment, how devotion to the state was made the citizen's prime responsibility, how poets sang about the glory of the fatherland, and how patriots regretted that they had but one life to lose for their country. They were familiar with Rousseau's social contract, with Montesquieu's analysis of the spirit of legal institutions, with Alexander Hamilton's project of a national economy and with the vision of Keynes. They learned how Bismarck unified the German national state, how Mazzini, Garibaldi, and Cavour stimulated Italian unity, and how Marx and Lenin proposed to change the world.

Once they returned, this elite, with their charisma and, in some cases, political genius, gave direction to the nationalism, including economic nationalism, of emerging countries. They wanted liberation from the bonds of imperialism, but at the same time, they would construct their new nation-states in the image of the developed nation-states. They would accept economic modernization but maintain their ancient cultural heritage. They would superimpose industrialism upon their predominantly agrarian economies while introducing agricultural reforms. They would be torn between the old and the new. This dilemma explains in part the unevenness of development in emerging nations, the constant crises, the spasmodic changes in leadership, and the air of discord and dissension. The pursuit of policies promoting economic nationalism are not always helpful, are often counterproductive.

This is a familiar story which many of the world's developed nations experienced more than two centuries ago. The differences are that today the world is much more integrated, and in the emerging nations, the experience is telescoped and more rapid. There is less chance for the successful pursuit of economic nationalism than in the earlier period. A competent and patient political leadership recognizes that nation-states that have given their people hope and rising standards are more apt to end in becoming modern democratic states. Indeed, the spirit of enterprise, independent judgment, desire for progress and change, knowledge of the world, and improved education are ingredients essential to these states. These are the very ingredients often lacking in a policy of economic nationalism. They are also the ingredients that should be promoted and cultivated by political and economic leaders of even one-party states with a genuine long-term interest in the development of their countries.

It is now generally accepted that central controls impede innovation, foster waste, and distort output. The various reform programs restrict central planning, expand the authority of enterprises over wages, prices, and product, and rely much more on the market and competition to guide production and pricing. A wider spread in wages is encouraged to reward diligence, productivity, and skill.

Reform is a sharp break with the past; it is complex and cannot be achieved at one stroke. Getting rid of consumer subsidies, adjusting prices and wages, and avoiding inflation or undue unemployment is difficult and risks serious social dislocation and discontent. Even if pursued vigorously, these reforms take time.

Reform is a bold and realistic step. The alternatives are slow growth, inefficiency, low quality, and lack of innovation in industry and agriculture. Leaders in many of these countries have recognized these problems for some years but have done little beyond exhortation and palliatives. One can assume that the bureaucrats and the political elite resist changes bound to threaten their positions and perquisites.

For better or, quite possibly, for worse, world leadership and elites, including most in emerging countries, share a common intellectual heritage. This heritage includes mercantilist, classical, neoclassical Marxian, Keynesian, and monetarist economic doctrines. Many of these doctrines are as relevant to developed and emerging countries today as they were in the past. They merit our attention.

A survey of these doctrines and ideas underscores important differences in their approaches and methods toward economic nationalism and government intervention into economic affairs. The emerging countries have a rich menu from which to select. Not all of the available selections, however, are equally healthy for a country's economy and its development. Some selections are very unhealthy.

Economic nationalism does place constraints on cooperation theory. These constraints are multidimensional and include cultural, economic, monetary, and political elements. They are not simply internal to the country; they are external. Their net effects are to reduce the attractiveness of cooperation theory as a basis for national policy. Nevertheless, a nationalist government's room to maneuver in promoting a policy of economic nationalism—no matter the skill and determination of its political leadership—is limited. What a country can do in today's interdependent world depends only in part on its size, location, resources, and the ethnic bases for its nationalism.

Urging cooperation theory and cosmopolitan and less government-interventionist economic policies on emerging nations and others in an interdependent world is not hypocritical, nor does it necessarily mean accepting one of the other programs of the superpowers.[7] On the contrary, it is a recognition of contemporary world reality and the shortcomings of parochial nationalist economic policies.

NOTES

1. A useful discussion of nationalism in English is presented by Louis L. Snyder, *Varieties of Nationalism: A Comparative Study* (Hinsdale, Ill.: Dryden Press, 1976); Karl Wolfgang Deutsch, *Nationalism and Social Communication: An Inquiry into the Foundations of Nationality* (New York: Wiley, 1953); W. H. Carr, *Nationalism and After* (New York: Macmillan, 1945); S. W. Baron, *Modern Nationalism and Religion* (New York: Harper, 1947); L. W. Doob, *Patriotism and Nationalism: Their Psychological Foundations* (New Haven: Yale University Press, 1964); C. J. H. Hayes, *The Historical Evolution of Modern Nationalism* (New York: R. R. Smith, 1931): F. O. Hertz, *Nationality in History and Politics* (New York: Oxford University Press, 1944); Hans Kohn, *The Idea of Nationalism* (New York: Macmillan, 1944); F. Znaniecki, *Modern Nationalities: A Sociological Study* (Urbana: University of Illinois Press, 1952); B. C. Shafer, *Faces of Nationalism* (New York: Harcourt Brace Jovanovich, 1972); Harry G. Johnson, ed., *Economic Nationalism in Old and New States* (Chicago: University of Chicago Press, 1967); Karl Wolfgang Deutsch and W. J. Poltz, eds., *Nation-Building* (New York: Atherton, 1963); E. M. Earle, ed., *Nationalism and Internationalism: Essays Inscribed to Carlton J. A. Hayes* (New York: Columbia University Press, 1950); A. Eban, *The Tide of Nationalism* (New York: Horizon Press, 1959); H. A. Gibbons, *Nationalism and Internationalism* (New York: Stokes, 1930); G. P. Gooch, *Nationalism* (New York: Harcourt, Brace, and Howe, 1920); F. H. Hinsley, *Nationalism and the International System* (London: Hodder and Staughton, 1973); O. Jaszi,

The Dissolution of the Habsburg Monarchy (Chicago: University of Chicago Press, 1929); Louis L. Snyder, *The Dynamics of Nationalism* (Princeton: Van Nostrand, 1964).

2. Hans Kohn, *The Idea of Nationalism* (New York: Macmillan, 1944).

3. See C. J. H. Hayes, *The Historical Evolution of Modern Nationalism* (New York: R. R. Smith, 1931).

4. Louis L. Snyder defines nationalism as "that sentiment of a group or body of people living within a compact or noncontiguous territory, using a language or related dialects as a vehicle for common thoughts and feelings, holding a common religious belief, possessing common institutions, traditions, and customs acquired and transmitted during the course of common history, venerating national heroes, and cherishing a common will for social homogeneity." Snyder, *Dynamics of Nationalism*, p. 25. In any given situation, one or more of these elements may be absent, as Snyder points out, without affecting the validity of the definition.

5. In the post–World War II period, events all over the world have moved swiftly to bring new troubles and to make old ones harder to manage. The new ones sprang up chiefly in those areas variously called developing, underprivileged, colonial, or emerging. They ranged in extent from the Western Hemisphere to the East, Near East, and Far East and in intensity from protest to revolt against things as they were, and some argue still are: the established order and former colonial powers. Indeed, the term *Third World* is intended to distinguish these developing nation states, many of them small, from two groups of technologically advanced nations: one, the so-called Western nations, largely influenced by the United States, and the other, Soviet socialist, influenced by the Soviet Union. Communist China, which used to be classified as a Third World country, might now be more accurately described as a fourth power in the balance of nations. See George Macesich, *The International Monetary Economy and The Third World* (New York: Praeger, 1981).

6. See Dudley Seers, *The Political Economy of Nationalism* (Oxford: Oxford University Press, 1983).

7. Seers, *Political Economy of Nationalism*, p. 12.

6   Bureaucratic and Political Elite: A Taste for Nationalism

ECONOMIC IMPLICATIONS

This chapter study draws on the economic implications of nationalism from the work of Harry G. Johnson, Albert Breton, Anthony Downs, and Gary S. Becker, and my own earlier work on economic policies in several countries.[1] It also benefits from conversations with Harry G. Johnson in the early 1960s on various topics dealing with the economics of nationalism.

Downs argues that political parties attempt to maximize the gains from political office by catering to the tastes and preferences of voters. In a multiparty democratic society, political parties remain in office only by satisfying these tastes and preferences for various types and amounts of government programs. In effect, political power is exchanged for desired policies in a political transaction between party and electorate.

The critical element in Downs's hypothesis is the cost of acquiring information. He uses this cost to explain reliance on persuasion in arriving at political decisions, the inequality of political influence, the role of ideology, electoral apathy, and the bias in democratic government toward serving producer rather than consumer interests.

Breton's analysis of economic nationalism identifies nationality with ownership by nationals of various types of property and considers such nationality as a type of collective consumption capital that yields an income of utility and can be invested in by spending public funds in the acquisition of such capital. From these assumptions, Breton derives a number of testable propositions about nationalism.

These propositions about nationalism imply, among other things, that nationalist policy is primarily concerned with redistributing rather than increasing income. The redistribution, moreover, is from the working class to the middle class. As a result, there will be a tendency to resort to confiscation rather than purchase when the working class is poor. Since manufacturing jobs and ownership are preferred by the middle class, nationalism will tend to favor investment in national manufacturing. Given its collective nature, nationalism will strike a particularly responsive chord from socialists. Furthermore, the blossoming and appeal of nationalism will be closely associated with the rise of new middle classes who have difficulty in finding suitable career opportunities.

Johnson develops and extends Downs's cost of information regarding voter preferences and extends the concept from Downs's established democracies to include emerging countries. Thus, the main obstacle to efficiency in the exchange between political parties and their electorate is ignorance on both sides about prospective gains from policies offered and about the cost of acquiring the information necessary to make the exchange efficient. This obstacle forces the political party to depend on pressure groups, lobbyists, and the communications media for its information about voter preferences. One consequence of this dependence is to give political parties a strong incentive to gain control over communications media as a means to establish control over the country. Indeed, the recent push by emerging countries for a "New Information Order" is consistent with Johnson's hypothesis.

Given that the average voter is motivated by rational self-interest not to acquire much information about the policies of political parties and their impact on personal economic welfare—well-informed or not—his or her influence on which party is elected is negligible. Ideology then steps in to play a key role in political affairs and to simplify a political party's problems of communicating with its electorate. Its policies can be summarized in symbolism or slogans. Thus the voter's problem is also simplified since one can vote by ideology instead of investing time in evaluating each party's record and promises on a range of policy issues. As a result, parties will tend to compete through ideologies.

According to the above sources in established democracies, the type of party system that emerges will depend on a variety of features including: (1) the distribution among voters of ideological preferences; and (2) the type of election system, whether by proportional representation or by plurality and geographical distribution of voter preferences. Thus, proportionality will tend to foster a multiplicity of ideologically differentiated parties. Plurality election will tend to promote a two-party system, except where ideological differences are associated with a geographical region. Actual policy in a multiparty system will tend to present a compromise among ideologies because coalitions must be formed to obtain power. In two-party systems, the relation of party ideologies will be determined by the distribution of voter preferences for ideologies. If the distribution of voter preference for ideologies is unimodal, there will be a grouping around a central ideological position, and party ideologies will not differ significantly. On the other hand, if voter preferences are multimodal, then voter preferences that will group around two or more ideological positions become very important. And if a party departs too significantly from its ideological position, it may alienate its constituents, who will tend not to vote. Worse yet, if party ideologies are significantly differentiated, the country itself will tend to be politically unstable and ripe for disintegration.

Matters are somewhat different when democracy is not well established. The incentive is for a political party to attempt to create a comprehensive and preclusive ideology to enable it to enjoy exclusive control of government. Emerging countries, observes Johnson, are particularly susceptible. This is reinforced when emerging countries experience a change in government and impose significant costs on those who have to wait for political office, in contrast with those holding permanent power and political office. Even in developed democracies, the change of office by political parties tends to be wasteful, while the economic and sociopolitical system tends to reabsorb ousted political officeholders without imposing great private losses on them. Consequently, it is the ability of the economic and sociopolitical system not to impose undue losses on political losers, as well as the acceptance of the "rules of the game" of democracies and their principles, that is important in cultivating workable democracies.

It is this nationalistic feeling that provides the foundation for the establishment of a preclusive ideology as a prerequisite for a single-party government. Johnson calls attention to the connection between the stridency of nationalism in emerging countries and their propensity to establish a one-party government. Even where the two-party system is maintained, the competition in ideology would tend to make both parties stress nationalism and nationalist policies if there were widespread nationalist sentiment among the electorate. Johnson succinctly observes that only if there is a sharp division of voter preferences, with some votes having the potential for serious disadvantages, will there be a significant political division on the issues and the likelihood of a threat to political stability.

Moreover, Downs underscores that the workings of political democracy will display a certain asymmetry between producer and consumer interests. The concentration will be on producer interests often at the expense of those of the consumer. Johnson extends this observation to nationalism and nationalistic policies. Since producer costs can be spread thinly over a mass of consumers, nationalist policies win political support more readily by promoting producer interests, even though the net benefits, for both consumers and producers, tend to be negative.

A TASTE FOR NATIONALISM

Thus far, our theoretical framework outlines the workings of the political democracy and party government integration into the framework of nationalism in emerging countries. We can draw on Becker's work on racial discrimination and Johnson's interpretation of nationalism as a cultivated preference, calling it a "taste for nationalism." This is identical with Becker's concept of a "taste for discrimination." That is, people who discriminate are willing to give up pecuniary returns for the nonpecuniary or psychic income derived from avoiding the group discriminated against—in Becker's study, blacks in the United States. Johnson substitutes "taste for nationalism" for Becker's "taste for discrimination." Accordingly, the taste for nationalism attaches utility to certain jobs or certain property owned by members of the national group, even though pecuniary return is forfeited in the exercise of such tastes.

The types of property and jobs to which such utility is attached are obviously the prestige jobs and socially significant property. These include, for example, the literary and cultural activities. Others include political and economic activities and properties with high prestige and incomes. The nationalist utility attached to the various properties, jobs, and cultural and other activities is derived internally from an emerging country's colonial era and externally by observing what takes place in more developed countries.

Nationalism is a collective consumption good or public good the consumption of which by one individual does not exclude its consumption by others. The problem is one of determining the optimum amount of nationalism to supply. The specific benefits of nationalism obviously go to those select nationals who acquire offices and property rights in which nationalism invests. This would include the bureaucracy, the elite, and producer interests. Thanks to the desire of cultural, linguistic, and communication interests to cultivate monopoly power, they are natural beneficiaries of a policy of economic nationalism. All of these interests are vulnerable to foreign competition.

Since everyone in the national state must consume the same quantity and quality of the public "nationalism" good, even though their preferences and tax payments for the good may vary, it is not surprising that there is considerable controversy regarding the output and resource input of public goods by the nation-state. Some consumers want more and some want less. Few will agree that the optimal quantity is truly optimal.[2]

As we have noted, collective decisions in political markets are complex. People can communicate their desires for public goods through voting behavior. Still, what a consumer-voter desires in a political market may be significantly different from what he ultimately receives. The correlation between a voter's choice and the expected outcome may be very weak. Efficient political decisions tend to affect everyone in the community, unlike decisions in a private market, which affect primarily the consumer and supplier of a given product or service.

If the demand for nationalism as a "club good" by the elite and bureaucracy is added to the demand by the general population for nationalism as a public good, it is likely that there will be an overproduction of nationalism. This will tend to allocate too many resources for the creation and preservation of the nation-state, including a formidable bureaucracy and military.

Thus, it is imperative that the bureaucracy and elite be discouraged and constrained from the use of nationalism to maximize their returns and advantages. One way is to structure the incentive system so as to prevent or limit the abuse of their authority. The method this study recommends is a system of well-defined guides within lawful policy systems. In effect, it argues for a system of rules that constrains the bureaucracies and elites from the discretionary exercise of power. The more closely constrained their actions are by rules or performance criteria, the less their power and prestige, and the less their interests will coalesce with the promotion of excess production of nationalism.

As a public good, economic nationalism appeals to the elite, the bureaucracy, and perhaps specific producer interests, whereas the costs are spread out over the mass of consumers. The political support for nationalist economic policies is obtained from the gains they promise to their constituents, even if the total net benefits to all concerned tend to be negative.

As a policy economic nationalism is encumbered by at least three biases.[3] First, it concentrates on industrialization, usually at the expense of agriculture. The objective here is to achieve a modern looking nation-state as quickly as possible. The bias for industrialization is usually specific about the types of industries to encourage. The selection is more on the criteria of what leading developed nations possess than on any comparative advantage and economic logic. A steel industry, an automobile industry, and a national airline are the more obvious choices.

The second bias is a preference for economic planning. There is the feeling that controls associated with planning enable a country to mobilize available resources more quickly to achieve other desired goals of nationalism. The Soviet Union's experience and its rapid postrevolution development into a world power recommend a similar course of national economic planning to some people. There is, in general, the perception that the processes of economic development are speeded up as a result of planning. Finally, the elite and the bureaucracy see planning as a direct means to exercise and enhance their power and prestige.

The third bias in a policy of economic nationalism is indiscriminate hostility to large multinational or transnational corporations. They are viewed as agents of colonialism and imperialism on the part of the advanced countries in which they happen to have their headquarters—as a threat to national sovereignty and independence. In effect, these corporations are viewed simply as an arm of the economic and political power of their parent countries. Since these corporations are more than likely independent entities, they are viewed suspiciously by both host and parent countries. The parent countries complain that such corporations should invest and produce more at home rather than send employment opportunities abroad, creating balance-of-payments problems for the country.

It may be that the nonpecuniary gains by the mass population from collective consumption aspects of nationalism offset the loss in primary income imposed on them by policies of economic nationalism, so that nationalistic policies do result in maximizing total satisfaction. In effect, it may also be that nationalistic policies are the simplest and cheapest means of raising real income in some emerging countries.[4] Economic nationalism may block economic growth to the extent that it becomes necessary to resort to even more extreme nationalistic sentiment and policy as the only means available to maintain the illusion of economic development.

Thus the economic significance of nationalism is to cultivate and extend property rights and jobs to nationals to satisfy their taste for nationalism. Confiscation and nationalization are ways to implement these policies. This would include property and, very likely, jobs. Investment is another route whereby public funds are used to purchase property and create jobs and activities on behalf of nationals. It would also include imposing tariffs and, in general, protecting the activities of nationals who would receive higher prices, which are, in effect, taxes imposed on the general consumer.

By reducing the efficiency of the country's economy, these by-products of economic nationalism will also reduce its real income. Disappointment with the economy's performance increasingly pushes the government into setting prices and wages to assure desired outcomes. This will typically lead to price and wage controls. Since wage and price controls inevitably fail, the system is increasingly driven into collective participatory planning where wages and prices are determined. This may, in fact, be desired by some people. Nevertheless, such an arrangement offers little chance that the market system will be allowed to play its effective and efficient role.

The inevitable failure of price and wage controls is readily demonstrated by considering some problems and consequences of prices for individual products and services, including wages. The effects of a fixed price for a product or service depend on the level at which it is fixed and whether it is a minimum or a maximum price.

To illustrate the issues, let us suppose we set up an administrative agency to fix prices. Now suppose this agency fixed the price of a commodity or service precisely at the level at which it would fall relative to other prices if there were no price controls, with the price establishment by free-market forces. In this case, the price control would have no effect, and our agency performed a needless exercise. Of course, the administrative costs incurred by this exercise would be borne by the taxpayer.

Now suppose that our agency sets a fixed price which is a maximum price, but it sets the price at some level lower than what the price would be if it were determined by free-market forces. Shortages would appear.

People would want to buy more of the commodity or service than they otherwise would, but less of the product or service would be produced than normally would be. Why should less of the product be produced at this lower price? The reason is simply that at this lower price, it becomes more profitable to produce other items whose prices are not fixed at this lower level. Now if more is demanded than supplied, then some system determines who among the people is going to get the product or service in question. This can be done by attaching another office to our price-administering agency, whose function will be to issue coupons or the product, or service can be given to old and regular customers of the suppliers, or it can be done according to the rule of "first come, first served." This is, of course, the familiar case of the queue, with the loss in time spent waiting one's turn.

If less of a product or service is produced because its price is fixed too low, it must be that fewer resources are employed. Now, what happened to those resources? They simply moved to other industries, producing products and services whose prices were not controlled. Ironically, since prices tend to be controlled in "essential" industries and not controlled in "unessential" industries, this means that price controls tend to cause fewer of the essential products or services to be produced and more of the unessential products or services.

However, the above need not be the case since the government can induce producers of the commodity or service in question to produce more at this lower price by offering them an incentive (subsidy). All this means is that producers now receive a higher price, raised "artificially" by the government subsidy. In general, the taxpayer will now bear not only the cost of the price-administering agency but also the additional cost of the subsidy.

Consider our last case, in which a minimum price is fixed at a level higher than that which would prevail in a free market. Now there will be initial surpluses. At the higher price for the product or service more will be produced. Instead of rationing consumers, it will now be necessary to "ration" the production of the product or service among the many producers who would be willing to produce at this higher price. Again, as in the case of consumers, this can be done by attaching to our price-administering agency an office whose function will be to allocate by quota production of the product or service in question.

In general, this has been a familiar problem with U.S. agricultural surpluses in the past. In this case, the taxpayer as a consumer will very likely pay the higher price for the product or service as well as the cost of the administering agency.

Selective price controls cannot avoid discrimination. If a producer's selling price is fixed, there is usually an obligation to control his costs. This means fixing more than the prices of a producer's more obvious inputs, such as labor and raw materials. It also means that such items as taxes, interest costs, and business costs must also be fixed.

Control over labor costs is the most difficult. Such elements of labor costs as fringe benefits, compensation for overtime work, shift differentials, and paid leave serve to complicate the already difficult task of setting wage rates. The U.S. federal minimum wage example will suffice to illustrate the difficulties in setting wage rates.[5]

The inverse relation between changes in the minimum wage and substitution (capital for labor) effects one would expect from economic theory appears to be confirmed. When information on evasion and violations of the minimum wage law is taken into account, considerable light is shed on the complexities of wage fixing. In effect, an increase in the minimum wage is equivalent to a reduction in the price of evasion and avoidance. The price of evasion and avoidance is the cost of evasion and avoidance minus the benefits of evasion and avoidance. The benefit has increased with the increase in the minimum wage. Other things being equal, one would expect evasion and avoidance of the minimum wage to increase. This also appears to be confirmed by the evidence.[6]

The minimum wage has had adverse effects on wage differentials.[7] These differentials serve a useful purpose in allocating labor services into various occupations. In fact, they are an essential part of the price mechanism. When they are subjected to an autonomous shock in the form of a government fiat, a compression of wage differentials occurs. The wages of those directly affected by the rise in the minimum wage rise more than the wages of those not so directly affected. Since it is not so easy to allocate labor services as it is other services and goods, the problem of production adjustments is aggravated.

Matters are further complicated by difficulties in defining exactly what it is that is being controlled. Failure to specify accurately the end product or service leads to the inevitable tendency to increase profit margins by cutting quality, particularly where shortages already exist. The problem is not simply one of quality deterioration. There is also a tendency for the variety of products to be reduced.

In light of domestic price and wage ceilings, there is always a tendency for a producer to sell abroad at a higher price. When the producer is allocated fewer productive resources than he desires, he may seek to increase his supply by imports. This inevitably leads to price controls and physical controls over imports, such as foreign exchange controls and import and export quotas. The general direction in which a country with such controls is pushed forces its government and bureaucracy to become the sole judge of the volume and direction new investment will take. Government and its bureaucracy dominate the field of new investments through profit and sales policies.

Even more important, failure to allow the market system to play its effective and efficient role almost assures that money and the monetary system will not be allowed to play a nondiscriminatory and autonomous role within the constraints of the rules-based policy system so necessary to assure the preservation of economic and monetary stability in the country.

Worse still, the pursuit of economic nationalism in today's inter-dependent world can be a threat to worldwide stability. For small and emerging nations in particular, it is a prescription for disaster, since they are most likely to be dependent on foreign trade and the goodwill of other nations. Promoting economic nationalism through various protective measures invites and encourages retaliation by others, as we would expect from our theory of cooperation. These activities serve to undermine the stability not only of the nation-state promoting economic nationalism but of world cooperation and prosperity as well.

NOTES

1. See Harry G. Johnson, ed., *Economic Nationalism in Old and New States* (Chicago: University of Chicago Press, 1967); Albert Breton, "The Economics of Nationalism," *Journal of Political Economy*, vol. 72 (1964),

pp. 376–86; Anthony Downs, *An Economic Theory of Democracy* (New York: Harper, 1957); Gary S. Becker, *The Economics of Discrimination* (Chicago: University of Chicago Press, 1957); George Macesich, *Commercial Banking and Regional Development in the United States: 1950–60* (Tallahassee: Florida State University Press, 1963); George Macesich, *Yugoslavia: The Theory and Practice of Development Planning* (Charlottesville: University Press of Virginia, 1964); George Macesich, "The Theory of Economic Integration and the Experience of the Balkan and Danubian Countries Before 1914," *Proceedings of the First International Congress on Southeast European Studies*, Sofia, Bulgaria (1966) and *Florida State University Slavic Papers I* (1967); George Macesich, "Economic Theory and the Austro-Hungarian Ausgleich of 1867," in *Der Österreichischungarische Ausgleich, 1967*, Ludovit Holitik, ed., (Bratislava: Slovak Academy, 1971); George Macesich, *Geldpolitik in einem gemeinsamen europäischen Markt* [Money in a common-market setting] (Baden-Baden: Nomos Verlagsgesellschaft, 1972); George Macesich, "Supply and Demand for Money in Canada," in *Varieties of Monetary Experience*, David Meiselman, ed. (Chicago: University of Chicago Press, 1971), pp. 249–96.

2. James M. Buchanan, *The Demand and Supply of Public Goods* (Chicago: Rand McNally, 1968); James Buchanan and Gordon Tullock, *The Calculus of Consent* (Ann Arbor: University of Michigan Press, 1962); Fred R. Gladbe and Dwight R. Lee, *Microeconomics: Theory and Applications* (New York: Harcourt Brace Jovanovich, 1980); Ronald Coase, "The Problem of Social Cost," *The Journal of Law and Economics* (October 1960), pp. 1–45.

3. Harry G. Johnson, "Ideology of Economic Policy in New States," in *Economic Nationalism in Old and New States*, Harry G. Johnson, ed. (Chicago: University of Chicago Press, 1967), pp. 129–30.

4. Harry G. Johnson, ed., *Economic Nationalism*, p. 15.

5. George Macesich and Charles T. Stewart, Jr., "Recent Department of Labor Studies of Minimum Wage Effects," *Southern Economic Journal* (April 1960); Marshall R. Colberg, "Minimum Wage Effects on Florida Economic Development," *Journal of Law and Economics* (October 1960); John M. Peterson, "Recent Needs in Minimum Wage Theory," *Southern Economic Journal* (July 1962); Yale Brozen, "Minimum Wages and Household Workers," *Journal of Law and Economics* (October 1962); and L. G. Reynolds, "Wages and Employment in the Labor-Surplus Economy," *American Economic Review* (March 1965).

6. Macesich and Stewart, "Recent Department of Labor Studies," pp. 288ff.

7. George Macesich, "Are Wage Differentials Resilient? An Empirical Test," *Southern Economic Journal* (April 1961).

EXERCISE 6-2. Complete this Benedictus.

EXERCISE 6-3. Complete in double counterpoint at the octave. Design the counterpoint in the first two measures so that it will make a successful counterpoint in the last two measures.

*EXERCISE 6-4. Write a two-part setting of "Gloria in excelsis Deo" for Sopranos I and II. Use triple meter. Length: 8 to 12 measures.

*EXERCISE 6-5. Write a two-part motet on the following text:
PU-er NA-tus in BETH-le-hem,
UN-de GAU-det Je-RU-sa-lem,
Al-le-LU-ia.
(A child is born in Bethlehem, therefore rejoice Jerusalem, alleluia.)

Sources for Further Study

Scores:

See the list of scores at the end of Chapter 3.

Readings:

Gauldin—16th c.: pp. 39–41; 55–60; 63–75

Jeppesen: pp. 152–174; 241–250

Merritt: pp. 104–120

Morley: pp. 292–294

Roberts and Fischer: 87–94

Smith: pp. 20–21; 36–37; 53–55; 65–70

CHAPTER

7

Two-Part Secular Music

Instrumental Duo; Canzonet

Instrumental Duo

Sixteenth–century composers wrote for instruments in much the same way as they wrote for voices, but some important differences may be found. Examine Ex. 7-1.

EX. 7-1 From *Musica à due voci*, 1598 by Giovanni Gastoldi (1550–1622)

Questions for Discussion

Compare Ex. 7-1 with the motet-style pieces, Ex. 2-1b, Ex. 3-1, and Ex. 6-1.

1. What do motet style and instrumental style have in common? Discuss melodic treatment, use of consonant and dissonant intervals, cadences, rhythm, imitation, range, length of phrases, and formal construction.
2. How do motet style and instrumental style differ?
3. What gives Ex. 7-1 its playful mood? What tempo would you suggest?
4. What instruments (other than recorders) could play the piece? Example 7-1 has been transcribed an octave above the original notation. What instruments of the period might have been used? Assuming that transposition is appropriate, what modern instruments could be used?

Observations

If supplied with appropriate text, much of the instrumental music of the sixteenth century would be virtually indistinguishable from music composed with text, except for keyboard and lute music. The same principles of melodic writing, use of consonance and dissonance, cadence construction, and use of imitation apply to instrumental and choral music alike.

The differences between instrumental and choral music are subtle. Phrase lengths tend to be shorter, repeated notes and quick figures more easily played than sung are encountered, a more extended range is possible, and sequences are more plentiful in instrumental music. The interplay of short motives occurs more frequently than extended points of imitation.

The Gastoldi duet, Ex. 7-1, demonstrates all of these traits. The repeated note figure introduced in m. 20, the close imitation beginning in m. 30, the playful figure beginning in m. 34, then treated to double counterpoint at m. 40, the "hopping" figure at m. 51, and the quick cascading instrumental figure beginning in m. 58 all give the piece its playful mood and at the same time suggest a sprightly tempo.

As is usual with most composers of the time, Gastoldi did not write the piece for specific instruments. It could be played successfully by various Renaissance winds and strings, especially recorders, cornetti, viols, or even two lutes. Modern winds, brass, or strings could be used for performance if the appropriate key and tessitura are chosen for the transcription.

Exercises

EXERCISE 7-1. Complete the alto recorder part.

Soprano
Recorder

Alto
Recorder

EXERCISE 7-2. Complete this canon for two cellos or viole da gamba.

*EXERCISE 7-3. Write a short duet based on the following subject for two trombones or sackbuts. Length: about 20 measures.

Canzonet

Morley has provided us with fine examples of secular vocal writing in his two-part canzonets, one of which is shown in Ex. 7-2.

EX. 7-2 "I goe before my darling" from *Canzonets to two voyces*, 1595, by Thomas Morley (1557–1602)

Questions for Discussion

1. How is the setting of the secular text in Ex. 7-2 different from the setting of the texts of the sacred choral pieces we have examined?
2. How and where has Morley used word painting?
3. How do Morley's cadences differ from those we have studied?
4. Is there anything new in the use of dissonance?
5. What is the formal design of this piece? How is it like a motet? How is it not like a motet?
6. How does Morley manage voice crossing?
7. How does Morley use accidentals in this piece?
8. How would you describe the implied harmonies?

Observations

Sacred texts were familiar enough in a liturgical setting that composers were not primarily concerned with the communication of the words themselves; it was more important for a motet to convey the mood and spirit of the text. But in the case of secular texts it was more important for the words to be understood. One way to accomplish this was to use more syllabic text setting, saving melismas for special or important words. Another was to repeat lines or phrases of the text. Yet another was to use rather obvious word painting.

"I goe before my darling" strongly suggests strict imitation, which Morley gives us in abundance. At "Follow thou to the bowre in the close alley" the imitation is "close"—a mere two quarters. The distance closes to just one quarter for "sweetly kisse each eyther," and the playful triple meter setting of the word "dally" feeds our imagination.

Cadences in motet-style composition most often were prepared by a suspension followed by a tenth, sixth, or third, and finally resolving in contrary motion to an octave or unison. In Morley's secular pieces we find some new cadential types: (1) authentic cadences with leap of a fourth or fifth in the bass (mm. 6, 15, 28–29, and 40–41); (2) cadences in parallel motion, third to third (mm. 8–9, 17–18, 32–33, and 44–45); (3) cadences in contrary motion, tritone to third (mm. 5 and 14). The remaining cadences (mm. 21, 25, and 36–37) are more regular except that the suspensions are not tied to accommodate the text.

The use of dissonance in Ex. 7-2 is the same as in motet style except for the harmonic use of the tritone in mm. 3, 5, 12, and 14. In all cases the tritone resolves immediately to a third. The harmonic impression is similar to that of the dominant seventh resolving to the tonic in tonal music.

The structure of the piece presents the scheme "aabcdcd." Each new idea is presented as a point for imitation, a trait common to motets as well. The phrases, however, are generally shorter than those of a motet, and cadences are therefore more frequent. Repetition with the voices switching roles as leader and follower is much more common to secular than to sacred choral music.

The piece is for equal voices, and voice crossings are a special feature. The effect of rapid and frequent crossing adds to the playful mood of the piece. Morley uses two methods to accomplish voice crossing: (1) one voice is stationary while the other leaps over or under it, and (2) the voices cross in contrary motion. Voices are not allowed to cross when they are moving in similar motion.

Rather than depending on the singers to apply the usual musica ficta, Morley indicates accidentals for leading tones at cadences. The E♭s (mm. 20, 30, and 42) are for harmonic coloring since they are not needed to avoid a tritone or to satisfy the "nota supra la" musica ficta condition (see Ex. 3-1, m. 29).

The short phrases and frequent cadences give an impression of tonal rather than modal harmony. It is in secular music that the newest style elements first appear; sacred music reflects changes in style much later. The implied harmonies in this canzonet approach modern functional harmony. A keyboard instrument such as a virginal could play the continuo accompaniment to the opening shown in Ex. 7-3 without destroying the character of the piece.

EX. 7-3 Continuo accompaniment for the opening of Ex. 7-2

Exercises

EXERCISE 7-4. Fill in the missing parts.

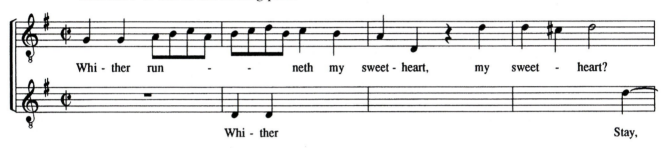

Whi - ther run - - neth my sweet - heart, my sweet - heart?

Whi - ther   Stay,

___ stay,___ stay,___ stay___ just for one more_____ kiss!

EXERCISE 7-5. Supply an appropriate meter and an appropriate clef. Add a signature if needed.

Rich man, poor man,   beg - gar man, thief, be ye

Rich man, poor   man,   beg - gar man, thief,

tink - er, tail - or, In - di - an chief?

tink - er, tail - or,   In - di - an chief?

EXERCISE 7-6. Name the contrapuntal device which is exemplified by Ex. 7-5.

*EXERCISE 7-7. Write a two-part canzonet on one of the following texts:

> a) Love learns by laughing first to speak,
> Then shyly gains cares passing great.
>> But I will laugh without that care,
>> And bid Love touch me if he dare.

> b) Away, thou shalt not love me!
> Away, thou shalt not love me!
>> So shall my love seem greater,
>> And I shall love thee better,
> Shall it be so, what say you?
> Why speak you not, I pray you?
>> Nay then I know you love me,
>> That so you may disprove me.

> c) Too much I once lamented,
> While love my heart tormented,
> Alas and Ay me, sat I wringing,
> Now chanting go I and singing.

Sources for Further Study

Scores:

In addition to the list of scores at the end of Chapter 3, the following sources contain secular vocal and instrumental duos:

Banchieri: Duos from *Cartella musicale,* 1614

Galilei: Duets from *Fromino,* 1568

Gastoldi: *Il primo libro della musica a due voci,* 1598

Lupacchino and Tasso: *Il primo libro a due voci,* 1559

Morley: *Canzonets to two voyces,* 1595. (There are nine instrumental fantasias in this collection.)

Sweelinck: *Rimes françcoises et italiennes,* 1612

CHAPTER
8

Three-Part Counterpoint

Motet; Canzonet; Fantasia

Motet

Counterpoint in three parts is richer both harmonically and rhythmically than counterpoint in two parts. Three-part textures also give the student many new challenges. Examine Ex. 8-1.

EX. 8-1 Hymn setting, *Sub tanto duci* by Palestrina (1525–1594)

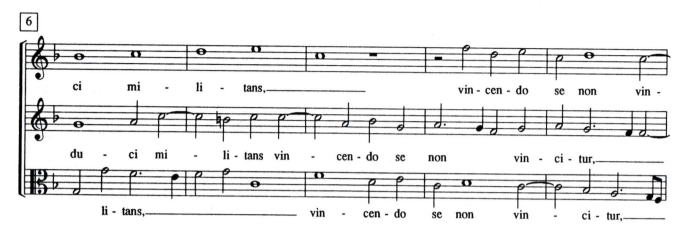

Under such a great leader, the warrior, by conquering himself, is not conquered. Dwelling with the leader, the soldier is not confounded by war.

Questions for Discussion

1. What musical entity can be constructed with three parts, but can only be implied by two?
2. How many two-voice combinations are present in three-part polyphony?
3. Omit the top part and analyze the piece as a two-part motet. What do you find?
4. What do you find if you omit the middle part?
5. What do you find if you omit the lowest part?
6. How is the motion distributed among the three parts? Where do you find only two parts?
7. Where are the cadences? What cadence types do you find?
8. How does the formal plan of this hymn setting compare with the formal plan of a two-part motet?

Observations

Harmonic Structures

Although two-part texture can imply triadic harmony, it takes at least three parts to create complete triads—with root, third, and fifth all present. Triads can also be implied in three-part texture if one chord member is doubled and one is omitted. A quick scan of the vertical sonorities in this piece shows that when all members of a triad are not present, it is usually the fifth which has been omitted, in which case the root is most often doubled. You will have found that most of the triads are in root position, some are in first inversion, and when a triad is used in second inversion, the fourth is treated as a prepared dissonance (suspension, passing tone, neighbor tone, etc.).

In three-voice textures there are three two-voice combinations to be considered: (a) lowest and highest voices; (b) lowest and middle; and (c) middle and highest. All three combinations follow the principles of two-voice counterpoint which we have discussed thus far, with one important exception: a perfect fourth or a tritone *between the upper two parts* may be used as if it were a consonance when the lowest part combines with them to make a triad or other appropriate sonority. In Ex. 8-1, m. 11, the tritone between E and B♭ in the upper two parts would not be used if the lower part were not present to create an appropriate triad. Example 8-2 shows where a fourth or tritone may be used between the upper voices in three-part textures.

EX. 8-2 Appropriate sonorities with fourth or tritone between the upper parts

| Chord position: | 8 5 | 6 3 | 6 3 | 6 3 | 6 3 | 8 5 |

Two other harmonic structures also are found in textures of three or more parts: (a) the 6/5 harmony, and (b) the so-called "consonant fourth." You will notice in Ex. 8-1, m. 7, that the C in the middle part makes a fifth with the lower part, and at the same time the D in the upper part makes a sixth. Both upper parts are consonant with the bass but are dissonant with each other. The C, however, is properly suspended against the D. The resulting harmony is a 6/5 chord which moves immediately to a 5/3 chord. In the final cadence of Ex. 8-1, m. 28, the F in the middle part creates a fourth with the lower part and then is treated like a 4-3 suspension. The preparation for the suspension is a "consonant fourth." Ex. 8-3 illustrates both of these structures.

EX. 8-3 **Other possible constructions: (a) the 6/5 harmony, and (b) the consonant fourth.**

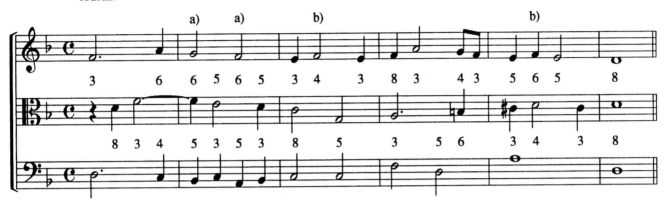

Rhythmic Considerations and Cadences

Three-part texture gains rhythmic variety from the distribution of motion among the parts. Considering each measure of Ex. 8-1, each part seems to have a rhythm which is different from either of the others, but there are places where two parts move in the same rhythm in opposition to the third (mm. 16-17), and still others where all move in nearly the same rhythm (m. 14). Two-part sections occur: (1) before the third voice enters, and (2) following cadences when one of the voices rests.

The cadences are at the end of each phrase of text, as we have seen before. The various parts may cadence at different times (mm. 11–12) or together (mm. 14 and 29). One voice may allow the others to cadence while it has a rest in preparation for a new phrase (mm. 21 and 24). As we have noted before, a "full stop" is reserved for the final cadence.

The cadence types familiar to you from harmony and analysis courses (with the exception of the half cadence) appear in Ex. 8-1: authentic (m. 29), plagal (m. 14), and deceptive (m. 18). Modal cadences are still used frequently in the sixteenth century, especially the Phrygian. Example 8-4 shows some examples.

EX. 8-4 **Phrygian cadences**

Three-part motets such as the Palestrina hymn setting, Ex. 8-1, exhibit the same formal characteristics as two-part motets; each phrase of the text begins with a new point of imitation and ends with a cadence. Overlapping may occur when one voice begins a new point of imitation while the others complete a cadence. This device helps to keep the music flowing smoothly.

Exercises

EXERCISE **8**-**1**. (a) Complete this three-part canon. (b) Continue the interval identification and label dissonant tones. (c) Identify all complete triads by root and quality.

EXERCISE **8-2**. (a) Continue the treble part in whole notes to create a first species counterpoint. (b) Convert the middle part to second species by changing the whole-notes to half notes and adding a half note to each measure but the last. (c) Using your solution to (a), convert the bass part to third species (all quarter notes except for the final measure).

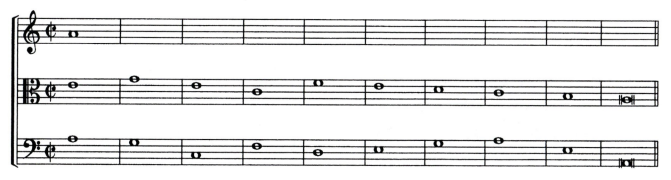

EXERCISE **8-3**. Add a treble part to this *Magnificat* verse.

*EXERCISE **8-4**. Provide the outer parts.

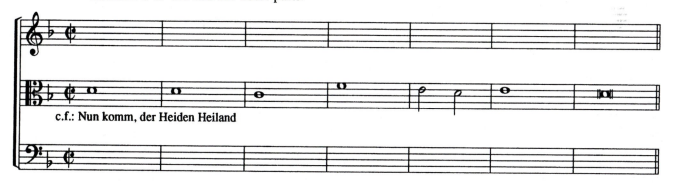

*EXERCISE **8-5**. Write a three-voice Kyrie eleison (about 12 measures).

Canzonet

In Chapter 7 we examined a two-part canzonet by Morley. Example 8-5 is one in three parts for comparison by his contemporary Thomas Weelkes.

EX. 8-5 Canzonet: "The nightingale, the organ of delight" by Thomas Weelkes (1576–1623)

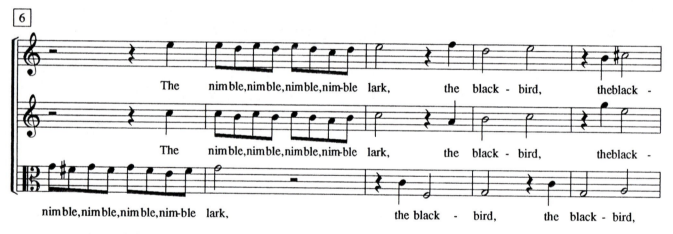

Questions for Discussion

1. After comparing this canzonet with the Palestrina hymn (Ex. 8-1), what observations can you make about three-part secular music compared to three-part sacred music?
2. Other than the text itself, what does Weelkes use to articulate form in this piece?
3. Discuss the word painting in the piece.
4. Describe the cadences and the key scheme.
5. What textural element is present here which we have not previously encountered?

Observations

The differences between secular and sacred music in three parts are the same as those we found in two-part music. Secular music exhibits a tendency toward shorter phrases, there is more interest in motivic development, text setting is more syllabic, more explicit word painting is used, cadences are more clear-cut, and harmonic progressions tend to be more tonal than modal.

If there were no text in Ex. 8-5, the form would still be quite clear because of the shifts in the texture. Each section presents a different arrangement of the voices, sometimes imitating from top voice down, sometimes from lower voice up, sometimes two together against the third, and sometimes all have the same rhythm. The strong cadences also help to delineate formal sections. Paired phrases approach the effect of periodic structure.

Birds were a favorite subject for sixteenth–century composers. The melodiousness of the nightingale, the nimbleness of the lark, the solemnity of the blackbird, and the distinctive song of the cuckoo are set with appropriate music by Weelkes. Objective word painting was considered suitable for secular music, whereas a more subjective type of musical representation of the mood and meaning of the text was considered more appropriate for sacred music.

A clear key scheme emerges as we look at the cadences. In spite of the lack of an F♯ in the signature, the piece is in G major. The nightingale gives us a G-major triad, and the phrase ends with an authentic cadence at "delight." The lark takes us briefly to C, the blackbird to D, and the thrush brings a half cadence in the tonic key, which is established by "the pretty choristers," ending in an authentic cadence in G at the word "bush." The phrase which introduces the cuckoo ends with a cadence to the dominant on "excell," and the cuckoo, using nothing but primary chords, brings us to the close with a ringing authentic cadence in the tonic, G major.

At m. 23, the texture is *homorhythmic:* all parts have the same rhythm. This phrase serves as an "island of homophony" in a sea of counterpoint. This is often referred to as *familiar style.* It provides some relief from constant polyphony and at the same time allows for clearer declamation of the text. Motets sometimes have sections in familiar style, but secular music makes far greater use of it. Canzonets and madrigals often begin with a homophonic texture.

Exercises

EXERCISE **8-6.** Supply the missing parts.

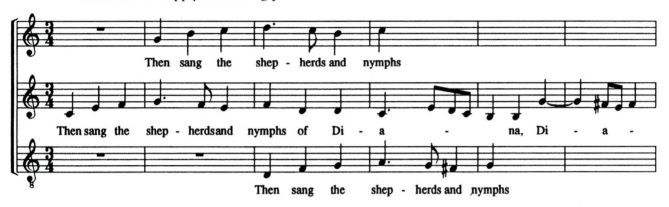

Then sang the shep - herds and nymphs

Then sang the shep - herdsand nymphs of Di - a - na, Di - a -

Then sang the shep - herds and nymphs

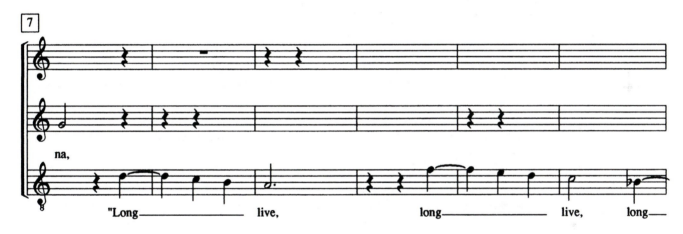

na,

"Long⸺ live, long⸺ live, long⸺

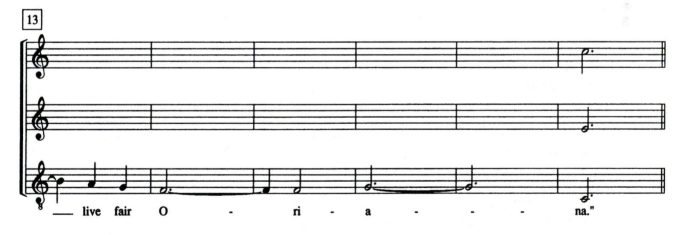

⸺ live fair O - ri - a - - na."

EXERCISE 8-7. Complete the following opening of a balletto. Set the verse in familiar style and the "fa la" in imitative style.

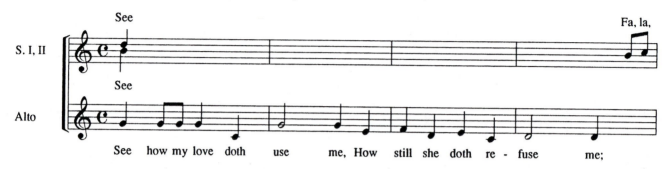

*EXERCISE 8-8. Set this Italian verse for three tenors in the style of a canzonet. The accented syllables are shown in upper case. The opening measures are given below.

> AHI, di-spe-RA-ta VI-ta,
> *Ah, life without hope*
> che fug-GEN-do il MI-o BE-ne
> *that, fleeing my beloved,*
> mi-se-ra-MEN-te CA-de in MIL-le PE-ne!
> *falls miserably into boundless distress!*
> DEH, TOR-na AL-la TU-a LU-ce AL-ma e gra-DI-ta
> *Oh, it returns to your pure and pleasant light*
> che TI vuol DAR a-I-ta!
> *for it desires your help!*

Fantasia

The fantasia is an imitative instrumental piece which resembles the motet in construction. Example 8-6 shows a three-part English fantasia.

EX. 8-6 Fantasia by William Byrd (1543–1623)

Questions for Discussion

1. How does this piece resemble a motet (such as Ex. 8-1)?
2. Where do the "points of imitation" begin? How many statements of the "point," which begins in m. 24, can you find?
3. What type of dissonance has Byrd used after m. 24 which we have not yet discussed?
4. How does this piece differ in construction from a motet?

Observations

Like the motet, the fantasia is made up of several sections, each beginning with a point of imitation and proceeding to a cadence. Each new point is different from its predecessor in melodic shape and rhythm. In our example, the first "point" or "subject" is characterized by a fall of a third and a syncopation. As the upper parts complete a cadence in m. 10, the bass part begins the second subject, characterized by a rising tetrachord. The third subject enters in m. 24 in close imitation between the lower parts. It consists of three notes descending stepwise to a cambiata figure and rising scale of eighth notes. It is developed extensively from there to the end, appearing no less than eighteen times in one form or another.

This figure ends with rising scale motion followed by a fall of a third. Several times the highest note of the scale makes a dissonance with one of the parts. The falling third which follows it disqualifies it as a passing tone or neighbor tone. It is, in fact, an escape tone or échappé. It appears in second and third species as shown in Ex. 8-7.

EX. 8-7 Escape tones

Each of the three subjects in the fantasia has been stated several times before a new subject is introduced. This pervasive development of the subject material is a special feature of the fantasia and its cousins, the ricercar and canzona (which are discussed in Chapter 14). This quasi-fugal treatment sets these forms apart from the motet.

Exercises

EXERCISE 8-9. Provide two upper parts for "The Browning" tune given in the bass.

EXERCISE 8-10. Complete the variation below using the following basic pitches:

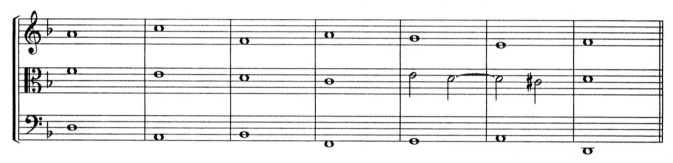

Variation:

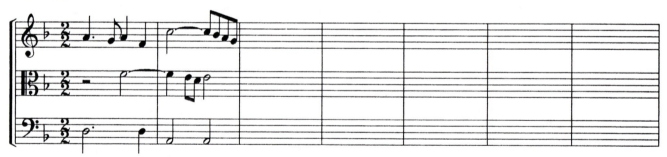

*****EXERCISE 8-11.** Using this as a beginning, write a short fantasia (15 to 20 measures) for the three brass instruments indicated.

*EXERCISE 8-12. Write two variations for three recorders on "The Carman's Whistle," one with the tune in the upper voice, the other with the tune in the middle voice.

Sources for Further Study

Scores:

MASSES AND MOTETS:

The Benedictus sections of masses by Palestrina, Lasso, Victoria, and others are often set in three parts.

Byrd: *Mass for three voyces*

Lasso: Three-part psalm settings

CANZONETS (SEE FELLOWS: ENGLISH MADRIGAL SCHOOL)

Morley: *Canzonets to three voyces,* 1593

Weelkes: *Ayres for three voyces,* 1598

Wilbye: Second set of madrigals to three, four, five, and six voyces, 1609

FANTASIAS:

Byrd: Fantasias for three parts

Gibbons: Fantasias for three parts

Josquin: "La Bernardina"

Readings:

Gauldin—16th c.: pp. 76–104; 120–134

Jeppesen: pp. 175–201

Merritt: pp. 144–166

Morley: pp. 42–52; 54–56; 78–84; 98; 173–185

Roberts and Fischer: 63–85

Salzer/Schachter: pp. 25–37; 71–77; 90–100; 110–113

Smith: pp. 71–95

CHAPTER

9

Four-Part Counterpoint

Dance Variations; Motet; Madrigal

Dance Variations

The *passamezzo* is a sixteenth–century Italian dance in duple meter based on a fixed succession of harmonies which form the basis for variations (see Ex. 9-1). It is similar to the pavan, but faster and somewhat lighter in character.

EX. 9-1 *Passo e mezzo* from *Opera nova di balli*, 1550

Questions for Discussion

1. What is the basic progression of the passamezzo? Make a chordal reduction in which each part is reduced to one pitch per measure except for m. 7, where there will be two or three harmonies.

2. How has the basic progression been elaborated? How have the basic pitches been melodically ornamented? Is there harmonic elaboration as well?

3. What principles of doubling have been used?

4. What principles of voice leading have been applied?

5. Compare these principles with those we have discovered in two- and three-part counterpoint. How do they compare with the principles you studied in harmony or theory classes?

6. How would you describe the texture of this dance variation?

Observations

Two harmonic patterns are associated with the dance, one called passamezzo antico (Ex. 9-2) and the other called passamezzo moderno. The antico version is the pattern used in Ex. 9-1.

EX. 9-2 Harmonic progression for the passamezzo antico

Melodic and Harmonic Elaboration

The passamezzo makes extensive use of melodic elaboration; it often uses harmonic elaboration as well. Note repetition in various rhythms is the simplest kind of melodic ornamentation used, as can be seen in mm. 2, 4, and 8. Scalewise filling-in of leaps is also common. The bass in m. 5 fills in the fifth between B♭ and F with stepwise motion, for example. Neighbor tones provide another simple form of melodic decoration exemplified by the B♭ in the soprano, m. 2. More florid ornamentation may use various figures in conjunction, such as a leap of a third or fourth to a consonant (or harmonic) tone, followed by a stepwise return, seen in the eighth-note figures.

Harmonic elaboration may occur from time to time, as in m. 2, where a D–minor triad is used quickly at the end of the measure to "elaborate" the F major preceding it. As the bass "fills in" the falling fourth between mm. 3 and 4, the E♭ is harmonized on the way to the half cadence in m. 4. The penultimate measure (m. 7) prepares the cadence and may be harmonized in several ways in sixteenth and seventeenth century dances based on the passamezzo antico: VI - iv - V as we find in our example, or i - iv - V, or simply i - V.

Doubling and Voice Leading

Nearly every vertical sonority in Ex. 9-1 is voiced with the root doubled. There are two notable exceptions: the G–minor harmony at the beginning and in m. 3, where the third is doubled. Doubling the third in the first measure allows for smooth voice leading to the F–major harmony in m. 2. The doubled third is encountered more often in minor triads than in major triads (where the third may be the leading tone). Some of the harmonies resulting from elaboration are in first inversion (the C–minor chord on the last quarter, m. 3, the G–minor chord above the B♭, m. 7), but the remainder are in root position. Second inversion triads are used in sixteenth and seventeenth century music in four parts only when the fourth above the bass is the result of a suspension (especially at cadences), a passing tone, or a neighbor tone.

Voice-leading principles are precisely the same as in two- and three-part counterpoint. Each of the upper parts must make acceptable two-part counterpoint with the bass. Fourths and tritones are permitted between upper parts if a proper harmony is created with the bass (see Ex. 8-2). Examples of these "consonant" fourths are indicated with brackets in Ex. 9-3.

EX. 9-3 "Consonant" fourths and tritones between upper parts. (Based on *Lachrimae* by John Dowland) (1536–1626)

In mm. 1 and 5 the fourth between E and A becomes consonant in the A–minor harmony. In mm. 3 and 7, the fourth between A and D is part of the D–minor triad, first inversion. The fourth between B and E in mm. 4 and 8 is part of an E–major triad. Note the parallel fourths in the inner parts in mm. 3–4. The tritone, B to F, is used as part of a diminished triad in first inversion.

The principles of proper voice leading and doubling you learned in harmony or theory classes apply here as well. These principles were solidified during the Renaissance and have served as guidelines throughout the "common practice period" (eighteenth and nineteenth centuries).

If Ex. 9-1 were considered along with the examples in Chapter 1, we would classify it as having a hybrid texture, similar to that of the chorale. The basic harmonic progression is very clear in spite of the polyphony generated by the process of elaboration. The melodic and harmonic embellishment technique was a favorite one for composers of variations in the sixteenth and seventeenth centuries. The English referred to the practice as making "divisions." You will find it a convenient way to approach the writing of four-part counterpoint in the exercises to follow.

Exercises

EXERCISE 9-1. Make a copy of Ex. 9-1. Make a harmonic analysis below the bass; label all dissonant (non-harmonic) tones.

EXERCISE 9-2. Write a new soprano for Ex. 9-1 using your own "divisions."

EXERCISE 9-3. Add some "divisions" to the alto, tenor and bass of Ex. 9-1.

*EXERCISE 9-4. Write your own passamezzo (three or four variations) based on the progression of Ex. 9-2.

*EXERCISE 9-5. Write a variation on "Greensleeves" for four instruments.

*EXERCISE 9-6. If possible, perform your variations in class; improvise divisions for the highest part.

Motet

The principles of four-part motet style are admirably exemplified by the Mass movement shown in Ex. 9-4.

EX. 9-4 Kyrie from *Missa O Magnum Mysterium* by Tomás Luis de Victoria (1548–1611)

Questions for Discussion

1. How is Ex. 9-4 formally organized? Discuss points of imitation, motivic development, cadences, and other factors which contribute to the unity, variety, and continuity of the piece.

2. How are dissonances used? Discuss the treatment of dissonant intervals when there are two, three, and four voices sounding together.

3. How is doubling handled when there are four parts compared to three?

4. What harmonic sonorities can result when the moving parts involve dissonances against the sustaining parts?

5. What observations can you make regarding voice leading?

6. What similarities and differences do you observe between four-part motet style and dance variation style comparing Ex. 9-4 with Ex. 9-1?

Observations

The Kyrie of a sixteenth–century polyphonic Mass is normally in three sections in response to the text; the first and third sections are settings of "Kyrie eleison," and the second section is a setting of "Christe eleison." Each section, as we have seen in two- and three-part motet style, begins with a point of imitation and concludes with a well-defined cadence. The overall structure is A-B-C, rather than the A-B-A ternary structure, which is more commonly found in the Baroque era and later. Victoria's Kyrie, Ex. 9-4, is typical, but it has special structural features which deserve comment.

Since the work from which this Kyrie is taken is a parody Mass, we can expect that the melodic and harmonic materials have been drawn from the motet *O magnum mysterium* (also by Victoria). But rather than discuss this aspect here, we will look at the formal organization of the piece itself.

The falling fifth is the strongest characteristic of the opening point, and it is imitated successively by each of the lower parts. The cantus is more exactly imitated by the tenor and the altus by the bassus, which has only the opening point and then falls to G for the authentic cadence at m. 12. The falling fifth is echoed after the opening in the cantus in mm. 4 and 8, and the altus in m. 5.

A four-note ascending scale serves as the point for the "Christe eleison," and the whole section reflects this stepwise movement. The bassus and tenor each have time for another iteration of the rising scale before the half–cadence in m. 19. Variety is achieved by reversing the order of voice entry from that of the opening section.

The tenor, cantus, altus, bassus order of entry in the final section contrasts with the other sections. A strong point of unity with the first section is established with the opening motive of the tenor, which inverts the first two intervals of the cantus in m. 1. The rising fifth is answered in the other voices, except that the cantus answers with a rising fourth in the manner of a "tonal response," looking forward to fugal practice in the Baroque era. In a *tonal* response the imitating voice will answer a rising fifth by a rising fourth and vice versa in order to preserve the tonality. In a *real* response, the imitating voice responds with a transposition at the fifth. (Tonal and real responses will be discussed more fully in Chapters 14 and 20). In Ex. 9-4, the re-entries in the upper three voices also develop the rising fifth or fourth. The final cadence, like the one at m. 12, is an authentic cadence to G.

A careful study of the dissonances will show that their treatment follows the principles we have discussed when there are two parts or three parts sounding with the possible exception of m. 6. Here, several dissonant figures are presented simultaneously. Considering cantus against tenor, the quarter-note D in the cantus makes a fourth, which can be considered a neighbor tone. In the case of altus against tenor, the tied D can also be considered as a long neighbor resolving like a suspension to the C♯. Cantus against altus is not as simple. The fourth, C to F, is heard as a consonance when it is part of the first inversion F–major triad. The D in the altus would have made a third with the F above as a proper preparation for the suspension to follow, but the E in the cantus acts like an accented passing tone, giving us a momentary second. The D is held into m. 7, making a suspension with the E in the cantus, and the altus dutifully resolves to the C♯ in preparation for the cadence. In m. 29, the G in the cantus makes a consonant fourth with the D in the bassus. This is one of the more common cadential figures in sixteenth–century motets of three or more parts.

The consonant fourths and tritones are indicated in Ex. 9-5, and the harmonies are indicated below together with the chord position and the chord member doubled. As we noted above, the most common doubling by far is the chord root. Third doubling is found occasionally in minor triads. Doubling of the fifth is rare when the third is present.

Triads are most often in root position when there are four parts sounding. First inversion triads are used occasionally. When the diminished triad is used, it is almost always found in first inversion. As we have previously observed, use of triads in second inversion requires that the fourth above the bass be treated as a properly prepared dissonance.

EX. 9-5 Excerpt from the final Kyrie of Victoria's *Missa O Magnum Mysterium*

Harmony:		gm	f#°	gm	gm	dm	b°	C	F	F	cm	D7	gm		D	gm
Position:		r	6/3	r	r	r	6/3	6/3	r	r	r	r	6/4		r	r
Doubling:		r	3	r,3	r	3	3	r	r	r	r	r	5		r	r

When two or three of the parts are involved in simultaneous passing tones, neighbor tones, or other figures involving dissonances against the sustaining parts, colorful harmonies may result. In m. 10, the B♭ in the cantus momentarily creates an augmented triad, the A which follows it creates a momentary half-diminished seventh chord, and in m. 11, the neighbor motion in cantus, altus, and bassus create another half-diminished seventh chord against the sustained A in the tenor. Note also the dominant seventh chord created by the suspension of the C♯ in m. 29 (indicated as D7 in Ex. 9-5).

All parts maintain contrapuntal independence. This insures proper voice leading. As we have observed in Ex. 9-1, oblique and contrary motion are used more often than similar and parallel motion, especially with regard to the outer voices. Note that nowhere in the examples in this chapter do all parts proceed together in similar motion. Note that leading tones resolve up, chord sevenths resolve down, common tones are usually sustained.

From the foregoing discussion it is evident that there is no difference between the dance variation style and the motet style in terms of the use of dissonance, chord doubling, and voice leading. Where these styles differ is in texture and formal design. In the dance variation, the polyphony results from the counterpoint generated by divisions based on a given set of harmonies, whereas in motet style, the harmony is a result of the interaction of melodically conceived parts which are often responding to the working out of points of imitation. The concept of polyphony based on a harmonic framework is the essence of the polyphonic music of the Baroque era, as we will see in subsequent chapters.

Exercises

EXERCISE 9-7. Complete the alto and tenor parts, ending with an authentic cadence on G. Indicate all passing tones, neighbor tones, and suspensions.

EXERCISE 9-8. Complete this double canon. Indicate dissonances as in Exercise 9-7.

EXERCISE 9-9. Write a four-part *Hosanna in excelsis* using the following opening motive. (Length: about 16 measures.)

Ho - san - na   in   ex - cel - sis.

*EXERCISE 9-10. Write a four-part motet on the following text.

HÆC DI-es quam FE-cit DO-mi-nus:
ex-sul-TE-mus et lae-TE-mur in E-a.

(This is the day which the Lord hath made;
we will rejoice and be glad in it. Ps. 118:24)

Madrigal

The term *madrigal* was first used in fourteenth–century Italy for a poetic form set in two or three voices. It has no direct connection with the more familiar Italian madrigal, which developed in the 1530s and reached its peak by the end of the century.

Arcadelt has left us many fine early madrigals in four parts. Example 9-6 is one of them.

EX. 9-6 Madrigal: "Lasso che pur homai" by Jaques Arcadelt (1505-1568)

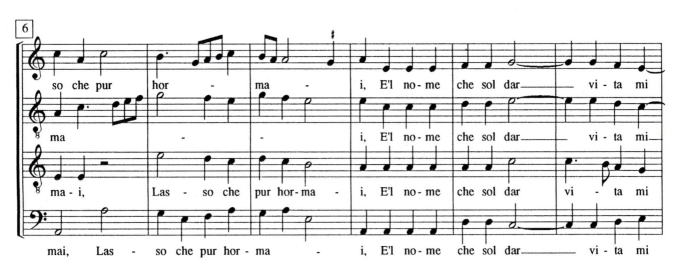

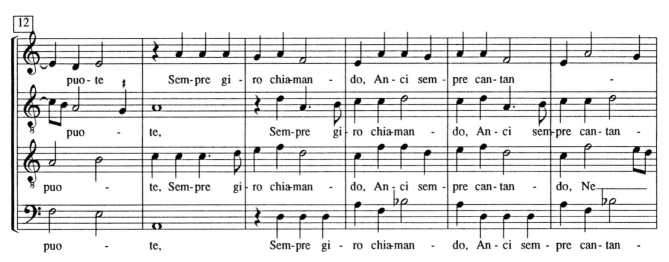

Alas, now I go around singing the only name that can give me life, and never shall I cease to do so. Therefore, sweet notes, render my song lovely so that it will be ever more clear, and hearing it will be ever more delightful to my lady.

Questions for Discussion

1. Considering Ex. 9-6 and Ex. 9-4, how would you compare four-part motet style with madrigal style?
2. Considering Ex. 9-6 and Ex. 8-4, how would you compare madrigal style to that of the canzonet?
3. Compare the treatment of dissonances, chord doubling, and voice leading in madrigal style to that of the motet.

Observations

Except for the obvious difference in texts, the style of the Victoria Kyrie and the Arcadelt madrigal are quite similar. As we have noted before, secular vocal music tends to use shorter phrases and greater motivic development than sacred vocal music. There is generally more note-against-note counterpoint in the madrigal than there is in the motet. Imitative sections alternate with more chordal, homophonic sections. After an imitative section in mm. 1-9 in Ex. 9-6, there is a section in "familiar style" up to m. 12. A lightly imitative passage follows, cadencing in m. 21, after which another chordal section appears. The remainder of the piece is imitative.

Madrigal style is essentially the same as the style of the canzonet except that the madrigal itself tends to be more extended and perhaps more serious than the canzonet. Italian composers considered the canzonet, the frottola, the villanella, and the balletto to be somewhat lower in class compared to the madrigal. The French chanson, predecessor to the madrigal, could be serious or gay, profound or silly, and might be very long or quite short.

In regard to the treatment of dissonance, chord doubling, and voice leading, there is little difference between the canzonet and early four-part madrigal and the sacred choral music of the same period. Composers of the later madrigals, however, were more daring in their treatment of dissonance, especially in the portrayal of strong emotions. The treatment of dissonance in four-part instrumental music is also somewhat more free than in motet style.

Exercises

EXERCISE 9-11. Complete this little piece in madrigal style. The opening is echoed by the tenor and bass at "A". Use familiar style at "B". At "C" all parts share the motive in imitation. Close with an authentic cadence.

*EXERCISE 9-12. Write a four-part version of "The nightingale, the organ of delight" by Weelkes, Ex. 8-4, using the following opening:

Sources for Further Study

Scores:

DANCES:

Attaignant: *Danceries*, 1550

Phalèse: *Antwerpener Tanzbuch*, 1583

Susato: *Danserye*, 1551

MASSES:

Four-part Masses by Palestrina (especially *Papae Marcelli, Ad fugam, Veni sponsa Christi*);

Josquin (especially *L'homme armé, De beata virgine, Pange lingua*);

Lasso; Victoria; and Byrd

MOTETS:

Four-part motets by Palestrina (especially *Lauda Sion, Super flumina Babilonis, Ego sum panis vivus*);

Josquin (especially *Ave Maria . . . virgo serena, Tu pauperum refugium*);

Lasso

CHANSONS:

Four-part chansons published in 1533 by Attaignant

Readings:

Fux: pp. 109–139
Gauldin—16th c.: pp. 135–177
Jeppesen: pp. 203–217
Merritt: pp. 167–207
Morley: pp. 225–231; 241–269
Roberts and Fischer: 97–107
Salzer/Schacter: pp. 402–427
Smith: 96–115

CHAPTER

10

Polyphony in More Than Four Parts

Texture and doubling are of primary concern when there are more than four voices in a piece. The compositions shown in Ex. 10-1–10-3 demonstrate how composers of the late Renaissance scored for five, six, and eight parts.

EX. 10-1 Madrigal: "The Silver Swan" by Orlando Gibbons (1583–1625)

EX. 10-2 German motet: "Ich sucht des Nachts" (Song of Solomon) by Melchior Franck
(1573–1639)

Upon my bed by night I sought him whom my soul loves;
   I sought him, but found him not; I called him, but he gave no answer.
"I will rise now and go about the city, in the streets and in the squares;
   I will seek him whom my soul loves." I sought him, but found him not.
The watchmen found me, as they went about in the city.
   "Have you seen him whom my soul loves?"
Scarcely had I passed them, when I found him whom my soul loves.

EX. 10-3 Canzona: "Sol-sol-la-sol-fa-mi" by Giovanni Gabrieli (1555–1612)

Questions for Discussion

1. What technical problems arise in scoring for more than four parts?
2. What gives "The Silver Swan" its incredible harmonic richness?
3. How is textural variety achieved in the motet by Franck?
4. How is Gabrieli's canzona organized?
5. Scoring for two quartets requires special considerations. What are some of these?

Observations

When scoring for two parts, composers needed to concentrate on just one set of harmonic intervals. When there were three parts, they not only had to deal with three sets of harmonic intervals, but they needed to consider the triads formed by the three parts. Four parts again compounded the number of interval sets to track, and doubling in triads became a primary concern. With five or more parts, doubling itself became compounded. Could the root be trebled? Would it be appropriate to double the third or fifth as well as the root?

In "The Silver Swan," Ex. 10-1, Gibbons gives us a useful compendium of doubling possibilities. The opening sonority has the fifth trebled. When the quintus moves to F, we have doubling of the root and fifth. When the bassus moves down to D, we have a momentary dominant seventh as the tenor moves through G to F, resulting in an inverted diminished triad with two thirds and two fifths. Measure 2 begins with a C–major triad with root and third doubled. The first inversion F–major triad at the end of the measure has two thirds and two fifths. Further inspection proves that with five parts, any chord member may be doubled, and on occasions, the root or the fifth may be trebled. There is even an example of a trebled third in m. 9. The chord is temporarily without a fifth, and the Ds are approached in three different ways. Harmonic richness is created by the frequent doubling of the chord third, the relatively low tessitura and active harmonic rhythm, the close voicing, the presence of seventh chords, and the smooth undulation of contrapuntal motion. Example 10-4 shows common chord voicings in multi-voiced textures.

EX. 10-4 Chord voicings in multi-voiced textures

Fifth	1	1	3	3	2	3	2	3	3	3
Third	1	2	1	1	2	2	3	2	2	2
Root	3	2	2	2	3	2	2	3	3	3

The motet by Franck, Ex. 10-2, is more homophonic than contrapuntal in texture. The impression of polyphony is created by the call and answer of various groupings of voices. It is the deployment of these groupings that gives the piece variety. A middle-register quartet is answered by a quartet in a lower register, and then all six voices join to complete the first line of text. This kind of shifting in voicing continues throughout the motet. Sometimes, as in mm. 20–23, two trios alternate. The texture becomes more contrapuntal at the major cadences, mm. 17–18 and m. 33 to the end. When all six parts are sounding the doubling tends to be more of root than fifth and more of fifth than third. Notes bearing accidentals are very rarely doubled.

The Gabrieli canzona, Ex. 10-3, like Ex. 10-2, makes use of various groupings of voices to create variety. In eight-part music, however, we usually find two quartets deployed in antiphonal fashion. Each quartet may function by itself or in ensemble with the other quartet. Imitation may occur between the two quartets as in mm. 9–17 where the second quartet imitates the first after one bar, or among individual parts as in mm. 57–62 where the falling or rising scale motive may be found in any of the parts. The piece is tightly organized around the development of a few short motives. The primary motives are presented clearly by two treble instruments in canon. We will call this "A." The tutti section where the two quartets imitate each other may be called "B." The change to triple meter gives us a new "call and answer," "C." As the meter changes back to duple meter we have a development of the "A" motives in the dominant key. At m. 33 we have a repeat of the "B" section, which is in turn followed by a repeat of the "C" section at m. 41. At m. 48 a more extended development of the "A" motives occurs. The extension allows a shift back to the tonic key. The concluding section combines a new idea, the falling scale in quarter notes, with motives from "A" and "B," ending with a grand plagal cadence. The scheme of the piece is ABC-ABC-A-Coda.

The use of repetition and development and the role of tonality in the structural plan which the Gabrieli piece exhibits are indications of some of the changes which will result in the dawning of the Baroque era; these will be discussed at length in the next chapter.

In spite of the complexities which multiple parts present, sixteenth–century composers are still careful to avoid parallel unisons, octaves, and fifths. Some of the techniques which avoid these are shown in Ex. 10-5.

EX. 10-5 Voice leading in multi-voice textures

Exchange of third   Movement within chord   Voice crossings

Harmony in Multi-Voiced Textures

As a rule, when the number of parts increases, the harmonic rhythm tends to become slower. This is especially true of contrapuntal passages. A quicker harmonic rhythm is possible in familiar style. The harmonic rhythm in "The Silver Swan" is generally two changes to the measure. In the Franck motet, the texture allows for a more rapid and variable rate of harmonic change. In the canzona by Gabrieli, the harmonic rhythm is slower in contrapuntal sections and faster in homophonic sections. Polychoral motets of the latter sixteenth and early seventeenth centuries designed for performance in large cathedrals required relatively slow harmonic rhythm because of the extremely "live" acoustics of the spaces in which they were performed.

Root movement in multi-voiced textures emphasizes fourths and fifths. Note the frequency of fourth and fifth leaps in the bass part in Ex. 10-2. Authentic and plagal harmonic relationships abound in polychoral music of the late Renaissance and early Baroque, especially those of the Gabrielis, Praetorius, and Hassler. The polychoral technique was perpetuated in the Baroque by Heinrich Schütz and others including J. S. Bach in the *B Minor Mass* and the *St. Matthew Passion.*

Exercises

EXERCISE 10-1. Complete this instrumental dance strain.

EXERCISE 10-2. Complete this Hebrew letter *incipit* for a set of *Lamentations*.

*EXERCISE 10-3. Complete Choir II for this antiphonal Hosanna.

Sources for Further Study

Scores:

FOR FIVE PARTS:

Josquin: chanson: *Parfons regretz;* motet: *De profundis clamavi*

Palestrina: Mass: *Repleatur os meum* (canonic); motet: *Alleluia tulerunt*

Victoria: motet: *Ascendens in altum*

Byrd: *Mass for five voyces;* motet: *Non vos relinquam;* fantasia: *The Leaves Be Green*

Dowland: *Lachrimae pavans*

FOR SIX PARTS:

Josquin: chanson: *Petite camusette*

Palestrina: motet: *Viri Galilai;* Mass and motet: *O magnum mysterium*

Victoria and Morales: Final sections of magnificat settings

Byrd: Two fantasias

FOR SEVEN PARTS:

Palestrina: motet: *Tu es Petrus*

FOR EIGHT PARTS:

Josquin: motet: *Tulerunt Dominum meum*

Gabrieli: canzoni á8 (especially *Sonata pian' e forte*)

Viadana: canzona: "La Padovana" from *Sinfonie musicali a otto voci,* 1610

FOR TWELVE PARTS:

Gabrieli: canzonas for twelve parts from *Sacrae symphoniae,* 1597

Readings:

Gauldin—16th c.: pp. 178–187; 205–243

Jeppesen: pp. 219–233

Morley: pp. 58–62; 232–240

Smith: pp. 116–132

PART THREE

Counterpoint in the Early Baroque (1600–1700)

CHAPTER

11

Stylistic Innovations

The Basso Continuo; the Emergence of Tonality; New Uses of Dissonance; Chromaticism

The short lament by Monteverdi, shown in Ex. 11-1, illustrates many of the innovations of the early Baroque.

EX. 11-1 "Lamento d'Arianna" by Claudio Monteverdi (1567–1643)

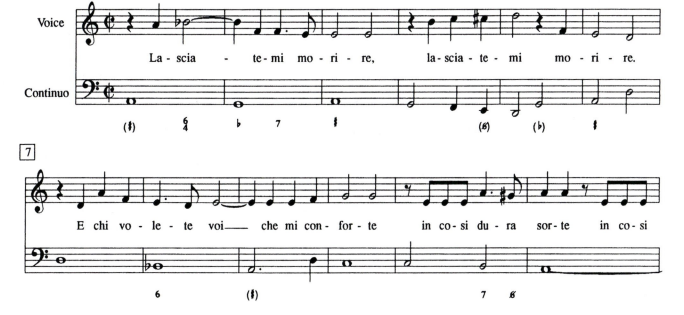

Let me die,
for who could comfort me in my hard fate, in my great torment?
Let me die.

Questions for Discussion

1. In what ways does Ex. 11-1 fit your definition of sixteenth–century counterpoint (see Chapter 3)?

2. In what ways does Ex. 11-1 differ from that definition?

3. How do the voice part and the bass part compare as to "role" and "character"? Are they of equal importance, or does one part serve as a support for the other? Which part seems to introduce the dissonances? How would you characterize the bass as a melody?

4. What is the purpose of the figures below the bass? What is meant by the numbers and the accidentals written below the bass part? Why are there parentheses here and there? If the figures are there to indicate harmonies, why not write them out for a keyboard instrument?

5. What is the tonal plan of the piece? How does the tonal plan relate to the structure of the melody and the text?

6. Can you explain the dissonances between melody and bass? Which of the dissonances agree with sixteenth–century practice? Which do not? What do these new dissonances have in common, and how are they related to the text?

7. How is chromaticism used in Ex. 11-1?

Observations

Monteverdi and the Sixteenth Century

One of the most important elements in your definition of two-part counterpoint in the sixteenth century is the preservation of melodic and rhythmic independence of the parts. Monteverdi adheres to this principle in "Lamento d' Arianna." We find also that conjunct moves still outnumber disjunct moves and that the most frequent kind of motion is oblique, followed in turn by contrary, similar, and parallel, just as we had seen in Renaissance music.

When we consider the harmonic elements, however, we find many differences between this piece and a two-part piece from the sixteenth century such as "Oculus non vidit" by Lasso (Ex. 3-1). Although there is still far more consonance than dissonance (3:1 in Ex. 11-1 compared to 4:1 in Ex. 3-1), the dissonances are much stronger: they often appear on strong beats, and some are approached by leap, which would certainly have been considered inappropriate during the Renaissance.

While both parts of the Lasso motet are of equal melodic interest, the voice part in Monteverdi's lament is of prime importance with the bass part assuming a supporting role. The bass part has very little melodic content, consisting mainly of chord roots. It has notes on nearly all of the downbeats while the melody often avoids the downbeats by using rests, tied notes, or continuing motion. The melody contains the tones of highest "color": the strong dissonances, the chromatically altered tones, the chord thirds. The bass, unlike the lower part of the Lasso motet, reaches its strongest cadences by a falling fifth.

The Continuo

You have undoubtedly recognized the lower part to be a "figured bass." The "basso continuo" or "thorough bass" was an invention of the early Baroque. Its original purpose was to provide a means of harmonic support for solo melody. The dramatic qualities of vocal declamation were enhanced by the continuo, which was seldom allowed to compete with the melody for the listener's attention in the early Baroque.

The figures are used as a shorthand notation or code which assists the continuo performer in the choice of harmonies. Like today's "lead sheet" chord symbols, the figured bass was only a rough indication; details were often left up to the player, who was expected to "realize" the harmonies on the spot. Writing out the harmonies would not only have been considered unnecessary and time consuming, it would have been an insult to the performer's skill. We have included figures in parentheses in order to give a more complete guide to the harmonies. See Appendix C for an explanation of figured bass symbols.

Tonality

The tonality of D minor is strongly established in Ex. 11-1. The opening section, consisting of two short phrases of three measures apiece, ends with a clear authentic cadence in the tonic. The second section, beginning in m. 7, modulates to A minor, and the final section, which is a repeat of the first, returns to D minor. This ternary plan is also expressed by the structure of the melody and by the text. The outer sections are nearly identical: the return begins in the middle of the measure (m. 14), and the word "morire" is shortened in m. 16 and lengthened for the final cadence. The tonal plan of a piece becomes increasingly important as a formal element during the Baroque period.

Dissonance

The dissonances in Ex. 11-1 are of particular interest. Only the suspensions in the bass in mm. 13 and 15 would be considered appropriate in the sixteenth century. All of the others are strong dissonance types developed in the early Baroque to express dramatic emotions through music. Easiest to recognize is the *appoggiatura,* which functions like a suspension which has not been prepared. A good example is to be found on the word "dura" in m. 11. The leap to the A in the melody which creates a seventh is then resolved to a sixth on the G♯. A similar effect is created in m. 8 on the word "vo-le-te." Some scholars prefer to call the E on beat one of m. 8 an *accented passing tone*. We prefer to consider this too as an appoggiatura because of its strong "leaning" or "sighing" musical gesture. The appoggiatura is a tone alien to the supporting harmony, which "resolves" to a note which is a member of that harmony before the next harmonic change occurs. It is accented because it occurs on relatively strong beats and coincides with a change of harmony.

Example 11-2 shows appoggiaturas, beginning with mild ones and continuing with successively stronger ones. Note that the force or strength of an appoggiatura is a function of the interval preceding it and the amount of time which elapses before the resolution. The remaining dissonances are more difficult to classify. The B♭ in m. 1 seems to anticipate the G-minor harmony to follow. When this figure returns in m. 15, the bass functions like a suspension, resolving within the measure. A similar anticipation of the harmony takes place with the word "voi" in m. 8 where the E makes a tritone with the bass, then becomes the fifth of the A-minor harmony in the next measure. In m. 2, the leap to the F which makes a seventh with the bass seems to function as a member of a minor seventh chord, G-B♭-D-F. The seventh resolves to a sixth on the word "morire." The Fs in mm. 5, 15–16, and 18 also resolve down. When the melody is supported by a continuo part, the 9-8 suspension (avoided in two-part sixteenth–century counterpoint) becomes possible as in m. 13.

EX. 11-2 Appoggiaturas of varying strength. (a) untied suspension (b) accented passing tone (c) small leap (d) large leap to a long note

Chromaticism

Chromaticism is not a new phenomenon in the early Baroque, but composers in the seventeenth century used it more freely than did their sixteenth–century predecessors. Monteverdi uses melodic chromaticism in mm. 4–5 and 17–18 for the word "lasciatemi" to represent Arianna's plaintive cry for death.

The most common use of chromatic alteration in the sixteenth century was for musica ficta in cadences and for avoiding the tritone. Melodic and harmonic chromaticism was reserved for music with strong emotional content (such as the madrigals by Rore and Marenzio). By 1600, the dominant-tonic function was well established, and the secondary or applied dominant was frequently used. In Ex. 11-1, the opening chord has the function of dominant, and a C♯ should be played in the continuo part. By m. 11, the piece has begun a modulation to A minor, and the G♯s in mm. 11, 13, and 14 act as leading tones. The B♭s in the melody, the bass, and the figures indicate what would now be considered the normal sub-dominant, a minor chord when the tonic is minor. By the eighteenth century we would expect to find the B♭ in the key signature.

Exercises

EXERCISE 11-1. Using the beginning given below, write out Ex. 11-1 with your realization of the continuo.

EXERCISE 11-2. Write a harmonic analysis for Exercise 11-1.

EXERCISE 11-3. Write a melody for this bass, then compose three variations to follow.

EXERCISE 11-4. Write a basso continuo for this melody.

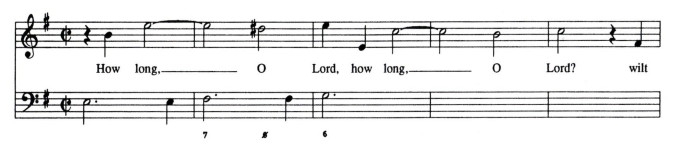

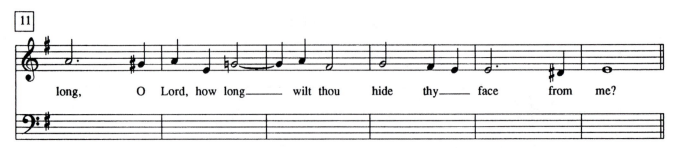

long,   O Lord, how long———— wilt thou   hide   thy——— face   from   me?

*EXERCISE 11-5. Write a short aria for voice and continuo in the style of Monteverdi using the following text:

>   PIAN-ge-te ME-cho a-MAN-ti ho ex-TRE-mo mio do-LO-re
>   ch'io PA-to a TUT-te l'HO-re TROP'po a MAN-do.

>   (Weep with me, ye lovers, for my grief is extreme;
>   and I suffer every hour for loving too much.)

Sources for Further Study

Scores:

Monteverdi: *Orfeo, Vespers, Ballo dell' ingrate;* Madrigals, Book VI

Several examples of early seventeenth–century monody appear in Vol. II of the *Harvard Anthology of Music* (HAM), Nos. 182–189

Viadana, *100 concerti ecclesiastici,* 1602 (those for a single voice and continuo)

Readings:

Crocker: pp. 223–254

Jeppesen: pp. 30–37

Schrade: pp. 38–47; 61–85; 124–134; 140–241; 276–278

CHAPTER

12

Continuous Variations

Ground Bass; Chaconne; and Passacaglia

Variation technique was highly developed during the sixteenth century. Works for keyboard and lute often used chant melodies, chorales, or popular songs as the basis for sets of variations. Composers also wrote variations based on chordal progressions or on a fixed succession of bass tones. In these pieces the music tends to flow continuously; the term *continuous variations* has been applied to such compositions. By the early seventeenth century pieces called "ground" are common in England, and on the continent the chaconne (ciaccona in Italian) and passacaglia (passacaille in French) are well established.

Examples 12-1–12-3 show continuous variation technique in the seventeenth century.

EX. 12-1 "A Ground in Gamut" for harpsichord by Henry Purcell (1659–1695)

EX. 12-2 "Ciaccona" from *Il primo libro di toccate* by Girolamo Frescobaldi
(1583–1643)

EX. 12-3 "Trio en passacaille" from *Messe du Deuziesme Ton* by André Raison
(1645–1719)

Questions For Discussion

1. What musical elements are varied and what elements are held constant in each of the examples?
2. How many variations are there in Ex. 12-2? How did you arrive at the length of each variation?
3. Write out the string of basic pitches in the ground bass used in Ex. 12-1. How has Purcell varied this set of pitches?
4. What are the basic pitches in the bass of Ex. 12-3? How has Raison applied variation to the recurring bass pattern?
5. Is there a similar pattern of pitches in the bass of Ex. 12-2?
6. Compare the handling of texture in the examples. Can you find instances of imitation?
7. Discuss each composer's use of tonality.

Observations

Before discussing the examples a few words must be said about the terms *ground, chaconne, passacaglia,* and *basso ostinato.* The English term *ground* has always referred to pieces with a recurring set of pitches or "theme" usually, but not always, found in the bass. *Chaconne* and *passacaglia* had their origins in triple meter dance tunes based on either a set of harmonies or a set of pitches in the bass. The terms seem to have been used interchangeably by composers in the seventeenth century, and so there are no real distinctions among them. The very same bass pattern may be called a ground by one composer, a chaconne by another, and a passacaglia by still another. The term *basso ostinato* is used to describe music with a recurring melodic phrase in the bass, and therefore it includes ground bass, chaconne, and passacaglia.

In all of the examples the melodic, rhythmic, and textural elements seem to change with each variation. There is a variety of tessitura, number of voices sounding at one time, rhythmic density, and complexity of contrapuntal motion. In some of the variations the rhythmic motion is confined to one of the parts, while in others it is distributed among the parts. At times the figuration is applied to the bass itself. Held constant in the variations by Purcell and Raison is the set of basic pitches in the bass and the regular cadences at the end of each variation.

This is true of the Frescobaldi example as well except that a recurring set of basic pitches is more difficult to find because of the amount of variation in the bass line. It is the recurring harmonic progression with its cadence that delineates the variations in Ex. 12-2. Authentic cadences to E minor occur each two measures—mm. 3, 5, 7 with raised third 9, 11, 13, 15. The final cadence to A comes as a surprise, and the first measure does not belong to the variation scheme. There are seven variations in all (or eight if the final two measures are counted).

Example 12-4 shows the basic pitches of Purcell's bass. You may have noticed its resemblance to the bass of Handel's *Chaconne in G Major* and the first eight measures of the bass in the Aria of Bach's *Goldberg Variations.* It begins with the familiar descending tetrachord used by many composers for continuous variations throughout the history of music.

EX. 12-4 Basic pitches of Purcell's "A Ground in Gamut"

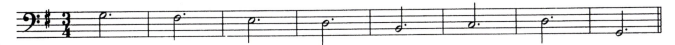

The last four notes support an authentic cadence which marks the end of all of the variations. Purcell often fills in the third between notes four and five with a passing tone on C (Ex. 12-1, mm. 4, 12, 20, and 36). Occasionally a neighbor tone is added (mm. 12, and 41–47). The melodic elaboration beginning in m. 33 is applied to the bass in the variation beginning in m. 41, and the scale passages in the final variation are shared by the bass and top part.

The pitch pattern used in the bass of the Raison example is shown in Ex. 12-5. Notice its resemblance to the first eight tones of Bach's *Passacaglia in C minor*. The pattern concludes with a half–cadence. A measure is added at the end of the piece to make a final authentic cadence.

EX. 12-5 Bass pattern in Raison's "Trio en passacaille"

The opening measures introduce the rising fifth motive in motet style before the bass enters. The actual variations begin in m. 3. Raison uses the same kind of decorative pitches to embellish the bass as we found in the Purcell example. The bass is embellished with passing and neighboring tones and associated harmony tones beginning in m. 11 and receives a new rhythmic motive in m. 23.

As we have said earlier, a basic pattern of pitches governing the variations in Ex. 12-2 is difficult to find. The harmonic progression with its authentic cadence, however, is more clearly the point of departure for the variations. Example 12-6 shows this progression with a bass line containing the most essential pitches.

EX. 12-6 Basic progression in Frescobaldi's "Ciaccona"

These pitches can be found in each variation, sometimes altered or displaced in rhythm, but not always in the lowest part.

Textural Variety

These compositions, like all good variations, employ a wide variety of textures. The Purcell example begins with the homophonic texture of melody with harmonic accompaniment. At m. 25 a little dialogue occurs between the melody and the upper part in the left–hand staff. At m. 33 the upper part is given continuous motion, set off from off-beat motion in the tenor and simple downbeats in the bass. At m. 41 the bass assumes the continuous motion with simple chords in the right hand for support. At m. 49 a new texture is achieved with syncopations in the right hand. The final variation features scale passages in imitative dialogue between the soprano and bass.

Example 12-2 displays a three-part texture for the most part with the motion divided equally between the outer voices. There is some contrapuntal motion given to the inner part, however, especially in mm. 4, 12, and 15–16. Our attention is captured by the imitative interplay of the ascending and descending scalewise motives shared by all parts. The harmonic texture is varied by the increasing use of chromaticism as the piece unfolds and by the striking use of cross-relations (the close proximity in different parts of C♯ to C♮ and D♮ to D♯ in mm. 5–6, G♯ to G♮ in m. 7).

The bass part in Ex. 12-3 assumes a more important role than the upper parts, which weave a decorative counterpoint above it but do not project a melodic identity. Imitation is used sparingly and in subtle ways. The right hand parts indulge in some rhythmic imitation, and the new motive introduced in the bass at m. 23 appears later in the upper part.

Tonality

It is interesting to compare Frescobaldi's use of tonality with that of Purcell and Raison. The "Ciaccona" was published in 1637, whereas the other examples come from the last decade of the seventeenth century. While there are strong progressions and definite authentic cadences in the "Ciaccona," it would be difficult to say what key it is in, and determining a mode for the piece is impossible. The early seventeenth century saw a great deal of experimentation in harmony. It was not until the latter part of the century that something like our present system of major and minor tonality emerged. We would have very little difficulty assigning Roman numerals to Purcell's ground. Its progression is clearly defined; it even has secondary dominant harmonies (V of V and V of IV). In spite of the modal signature, the "Passacaille" is a model of "common practice" diatonic harmony: i V i₆ iv V iv₆ iv V.

Exercises

EXERCISE 12-1. Using the following basic pitches, write two variations by adding "divisions" to the upper two parts.

EXERCISE 12-2. Add three upper parts to this bass, then compose two variations.

(after Pachelbel)

EXERCISE 12-3. Compose a set of eight to ten variations for keyboard on this progression.

Allegro   after Monteverdi

EXERCISE 12-4. Write three variations on "La Folia" for two violins and cello using this beginning.

Andante

*EXERCISE 12-5. Write a lament on the text "I was more true to love than love to me." Score for voice and continuo, and use this chaconne bass.

*EXERCISE 12-6. Write a fanfare passacaglia for antiphonal brass quartets using the last phrase of the chorale "Ein feste Burg" ("A mighty fortress") as the theme.

Sources for Further Study

Scores:

Corelli: Violin Sonata Op. 5 No. 12, the *La Folia* variations

Couperin: Passacaglia from *Pièces de clavecin*

Frescobaldi: *Follia* for organ

Monteverdi: *Zefiro torna* from *Madrigals,* Book IX; *Lamento della ninfa* from *Madrigals,* Book VIII; "Pur ti miro," duet from *L'Incoronazione de Poppea*

Pachelbel: Chaconne in D Minor for organ

Purcell: "A New Ground" for harpsichord, "Ah! My Anna" and "When I Am Laid in Earth" from *Dido and Aeneas*

Readings:

Benjamin: pp. 300–302

Crocker: pp. 241–244

Gauldin—18th c.: pp. 244–256

Kennan: pp. 270–278

CHAPTER

13

Trio Texture

Two Trebles With Continuo

Composers in the early Baroque were very fond of writing music for two trebles and continuo. This trio texture is found in opera, church music, vocal chamber music, and instrumental chamber music. In the middle and late Baroque, composers used it in the trio sonata, perhaps the most favored genre of chamber music. Examples 13-1 and 13-2 show how trio texture is used in the early and late seventeenth century.

EX. 13-1 "Fugge il verno dei dolori" from *Scherzi musicali* by Claudio Monteverdi (1567–1643)

spie - ta - - ta A dar fi - ne a li miei gua - i.

spie - ta - - ta A dar fi - ne a li miei gua - i.

spie - ta - - ta A dar fi - ne a li miei gua - i.

The winter of sorrows now has fled,
The spring of love has returned
All adorned with pretty little flowers
But you return no more, ungrateful Phyllis, pitiless one,
To bring an end to my sorrows.

EX. 13-2 Grave from *Sonata da camera à tre* by Archangelo Corelli (1653–1713)

Questions for Discussion

1. How do the upper parts interact with each other? How do the upper parts interact with the bass?
2. What is the tessitura of each of the three parts?
3. How do Monteverdi and Corelli make use of sequence?
4. Discuss tonality in each example. Where are cadences located and what kinds are used? What vestiges of modality can you find?
5. Discuss the types of dissonances encountered in each piece. Discuss harmony in each piece, especially Ex. 13-1, m. 7 and 19, and Ex. 13-2, m. 8, last beat, and m. 16, first beat. Where are secondary dominant chords located?
6. How is Corelli's piece different from Monteverdi's (other than the performance medium)?

Observations

Imitation and the Role of the Bass

Trio textures during the early and middle Baroque generally consist of two treble parts which engage in imitative interplay supported by the continuo with an independent bass line. In the late Baroque, the bass was given greater opportunity to join in the imitation, especially in the fugal movements of the solo and trio sonatas. This type of movement will be discussed in detail in Chapter 23.

In both of the examples above the upper parts are trebles, two violins or two soprano voices, supported by cello or bass voice and continuo. The upper parts share motives or move in parallel rhythm against the bass. The imitation in the ritornello of Ex. 13-1 begins immediately and involves the bass as well as the trebles. At m. 7, however, the violins move in parallel rhythm to the cadence. Parallel rhythm dominates the vocal section with a few measures of counterpoint at the words "Filli ingrata Dispietata." At that point the sopranos move in thirds against the descending bass.

Imitation is even more pervasive in Ex. 13-2. After the first measure, consisting of parallel thirds, nearly every note of the violin parts is involved in imitative interplay. The cello moves independently of the upper parts most of the time, but there are a few places where it too takes part in the imitation (the cello in m. 10 echoes the motive in Violin I, m. 9, for example).

In the Monteverdi example, the upper parts have a tessitura which generally stays within the treble staff. They are close together and often quite distant from the bass, which occupies nearly two octaves. In the Corelli example, the violin parts are somewhat higher, and they too keep their distance from the bass. This spacing allows for a real distinction between the bass and the melodic parts to be maintained, and the harmony provided by the continuo fills in the space in the middle register.

A common feature of trio sonatas is the frequent crossing and recrossing of the treble parts. Notice that most of the time one voice is stationary as the other crosses over it. Crossing when two parts are in contrary motion is used occasionally, but crossing when both voices move in the same direction is rare and should be avoided by the student. Example 13-3 shows some examples of voice crossing.

EX. **13-3 Voice crossing**

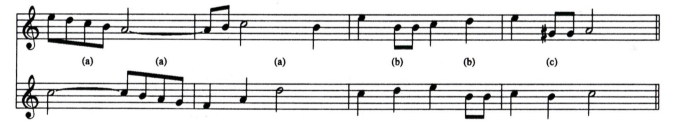

(a) One voice crosses while the other is stationary

(b) Two voices cross in contrary motion

(c) Two voices cross in similar motion (rare - not recommended)

The Sequence

Motivic development through sequence is a favorite technique of Baroque composers. Both examples are rich in this device. The ritornello of Ex. 13-1 begins with a five-note motive in the first violin which is taken by the cello and developed immediately in sequence. It reappears in Violin I in m. 4 and is sequentially repeated. In the vocal section, the opening phrase is given sequential treatment (mm. 11–12 is a varied sequence of mm. 9–10). The next phrase is similarly treated. Following the opening phrase of Ex. 13-2, the cello has a rising four-note scale which is repeated in sequence a fifth lower. This serves as the harmonic support for the upper parts which exchange motives in invertible (or double) counterpoint. Measure 7 in Violin I is repeated down a third in the next measure, and all parts join in sequential development in mm. 11–12. While the sequence is a very useful compositional device, it wears thin if used too many times in succession without being varied. In Baroque music we find that after a melodic pattern has been presented, two or three unvaried sequential repetitions may be used; longer sets of sequences require some variation in the pattern. Notice that the melodic and harmonic sequence beginning on the last beat of m. 10 repeats the figure only three times before a new sequence is presented.

Corelli often uses chains of suspensions in sequence. In Ex. 13-4, which is modeled after Corelli, there is a sequence of 2-3 suspensions. The sequence moves up as each voice crosses above the other, then down as the crossing is abandoned. The bass is typical of the bass lines found in many of Corelli's fast movements.

EX. 13-4 Suspension chains

Tonality vs. Modality

During the seventeenth century the signature of a piece was not a reliable indicator of the tonality. The cadences in the Monteverdi example indicate G as the tonic in spite of the lack of a sharp in the signature. Corelli's trio sonata movement is clearly in G minor, even though there is but one flat in its signature. It was not until the eighteenth century that signatures became firmly bound to their respective keys (especially the minor keys). In Ex. 13-1, we find a half–cadence in G major at m. 4 and authentic cadences in G major at mm. 8, 10, 12, 14, and 24. Another half–cadence in G appears at m. 22, and temporary cadential moves to C major and A minor take place in mm. 16 and 18 respectively. The cadences in Ex. 13-2 are as follows: half–cadence in G minor at m. 4, authentic cadence in B♭ major at m. 9, authentic cadence to C minor in m. 12, and authentic cadence in G minor in the final measure.

There is a lingering hint of modality in the Monteverdi example, especially at the beginning where F♮ is used in the upper part. This suggests the Mixolydian (Mode VII). The only vestige of modality in the Corelli example is the modal signature.

Dissonances

As we have seen in Ex. 11-1 and Ex. 12-2, composers in the early seventeenth century experimented with bold new dissonances including appoggiaturas, escape tones, anticipations, cross–relations, and other dissonant figures which passed out of use by the eighteenth century. Monteverdi's little scherzo uses several of these as well as the more mild passing tones, neighbor tones, and suspensions. The D in Violin II, first beat of m. 7, would seem to be a mistake in the eyes of composers a hundred years later. However, a C or an E would have resulted in parallel octaves. The D seems to be there in order to add a little "bite" to the harmony. It could be called an *acciaccatura,* a term usually found in connection with keyboard music where a non-harmonic tone is sounded simultaneously with its neighboring chord tones without having been prepared. Other dissonances to be observed are: the untied and scarcely prepared suspension in m. 8, Violin II; the escape tone in Violin I, same measure; and the tritone between bass and soprano in m. 19. The diminished triad in root position which results can be tolerated in three parts when the tritone resolves as it does here by contrary motion.

The dissonances encountered in Ex. 13-2 are not remarkable except for the large number of suspensions, a strong trait in Corelli's music. The harmony is rather chromatic because of the liberal use of secondary dominant harmonies: V of iv occurs in mm. 2, 5, 10, and 12; V of III appears in mm. 8 and 9. There is a V of vi in m. 11, a diminished seventh chord in m. 8, which acts as a dominant to the V of III in m. 9, and another in m. 16, which precedes the final cadence. On the downbeat of m. 16 the A♭ in the top part creates a Neapolitan sixth chord. Since nearly all of the cadences in Ex. 13-1 are authentic, those outside of the tonic could be considered as employing secondary dominant chords. The presence of C♯ indicates a dominant function to D, G♯ indicates a dominant to A minor, and an F♮ added to G and B indicates a dominant function to C.

Comparison of the Examples

Several similarities between the two examples have been noted above. Some of the differences are:

1) The phrases in the Corelli example are longer than those in the Monteverdi example, and consequently there are fewer strong cadences.
2) There is a much larger amount of voice crossing in the trio sonata movement, a typical trait for the genre.
3) The continuo part in Ex. 13-2 is more independent of the treble parts.
4) The harmonic rhythm is more regular and moves somewhat faster in the Corelli than in the Monteverdi example.
5) The Corelli movement is more chromatic than the Monteverdi piece.

Exercises

EXERCISE 13-1. Complete the bass for this ritornello.

EXERCISE 13-2. Complete the upper parts in the imitative texture of a trio sonata.

*EXERCISE 13-3. Write a short gigue-like dance using this beginning (nine to ten measures).

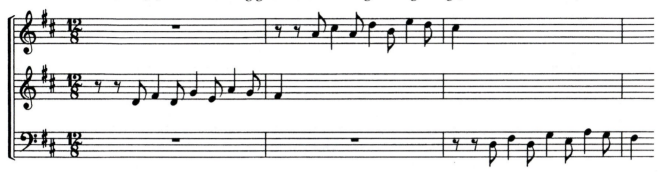

*EXERCISE 13-4. Write an "Alleluia" for two sopranos and continuo (twelve to twenty measures).

Sources for Further Study

Scores:

Monteverdi: *Scherzi musicali; Madrigals,* Book VII

Schütz: *Kleine geistliche Konzerte, Symphoniae sacre I*

Seventeenth century trio sonatas by Vitali, Corelli, Purcell, Marais

Eighteenth century trio sonatas by Loeillet, Telemann, Handel, Bach, Vivaldi, Hotteterre

Readings:

Crocker: pp. 238–240; 248–249; 271–274

Kennan: pp. 192–197

CHAPTER

14

Predecessors of the Fugue:

Canzona; Ricercar; Fantasia; and Choral Fugato

The fugue has a distinguished ancestry with roots in Renaissance vocal and instrumental forms. The motet and chanson led to the *canzona,* their instrumental counterpart. The *ricercar* began as an improvisatory instrumental piece but later developed into a composition which "searched out" the contrapuntal possibilities of its themes or "subjects." In England the *fantasia* exhibited traits of both the canzona and ricercar. In Germany the motet developed into the fugue-like chorus found in cantatas and passion settings.

Examples 14-1–14-4 show each of these genres. Our example of the canzona is from the late sixteenth century, the ricercar from the middle of the seventeenth century, and the fantasia from the late seventeenth century. Example 14-4 is a short choral fugato from the latter half of the seventeenth century.

EX. 14-1 Canzona by Florentio Maschera (1540–1584)

EX. 14-2 Ricercar on D by Johann Kaspar Kerll (1627–1693)

EX. 14-3 Fantasia in G Minor by Henry Purcell (1659–1695)

EX. 14-4 Chorus: Wir haben keine König from *St. John Passion* by Heinrich Schütz

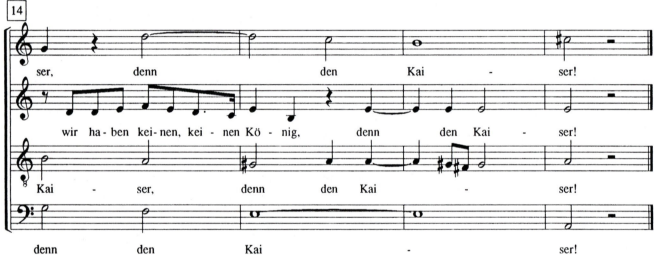

We have no king but Caesar.

Questions for Discussion

1. Although the examples represent a span of more than a century, they have certain traits in common which are also shared by the fugue. What are these traits?

2. How is the opening motive or subject developed in each example? What governs the order of entries and their starting pitches?

3. Describe the presentation and development of secondary motives.

4. Compare Purcell's fantasia to the fantasia by William Byrd, Ex. 8-6. What traits do they have in common, and how do they differ? What details in Purcell's fantasia would be considered inappropriate in the Renaissance?

5. Trace the development of *tonality* exemplified by these compositions.

Observations

Exposition and Development

A fugue begins with an *exposition;* one of the parts presents a subject, after which each of the other parts in turn joins the texture by presenting the subject in its own register. This is true of all four examples except that the opening motive of Ex. 14-1 might not be considered as a "subject" because of its simplicity and brevity, and it is quickly imitated in the alto part after only three notes have sounded. The repeated pitch in long-short-short rhythm was the customary opening in the French chanson of the mid-sixteenth century, and so the canzona, which began as an "instrumental chanson," typically began with this motive until the middle of the seventeenth century when distinctions between the canzona, ricercar, and early fugue became blurred. The solo music which begins each of the other examples has enough character to qualify as a fugue subject. It is interesting to note that all four examples begin with the long-short-short rhythm.

All of the examples develop the opening motive or subject to some extent. A typical Baroque fugue continues to develop its subject until the end. *Episodes,* or passages in a fugue that do not contain complete presentations of the subject, are usually related motivically to it.

Order of Entries

If we consider the soprano and tenor as "high" voices and the alto and bass as "low voices," we find that in each example the entrances alternate between high and low voices: Ex. 14-1 begins with T-A-S-B, Ex. 14-2 with S-A-T-B, Ex. 14-3 with S-A-T (the lowest voice begins in the tenor register), and Ex. 14-4 with T-B-S-A. Other possibilities for four-parts might be A-S-B-T, A-T-B-S, or B-T-A-S; for three-parts, T-A-S or A-T-B. An opening with T-S-B-A would be quite unlikely. Notice that the first and third entries begin with the same pitch classes but are not in the same octave. This is true of the second and fourth entries as well. The first and second entries begin on different pitches, if the first voice begins on the first scale degree, the second will begin on the fifth and vice versa. If the fifth degree appears in the opening motive, it is "answered" by the first degree in the voice entering second. It is convenient to call the first and third entries the "subject" and the second and fourth (when present) the "response" or "answer".

Real and Tonal Responses

Responses are called *real* if they are a simple transposition of the subject. When responses are altered in order to "answer" a fifth degree tone in the subject with a first degree tone, they are called *tonal* responses. In the opening of the canzona the E in the tenor is answered by an A in the alto, making it a *tonal response.* The A-D in the subject of the ricercar is answered by D-A, another example of a tonal response. The fantasia begins with 1-5 of the scale and is answered by 5-1 in the response. Only the Schütz example has a real response to the subject. The tonality at the opening is vague until the cadence in m. 4, and consequently we have no strong feeling of diatonic orientation until that point.

Techniques of Development

Each of the examples develops its opening motive or subject in a different way. In the canzona the opening motive is overlapped by the imitative response. It is freely developed until the cadence to C in m. 10, where a new motive is presented in the bass. This motive is similar to the opening motive, but it begins with quick repeated notes, then continues with slower-moving descending steps. This new motive is immediately imitated by the other voices and developed until the cadence to A in m. 18. Another new motive is presented here, again by the bass. This motive is characterized by syncopation followed by a descending scale in eighth notes. Although all parts engage in the imitation, a three-part texture is maintained until the end of m. 21 where a bit of first species counterpoint in all parts leads to a cadence on E in m. 21. At this point the opening motive reappears and is developed further and combined with elements of the second motive until the cadence in m. 35. A repetition of the music of mm. 18–35 appears next, leading to a short codetta which contains the final presentations of the opening motive and ends with a plagal cadence on A.

The ricercar has a subject which is never really abandoned throughout the piece. Following the initial presentation in all voices it is treated to overlapping imitation beginning in m. 18. This overlapping of subject entries is called *stretto.* An episode which develops a new motive begins on the upbeat to m. 24 and is joined by the subject in m. 27. Both the subject and the second motive appear in various voices until the end of the piece. A musical idea designed as a counterpoint to the subject is called a *countersubject.* In the mature Baroque fugue a countersubject would normally appear first in the exposition.

Purcell's fantasia shares some traits with William Byrd's fantasia, Ex. 8-6, written some eighty years earlier, but it also looks forward to the eighteenth-century fugue. Both fantasias develop their initial idea in all parts. Byrd's fantasia, however, moves to a new motive sooner, develops it, then moves on to a third motive, which is developed more extensively than either of the other motives. The only strong cadence is the final one. In Purcell's fantasia, the opening subject is presented ten times in various voices and in various keys until the authentic cadence in G minor at m. 37. The last two presentations are in stretto, mm. 32–35. The second section of the piece deals with a new theme, which appears both in its original and its inverted form (often in mirror fashion), and it too is presented in stretto (m. 60, and again in m. 68). The opening subject does not appear in this section. The sectional form recalls the canzona, and the playful development of motives recalls the ricercar. The use of inversion and stretto as well as the pervasive modulation will become trademarks of the mature fugue.

Purcell's Fantasia and Renaissance Practice

Several details in Purcell's fantasia would be considered inappropriate when measured by the standards of the Renaissance as we have observed them in the music of Lasso and Palestrina. Purcell's harmony is far more chromatic. From the beginning in G minor, modulations take us as far as to F minor in the first section and A minor in the second, four moves apart on the circle of fifths. Where we find mostly major and minor triads in root position in Ex. 8-6, the vertical sonorities used by Purcell in Ex. 14-3 include triads in first and second inversion, and dominant and diminished seventh chords. Note for example the diminished seventh chord in 4/2 position, m. 10, which serves a dominant function to the following D–minor triad in first inversion; the augmented triad, m. 18, caused by the anticipation of the F–minor harmony in the next measure; the F♯ diminished 6/5 chord, m. 34, which prepares the authentic cadence in m. 37; the root-position diminished chord on A, m. 44; the curious A–minor seventh chord, m. 59, beat four; and another root–position diminished chord in m. 67.

The English had always been daring in their use of the cross relation, and there are examples of it here, especially in m. 60 between E♭ and E♮, leading tone to F in the cadence on beat three. Purcell makes use of many tritone leaps (see particularly mm. 59, 60, and 63 in the top part). They often involve an unaccented appoggiatura or "leaning tone." Purcell occasionally leaves active tones unresolved, as in m. 12, where the F♯ is not resolved in the expected octave but in an octave lower, on beat four. The minor-major seventh chord which is traced by the bass in m. 12 would have been avoided by composers at the time of Palestrina.

Purcell's escape tones occasionally contain a leap larger than a third (see m. 20, top part and m. 21, middle part). Sometimes the resolutions of his suspensions are delayed or decorated by an intervening tone (see mm. 45 and 71, top part). The anticipation has become commonplace in strong cadences, as can be seen in m. 36. In the Renaissance, the G on beat four would have been replaced by another A.

The Choral Fugato

Like the motet, the choral fugato begins with imitative entries, but instead of presenting new ideas for imitation, the choral fugato continues with the development of the opening idea. The Schütz chorus is a model for short fugal choral movements that appear in passion settings, oratorios, and some cantatas. It has a single subject which is developed throughout by all voices equally. The agitation of the text ("We have no king but Caesar") is sustained by the continuous repetition of the quick-moving subject. The downward-moving half-note motive serves as countersubject throughout the piece.

The Trend From Modality to Tonality

The four examples give convincing evidence of the gradual shift from modality to tonality from the late sixteenth century to the late seventeenth century. Maschera's canzona, written at the end of the sixteenth century, begins and ends in the untransposed Aeolian mode. Its internal cadences are on A, C, and E. The only accidentals used are the customary leading tone and its neighbor, G♯ and F♯, an occasional C♯ which serves as a leading tone to D, and an F♯ which helps to strengthen the cadence to E in m. 25. Kerll's ricercar, a mid-seventeenth century work, establishes D as the tonic and rarely strays from it. Only the cadence in m. 30 to A minor ventures away from the tonic, and the "dominant pedal on A" (mm. 34–36) assures a strong return to the tonic. We have, however, not yet reached the full development of the major-minor system in this piece. There is no flat in the signature, and the B♮s and C♮s of the Dorian mode are almost as numerous as the B♭s and C♯s which would indicate the key of D minor. The Schütz example, written just after the mid-seventeenth century, is vague in tonality until the cadence to A minor in m. 4, but the next set of subject entries modulates to G in m. 9. The return to A comes quite suddenly in the final three measures. The unsettled tonal focus seems appropriate for the agitated disclaimers by the High Priests at this point in the Passion.

Its title tells us that Purcell's fantasia, dating from the end of the seventeenth century, is "in G minor." The signature, the subject, and the cadences at the end of each section agree to this. The tonal stability of the exposition (mm. 1–7) allows for the extensive modulations to follow. Purcell uses a technique at the close of the piece which was to become a favorite one with later composers, especially Bach, in the re–establishment of the tonic in the final measures of a fugue: there is a harmonic move toward the subdominant, in this case C minor, before the final cadence. Purcell's harmony is strikingly chromatic. There is an abundance of secondary dominant and diminished seventh chords contributing to an impression of constant modulation.

Exercises

EXERCISE 14-1. Complete this canzona exposition.

EXERCISE 14-2. Complete this three-part keyboard fantasia to the end of the bass entry.

*EXERCISE 14-3. Write a choral fugato on the text "Laudate Dominum" using this beginning.

*EXERCISE 14-4. Compose a ricercar for organ on this subject. Use its inversion in your development.

Sources for Further Study

Scores:

Canzona: Willaert (in *Musica Nova*), Andrea and Giovanni Gabrieli, Frescobaldi (especially those in *Fiori musicali*), and Scheidt

Choral fugato: Choruses from oratorios by Carissimi; cantatas by Weckmann, Lübeck, and Tunder; passion settings by Schütz

Fantasia: Byrd, Gibbons, Bull, Frescobaldi, Purcell

Ricercar: Willaert, Andrea Gabrieli, Frescobaldi, Froberger

Readings:

Crocker: 243–248

Horsley: pp. 135–136; 163–165; 212–226

Mann: pp. 28–30; 34–36

Compare your definitions for canzona, fantasia, and ricercar with those given in your music dictionary.

PART FOUR

Counterpoint in the Late Baroque (1700–1750)

CHAPTER
15

Review of Basic Concepts and Introduction to Eighteenth–Century Counterpoint

This chapter can serve as a review of the basic concepts we have discussed thus far. At the same time, it will be useful to students who are beginning their study of counterpoint with eighteenth–century style. Students who are beginning at this point should first read Chapters 1 and 2.

The short round shown in Ex. 15-1 is characteristic of late seventeenth–century style, especially that of Henry Purcell (1659–1695). Become familiar with it by singing it in class, then consider the questions which follow. If you encounter terms which are unfamiliar to you, consult the Glossary.

EX. 15-1 Round: "A Musical Complaint" by the author

Questions for Discussion

1. How is a round such as this normally performed? Is it a canon?
2. Describe the melodic contours of each part. Describe the texture. What is the apparent harmonic rhythm?
3. Rewrite the round without the decorative pitches so that each part has a half note and a quarter note in each measure. Make a Roman numeral analysis of your reduction. Is it tonal, modal, or something in between?
4. What intervals do you find in your reduction between the bass and the upper part (or "ditty")? Between the bass and the middle part (or "meane")? Between the upper two parts?
5. Now compare your reduction with the original example. What types of decorative or non-harmonic tones do you find? What nonharmonic types of figures are not represented in the round? Give an example of each type. How are the dissonances treated?
6. What is a passacaglia? Why would the bass part make a good theme for a passacaglia?
7. This round was conceived originally for men's voices. How is the harmony affected if one part is sung by male voices and the other two by female voices?
8. What would you have to consider if you were to write a fourth part?

Observations

A *round* is a circular type of canon: each voice, beginning in turn, continues to the end, then repeats from the beginning. It is customary to repeat as many times as there are voice parts. In this round the first voice sings line one, then the second voice begins as the first voice sings line two. The third voice enters as the first and second voices move down. The first voice begins again as the second and third voices move down. The numbers at the ends of the lines indicate the next line to be sung.

Each line of the round has a different melodic contour. The top line rises to its center, then falls. Line two falls to the center, then after a leap falls back to the note from which it began. Line three falls with gentle undulations from beginning to end. Each line reaches its highest and lowest pitches only once. No pitch is over-used in any of the parts. The active tones generally resolve to their expected destinations: G♯ to A (ti-do), D to C (fa-me). The tendancies of F to E (le-sol) and B to A (re-do) are also observed for the most part. After a leap, the melody turns back with stepwise motion. These characteristics are common in the music of the eighteenth century, as you will see in the examples in the following chapters.

The texture of Ex. 15-1 is a hybrid combining polyphonic and homophonic characteristics. As we expect in polyphonic music, the parts maintain a degree of independence both in rhythm and melodic motion. No two parts in Ex. 15-1 have the same rhythm at the same time. The "ditty" (old English for tune, and sometimes used to mean cantus firmus), however, is the principal melody, and the "burden" (old English for bass) provides the harmonic roots. The "meane" (old English for the alto or middle part), while melodically sound in its own right, provides the completion of the harmonies. The harmonic rhythm is very stable; two harmonies per measure, except for the last.

Basic Pitches; Harmonic Progression, Decorative Tones

If the decorative pitches, both harmonic and nonharmonic, are removed, the basic structure as shown in Ex. 15-2 emerges. Note that the progression, which consists of i - v, sequenced down a third, VI–III, concluding with an authentic cadence, ii₆-V -i, is varied and diatonic. It proclaims the tonality of A minor; but the G♮s in m. 1, part two, can be considered as a remnant of modality, suggesting the Aeolian mode. Our modern melodic minor is really an amalgamation of the Dorian, Phrygian, and Aeolian modes. The Dorian gives us the raised sixth of the melodic minor, the use of musica ficta gives us the raised seventh. The Aeolian gives us the lowered forms of the seventh and sixth degrees, and it is quite likely that the Phrygian gives us the lowered second of the Neapolitan sixth harmony, most commonly found in music in the minor. The Phrygian cadence is often found at the end of the slow third movement in Baroque sonatas.

EX. 15-2 Basic structure of Ex. 15-1

The intervals formed between the parts in Ex. 15-2 are all consonances except for the fourth between parts two and three in m. 3. This is the familiar cadential $^{6-5}_{4-3}$ configuration. The use of consonances in note-against-note counterpoint (first species) was the rule in the Renaissance, and it is still generally true in the eighteenth century, although occasional use of accented passing and neighboring tones and appoggiaturas can be found in note-against-note counterpoint as well.

Example 15-3 shows the decorative harmonic and nonharmonic tones in the round. These include an appoggiatura (although not dissonant with the other parts, it is not a member of the basic harmony) in m. 1, a decorative harmonic pitch in m. 2, a suspension, a neighbor tone (or auxiliary tone), and an escape tone (or échappée) in m. 3.

EX. 15-3 Decorative harmonic and nonharmonic tones in Ex. 15-1

Although there are none here, passing tones are still the most common type of dissonance to be found in the eighteenth–century music. Also not represented in the round are the double neighbor (or neighbor tone group), the anticipation, the accented passing and neighbor tones, and the cambiata (found only rarely after 1650). Ex. 15-4 shows the types of non-harmonic tones normally encountered in eighteenth–century music.

EX. 15-4 Decorative figures involving nonharmonic tones

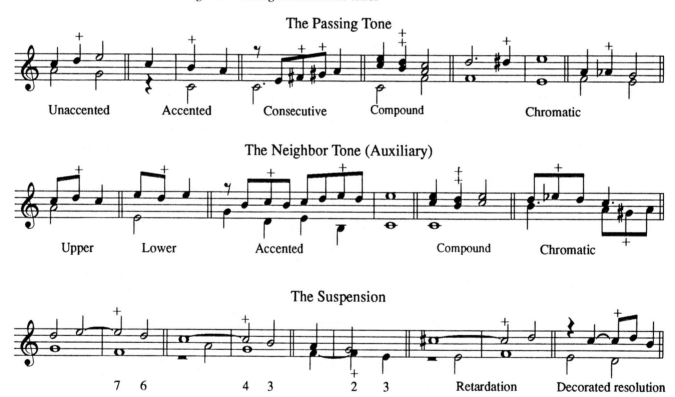

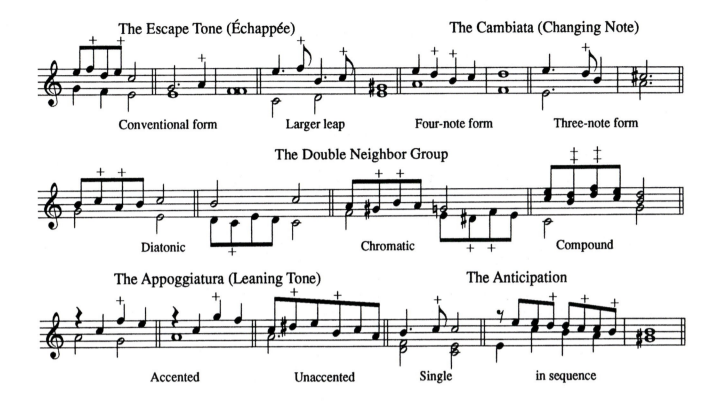

Basso Ostinato Variations

Variations over a repeating bass line were very common in the seventeenth century and continued to be popular with eighteenth-century composers. Although variations of this type go by a variety of names, they are essentially the same. Of these names the ground, the chaconne, and the passacaglia are most commonly used. Names such as *La folia* and *Romanesca* indicated a specified series of tones or harmonies. A good passacaglia bass should be a strong melodic line supporting a strong harmonic progression. A harmonic sequence adds both variety and unity. The bass of our round has all of these characteristics.

Invertibility

When men sing the round there will be no change in the position of the harmonies throughout the singing. If women sing two parts and men sing the third, the lines will be either in the indicated octave or an octave higher. When a shift of the position of the voices results in a proper set of intervals, we have *invertible counterpoint*. This is true until the men sing line one while the women are singing lines two and three. As the men sing the note B in the first and third measures, $\frac{6}{4}$ chords are created, which would normally be avoided.

Voice Leading and Doubling

The principles of voice leading you learned in theory or harmony classes are based on eighteenth-century practice, and they are just as true for contrapuntal as for homophonic music. The most important principles are:

1) Parallel motion is best when the intervals are thirds, sixths, or tenths.

2) Parallel unisons, fifths, and octaves are avoided, as are parallel seconds, sevenths, ninths, and other dissonant intervals.

3) Leaps of augmented or diminished intervals are usually avoided but may be used when the tones are members of a diminished triad or a dominant or diminished seventh chord.

4) Leading tones resolve up by step, and chord sevenths resolve down by step.

5) Altered pitches normally resolve by half step in the direction of their alteration.

6) A tone belonging to two adjacent harmonies is usually retained in the same voice.

7) In music for three or more voices, it is best to avoid moving them all in one direction.

8) Most dissonances should be approached and left by step. Exceptions include the appoggiatura, which is approached by a leap, the escape tone, which is left by a third (or occasionally a larger interval), and the leap of a third in the double neighbor group and the cambiata.

Chord doubling in three parts is seldom a problem except that leading tones, chords, sevenths, and most altered tones should not be doubled. This is true as well in four parts. If you were to add a fourth part to our round, you would need to consider carefully which chord tones to double. In four parts the normal doubling is of the root. Doubling the fifth is permitted occasionally. The third is usually not doubled, especially in major chords, and it is definitely avoided if it is a leading tone. If the third is to be doubled it is best when approached in contrary motion by step. In triads and seventh chords the fifth may be omitted. It is best not to omit the third except when all parts move to the root in a cadence.

If you added a fourth part to the Ex. 15-1 it is likely that it would need to cross over the existing parts. Crossing of parts is common in ensemble music of the Baroque, especially the treble parts in a trio sonata. It is best, however, to avoid part crossing in music for clavichord or harpsichord.

Chord spacing may be close or open, but the distance between any two upper parts in four-part music should not normally exceed an octave.

Exercises

EXERCISE 15-1. Using Ex. 15-2 as a starting point, add new decorative pitches of various kinds to all three parts in order to create a contrapuntal texture.

EXERCISE 15-2. Write a short passacaglia for two parts using the bass line of Ex. 15-2. Begin with one or two notes against the bass, then increase the average number of notes in later variations.

EXERCISE 15-3. Compose a fourth line for Ex. 15-1 using the text "But the last of the parts will pass you by." You may allow your new part to cross the others.

*EXERCISE 15-4. Write a four-variation passacaglia for two violins and continuo using the bass line of Ex. 15-2. Use some imitation between the violin parts. In the last variation add some decorations (divisions or diminutions) to the bass.

*EXERCISE 15-5. Write a round of your own in the style of Ex. 15-1.

CHAPTER
16

Polyphonic Style in 1700

Melodic, Harmonic, and Temporal Considerations; Polyphonic Textures

In the era of Lasso and Palestrina there existed a relatively unified musical language. The early Baroque was characterized by innovation and experimentation. By 1700, however, one could distinguish between the music of France, Italy, Germany, and England, and individual composers developed traits by which they could be identified. In spite of this diversity it is possible to make some generalizations about the mature Baroque style. Example 16-1 exhibits traits shared by composers of the first half of the eighteenth century.

EX. 16-1 Adagio from Sonata for Violin and Continuo Op. 5, No. 5 by Arcangelo Corelli (1653–1713)

Questions for Discussion

Melodic Considerations

1. What is the proportion of conjunct to disjunct motion in the unornamented violin part? What intervals are used in leaps? How does the melody behave after large leaps?

2. Apply Question 1 to the bass part.

3. How are the motives developed?

4. How can you recognize the cadences? If the ornamented version of the melody were to be played on a flute, where would the performer take breaths?

5. Describe the melodic contours in the violin part. What observations can you make about register changes? What is the range of the violin part?

6. What types of decorative or nonharmonic pitches do you find in the unornamented melody? In the ornamented version? Describe the decorative (structurally less essential) pitches in the bass line.

7. How are melodic unity and diversity kept in balance?

Harmonic Considerations

1. Describe the harmonic rhythm (the rate of change of harmony).
2. What intervals between the unornamented violin part and the bass are used most frequently? How are sevenths, fourths, seconds (ninths), and tritones used? What is the approximate ratio of consonances to dissonances?
3. Describe the palette of sonorities to be played by the continuo instrument. (See Appendix C if you are unfamiliar with figured bass symbols). Describe the function of any chromatic harmonies you encounter.
4. What types of cadences are used in this piece? What can you say about the key of the piece?

Temporal Considerations

1. The meter is strongly established by the continuo in the opening measures. Where and how has the metrical pulse been altered?
2. How are rhythmic stability and rhythmic variety kept in balance in this piece?
3. How does Corelli achieve the constant feeling of "forward motion"?
4. If this movement were part of a suite, what would it be called?

Observations

Melodic Considerations

The adagio, Ex. 16-1, is the third movement of a solo sonata. The *arioso* (or lyrical) melody has many traits which are common to Baroque melody in general, especially music of slower tempo. A more complete picture of Baroque melodic style will emerge with the study of pieces of a faster tempo as well, such as the opening and closing movements of concertos, toccatas, courantes, and gigues. Example 16-1, however, will give us a solid point of departure.

Conjunct motion exceeds disjunct motion in the unornamented violin part, but by only a small amount. There is more stepwise motion in the ornamented version. Leaps in the simple version include the augmented second, major, minor, and diminished third, perfect and augmented fourth, perfect fifth, major and minor sixth, diminished and major seventh, and perfect octave. The ornamented version includes the diminished fourth, diminished fifth, and minor seventh as well. We can gather from this that leaps of any size may be encountered in Baroque music. The tendency to turn back after large leaps is still honored, but not at all times. The major seventh leap from m. 3 to m. 4 is due to the register change for the sequence. The falling seventh leap found in mm. 17 and 20 in the ornamentation is followed by the downward step of the cadence. In these cases the upper note of the seventh was reached by arpeggiation. The leap of a diminished seventh from m. 26 to m. 27 (also mm. 32–33) is followed by a descending third. Here, the E♭ will be resolved by the D on beat three of the next measure, while the F♯ is the destination of the G on the downbeat of m. 26 as shown in Ex. 16-2. This is an example of *compound melody* in which the melodic line is broken by leaps in order to give the impression of two (sometimes more) strands of melody.

EX. 16-2 Examples of compound melody

(a) from Ex. 16-1, mm. 26-27   (b) from Ex. 12-3, mm. 19-21

Polyphonic equivalent

In compositions with continuo, the bass part serves more of a harmonic than a melodic function. Its rhythm is likely to be slower and more even than the melodic parts its supports, as we have seen in Ex. 11-1 and Ex. 13-2. The same holds true for Ex. 16-1. The bass contains more disjunct than conjunct motion due to the movement between root and third within measures and the root movement at cadences. Arpeggiated motion involves leaps of thirds and octaves, while cadential movement involves leaps of fourths and fifths. The movement from the root of one chord to the third of another, as in mm. 3–4 and 5–6, sometimes causes more unusual leaps such as the diminished fourth or the tritone. Leaps involved in register changes can be large (the major tenth in the cello part, m. 21).

Motivic development in the Baroque is accomplished by repetition, real and tonal sequence, inversion, and variation. In our example, the opening motive is twice restated as a sequence, first up a sixth, then up an additional fourth with cadential extension. The next phase, beginning in m. 10, describes a falling scale. The ornamentation adds sequential decoration to this. The phrase beginning in m. 15 also describes a downward scale but is varied by new "divisions" (also called "diminution") and immediately treated to sequence a step lower. The downward scale again provides the skeleton for the phrase beginning in m. 21, and again there is sequential treatment with extension to the half–cadence in m. 27. The final phrase, mm. 28–31, is repeated in varied form, mm. 32–35 with the extension that brings the final cadence. The bass has its own motives, which it develops independently. We have spoken of the root-third-root motive above. It is inverted in m. 2 to third-root-third. This pattern is repeated in varied sequence until the cadence in m. 10. Measures 15–17 are sequenced in mm. 18–20, after which sequences of a measure each parallel the sequences in the violin part.

The cadences can be recognized by: (a) the bass movement; (b) the figure consisting of a dotted-note trill and anticipation at the end of a phrase; and (c) a new set of sequences signaling the beginning of a new phrase. A flutist playing the ornamented version of the melody would probably take a breath at the end of each sub-phrase where the register changes occur. Other logical places would be before each of the half notes with ties. It is not surprising that these are also the cadence points.

The melodic contour of the first phrase rises through the three sequences, then settles for the cadence. The phrases which follow begin on higher notes and descend to their cadences. One exception is the rising motion in the phrase which begins with the upbeat to m. 28. Tension is created by the augmented second, which leaves the E♭ temporarily unresolved, but the tension is relaxed when the melody finally reaches D in m. 31, providing the delayed resolution. The changes of register at the beginning provide dramatic color and set up the prevailing downward motion to follow. This gives the melody a range of two octaves. The tessitura is rather high, with much of the music to be played on the E string of the violin.

In Chapter 11 we discovered a number of uses of dissonance besides the passing tone, neighbor tone, double neighbor, suspension, and cambiata, which were common in the Renaissance. The appoggiatura, the escape tone, the anticipation, and accented passing and neighbor tones were added to this list and became common in the seventeenth and eighteenth centuries. Our example contains all of these with the exception of the cambiata. The ornamentation contains many added passing tones and neighbor tones to embellish the basic pitches. It also employs the arpeggio figures mentioned earlier. The anticipation is still used mainly at cadence points, often coming after a trill, as in mm. 9, 14, 17, and 20, and in the ornamented version in mm. 34 and 35.

Suspensions are often given embellished or decorated resolutions. The term *delayed resolution* has been used for these suspensions, but we prefer to use the term *embellished resolution* since the resolution tone itself is not often delayed in time. We have already encountered embellished resolution of suspensions in sixteenth–century style (see Ex. 5-7). Ex. 16-3 shows several types of embellished resolutions of suspensions in Baroque style. Notice that the resolution marked 4 is actually delayed, since we expect to find it on beat two.

EX. 16-3 Examples of embellished resolution of suspensions in Baroque style

1) lower neighbor to the suspension
2) escape tone (upper neighbor to the suspension)
3) intervening harmonic pitch
4) delayed resoultion

In the Corelli adagio movement there are examples of type 1 in mm. 22 and 23, and type 2 in mm. 16 and 19. An example of the type 3 occurs in m. 31, but the expected resolution is not forthcoming in the violin part until m. 34 (although a point could be made for the resolution having been transferred to the bass in m. 32). An example of type 4 may be seen in Ex. 16-2 where the E♭ in m. 26 is not resolved until beat three of m. 27.

Decorative pitches in the bass of the Corelli movement are mostly passing tones.

In fugal movements, however, where the bass has a greater opportunity to join in the imitation, any of the dissonant figures may be used.

Baroque melody in general is characterized by the use of a limited number of rhythmic and melodic patterns or motives in a single movement. Diversity is achieved by the use of development and variation rather than the introduction of contrasting ideas. Corelli achieves a balance in this movement through sequences and varied repetitions. It is constructed from a small number of motives, and the movement sustains a single texture throughout.

Harmonic Considerations

Harmonic rhythm was one of the most important concerns of Baroque composers. Once set at the beginning of a movement, it remains stable through the movement. A slight quickening of the harmonic rhythm at cadence points is frequently encountered. Our example adheres closely to these principles; the harmonic rhythm is mostly one harmony per measure, and the rate of harmonic change is slightly increased at the cadences. In faster music, the harmonic rhythm may also be faster (two to four changes per measure), but there is little variation in the rate of harmonic change within the piece or movement.

The intervals found most frequently between melody and bass are thirds, sixths, and octaves (and their compound equivalents). The consonance to dissonance ratio is slightly more than 2:1. This compares to ratios of 3:1 or even 4:1 in the Renaissance. The larger number of sevenths and fourths is due to the frequent suspensions used by Corelli. Tritones and diminished sevenths appear often as members of dominant and diminished seventh chords.

By the eighteenth century, composers could choose from all diatonic triads and their inversions and all types of seventh chords. Although rare, the augmented triad could be found in pieces in minor as a result of an accented dissonance such as an appoggiatura or a suspended leading tone. The $III+_6$ involves no dissonances measured from the bass tone which can be seen in the except from a prelude by J. K. F. Fischer (Ex. 16-4).

EX. 16-4 From *Ariadne Musica,* Prelude No. 6, by J. K. F. Fischer (c. 1662–1746)

Purcell provides us with another curious use of the augmented triad in Ex. 14-3, m. 18.

Secondary dominant chords were used extensively (both dominant seventh and diminished seventh types). The Neapolitan sixth chord was in use by the middle of the seventeenth century. An example appears in Ex. 16-1, m. 13, beat one, in preparation for the cadence in D minor. Although there are no examples of the augmented sixth chords in Ex. 16-1, these too are part of the Baroque harmonic palette. Like the Neapolitan sixth chord, the augmented sixth chords are more common in minor keys.

The third movement of a sonata such as this one by Corelli is usually quite short. The final cadence is most often what can be called a *Phrygian cadence,* since the final pitch in the bass is approached by half step. It has the sound of a half–cadence, but the final movement is often in the relative major which does not provide a harmonic resolution. Interior cadences in our example are a half–cadence in G minor, m. 10; an authentic cadence to D minor, m. 15; authentic cadences to C minor in m. 18, and Bb major in m. 21, another half–cadence in G minor, m. 27, and authentic cadences to G minor im mm. 31 and 35. The last of these is extended to provide the customary Phrygian cadence for the ending. It is difficult to name a key for this piece for several reasons: it begins with a triad on Eb and does not have a full cadence before modulation takes place; the signature is a vestige of model practice and does not indicate the tonic; and the open quality of the final cadence leaves the key in doubt. In spite of this the functional home key appears to be G minor.

Temporal Considerations

The metrical pulse is established as three to the measure but is altered at several cadence points by the *hemiola.* The Baroque hemiola is most often a rendering of two 3/4 measures as if they were one 3/2 measure. Example 16-5, taken from a sonata for two flutes or recorders, illustrates the cadential hemiola (marked with brackets).

EX. 16-5 Largo from Sonata in F Major for two flutes or recorders by Jean-Baptiste Loeillet (b. 1688) (Note: Original time values have been divided by two.)

In the Corelli movement, Ex. 16-1, hemiolas occur in mm. 13–14, 16–17, 19–20, and 35.

Rhythmic stability is kept by the continuo, which allows for a great deal of rhythmic variety in the solo part, especially the ornamented version. The regular downbeats in the bass provide opportunities for frequent suspensions in the solo.

All but the first phrase of Ex. 16-1 begin on a half-note upbeat and end on a downbeat. This movement towards the downbeat from an upbeat creates the strong feeling of forward motion in the piece. This is a common trait of Baroque music. It can be seen in Examples 11-1, 12-2, 12-3, 13-2, and 14-3 (beginning in m. 37) and Ex. 14-4 (beginning in m. 6). The rhythmic motive in the opening phrase of the melody is the figure associated with the sarabande, one of the traditional movements of the Baroque suite.

Polyphonic Textures

We have examined thus far two types of polyphonic textures in Baroque music: (a) textures with continuo and (b) imitative textures. Two other general categories must be added to round out our survey of Baroque polyphony: (c) compositions employing a cantus firmus, and (d) "free counterpoint" which has neither cantus firmus nor continuo. The following genres can be assigned to the four categories:

Textures with Continuo	Imitative Textures	Cantus Firmus	Free Counterpoint
solo and trio sonatas	fugues	chorales	dances from suites
opera and cantata arias	fugal choruses	chorale preludes	toccatas
oratorio arias	fugal sonata movements	chorale variations	sonatas without continuo
recitatives	canons and inventions	motets	preludes
concertos	gigues	works based on	ritornellos
	ricercars, canzonas	plainchant	
		chaconnes, passacaglias	

Some special genres belong to more than one group, such as the canonic chorale variation and the aria over a ground; an overture makes use of the continuo, but the middle section is usually fugal.

Exercises

EXERCISE 16-1. Choose a short piece by Bach or Handel and apply the questions at the beginning of this chapter to it.

EXERCISE 16-2. Review the table in Exercise 2-4. Fill in the right-hand columns for the Baroque period.

*EXERCISE 16-3. Draw up a list of style traits you have found in Baroque music and compare it with the principles discussed in Chapter 3.

Sources for Further Study

Scores:

A variety of examples of music written around 1700 can be found in the following anthologies:

> Berry and Chudakoff: pp. 3–70
> Hardy and Fish, Vol II: pp. 59–67; 92–115; 121–124; 145–146
> *Harvard Anthology of Music,* Vol II: pp. 126–186 (Nos. 246–270) including the notes
> Parrish, *Treasury of Early Music:* pp. 253–303

Readings:

> Crocker: pp. 297–316
> Gauldin—18th c.: pp. 1–22
> Jeppesen: pp. 38–48
> Kennan: pp. 1–3

CHAPTER

17

Cantus Firmus Compositions

The Chorale Prelude

Johann Sebastian Bach's works based on chorale melodies represent the culmination of a tradition which began in the Reformation with Johann Walter (1496–1570) and others. By 1700, several distinct types had developed. Four of these are illustrated in Examples 17-1–17-4. Bach's chorale harmonizations, transposed to the appropriate keys, have been printed above the chorale preludes for ease in comparison.

EX. 17-1 Chorale prelude on Danket dem Herrn by Dietrich Buxtehude (1637–1707) (Verses 1, 2, and 3)

Versus 1

Versus 2

Versus 3

EX. 17-2 ''Christ lag in Todesbanden'' from *Orgelbüchlein* by Johann Sebastian Bach (1685–1750)

Chorale harmonization

EX. 17-3 "Ich ruf' zu dir, Herr Jesu Christ" from *Orgelbüchlein* by Johann Sebastian Bach

EX. 17-4 "Wenn wir in höchsten Nöthen sein" from *Orgelbüchlein* by Johann Sebastian
Bach

Chorale harmonization:

Questions for Discussion

1. How is the chorale tune used in each of the examples?
2. Compare the textures in the examples. How is the melody set apart from the accompanying voices? How can the organ be used to enhance the textures?
3. How are motivic patterns used in the accompanying voices?

4. How has Buxtehude harmonized the chorale in each verse? What reasons can you give for the differences in harmonization from one verse to another?

5. How do Bach's chorale harmonizations compare to the harmonies he uses in these preludes?

6. What techniques does Bach use to insure that we hear the chorale tune in spite of the ornamentation in Ex. 17-4?

7. What other types of compositions are based on or make use of chorale melodies?

Observations

Buxtehude gives us the unadorned chorale melody first in the highest voice, then in the middle voice (played by the pedals), and finally the lowest voice. This arrangement was common in chorale variations for keyboard throughout the seventeenth century. In Examples 17-2–17-4, the tune is in the highest part. Bach does, however, give the chorale tune to other voices in a few of the preludes in the *Orgelbüchlein*. The chorale "Christ lag in Todesbanden" is presented in basic quarter-note rhythm and given a slight amount of ornamentation. The first three phrases of "Ich ruf' zu dir" are ornamented, but the remainder of the tune is curiously unornamented. It seems likely that Bach intended the performer to continue the ornamentation until the end. The chorale melody has been highly ornamented in Ex. 17-4, and the first four notes of the tune provide the motivic material for the accompanying voices.

In all of our examples, the cantus firmus is set apart from the accompanying voices by rhythm. In all but the last example the chorale melody moves slowly and steadily against the faster-moving contrapuntal accompaniment. When the tune is highly ornamented, as in Ex. 17-4, the accompaniment moves in slower notes and provides a steady rhythmic support for the ebb and flow of the freely moving melody. The texture of each example is different. In Ex. 17-1, a freely imitative duet is set against the cantus firmus. In Ex. 17-2, a four-note motive appears in one or more of the voices on nearly every beat creating a dense imitative texture. In Ex. 17-3, there are three layers of movement—melody with some ornamentation, inner part in sixteenth notes creating a rich harmonic texture, and bass moving in steady eighth notes. In Ex. 17-4, the highly ornamented chorale tune is supported by a slower-moving imitative texture based, as we have observed above, on the opening notes of the chorale. These pieces were written for organ with at least two manuals and a full set of pedals. A solo stop in the pedals will enhance the melody in verses 2 and 3 of Ex. 17-1. All three parts can be given different registrations in Ex. 17-3. A solo stop for the right hand will serve well in Ex. 17-4 with the left hand and pedal parts given a less distinctive registration. A single manual alone can be used for verse 1 of Ex. 17-1, and one manual with pedals is sufficent for Ex. 17-2 where the rhythm sets the melody apart.

Bach begins with a harmonic progression and elaborates it with the counterpoint; Buxtehude's harmony seems more to be a result of the contrapuntal motion. Verses 1 and 2 follow the same tonal plan but differ in the use of decorative harmonies. Both move from G minor to B♭ major from mm. 1–3, but in different ways. Verse 1: iv i ii° V i V$^6_5$/III; verse 2:i v ii°$_6$ III VI ii°$_6$ V/III. [Note: V/III indicates a secondary dominant relationship, **V** of III]. Verses 1 and 2 both reach a cadence to the dominant in m. 6. All three verses conclude with a plagal cadence on G with Picardy third. Verse 3 has a number of harmonic differences because of the placement of the cantus firmus in the bass. In m. 6, a D major chord would be inappropriate with A in the bass (which would create an inconclusive $^6_4$ chord). The progression in mm. 9–10 has a modal flavor: VII$_6$ v iv. The final cadence is vii°$_6$ to I with cadential extension which recalls the plagal cadences in the other verses.

Bach retains very nearly the same harmonies and voice leading in the prelude on "Christ lag in Todesbanden" as he uses in the chorale harmonization. The double-neighbor motive fits very nicely in places where the chorale setting has downward-moving eighth notes. Bach sometimes adds embellishing harmonies; in the prelude, a ii°$^6_5$ embellishes the V/V in m. 2, for example.

In "Ich ruf' zu dir, Herr Jesu Christ," the texture of the prelude invites a completely reworked harmonization. Several of the cadences are different: there is a half–cadence in the prelude and full cadence in the chorale in m. 4; authentic cadence to C minor in the prelude and E♭ major in the chorale in m. 8; and an authentic cadence to A♭ major in the prelude and half–cadence in B♭ minor in the chorale in m. 11. The inner part creates a rich harmonic texture with its use of arpeggios, neighbor tones, leaning tones (unaccented appoggiaturas), and anticipations. It is an excellent example of compound melody. Each note of one group moves logically to its successor in the next group.

The cadential plan in Ex. 17-3 agrees closely with that of the chorale setting. Individual harmonies, however, respond to the needs of the imitation in the accompanying parts. The chief attraction of this prelude is the incredible variety and fluency of the ornamentation. Bach uses many ways to draw our attention to each note of the original cantus firmus. Among them are: (1) locating the note *on* the beat rather than between beats, (2) giving the note longer durations, (3) shifting to longer or shorter time values with the note, (4) leaping from or to the note, (5) giving the note special embellishments such as trills and mordents, (6) preceding the note with an appoggiatura, (7) initiating a sequence with the note, (8) turning about the note with neighbor or double-neighbor figures, and (9) avoiding the note until its time has come to be heard.

Thus far we have considered chorale preludes of four different types: (a) cantus firmus in long notes with free imitative counterpoint, (b) chorale melody accompanied by motivic elaboration, (c) chorale with layered texture, and (d) highly ornamented chorale melody. Several additional types exist, some of which will be discussed in later chapters: (e) canonic chorale preludes, (f) preludes with fugal treatment of the opening phrase of a chorale; (g) motet-style chorale preludes; and (h) preludes where the chorale is superimposed periodically upon unrelated music. Chorale preludes are generally shorter pieces which can stand alone. Other genres which make use of chorales include chorale variations, large fugues based on a chorale, and the chorale concerto or chorale fantasia found in cantatas.

Exercises

EXERCISE 17-1. Complete the beginning of the chorale prelude below as a motivic embellishment type using the given chorale harmonization as a guide. Continue the motion until the fourth beat of m. 2.

Jesu meine Freude

EXERCISE 17-2. Complete the beginning of the chorale prelude below as a layered type using the given chorale harmonization as a point of departure. If possible, continue the patterns in the lower parts.

Liebster Jesu, wir sind hier

EXERCISE 17-3. Complete the beginning of the chorale prelude below as ornamented cantus firmus type using the given chorale harmonization as a guide.

Vater unser in Himmelreich

*EXERCISE 17-4. Write a four-part chorale prelude of the motivic embellishment type on the following hymn tune. Use the figured bass as a guide for your harmonization.

Stuttgart

*EXERCISE 17-5. Write a chorale prelude on the canon below with the leader in the top part, the follower in the pedals, and a figured contrapuntal part between. You may wish to write the follower an octave lower.

Tallis Canon

*EXERCISE 17-6. Write a chorale prelude of the ornamental cantus firmus type on "America" ("My country, 'tis of thee").

Sources for Further Study

Scores:

Bach: *Das Orgelbüchlein, Schübler chorales*
Böhm: *Keyboard Works,* Vol II, ed. by Wolgast
Buxtehude: *Organ Works,* Vol II, Peters edition
Pachelbel: *Organ Works in DTB,* Vol IV
Walther, Johann: *Organ Works in DDT,* Vol. 26–27

Readings:

Gauldin—18th c.: pp. 141–154; 229–243
Kennan: pp. 249–269
"Organ Chorale" entry in your music dictionary or encyclopedia (the *New Harvard Dictionary of Music,* p. 589; and the Norton/Grove *Concise Encyclopedia of Music,* p. 152)

CHAPTER

18

Invention

Bach's Two-Part Inventions

Bach's two-part "inventions" were first called *Praeambles* and were written as keyboard exercises and lessons in two-part composition. Today they are still extremely useful for both purposes. Two of them are shown in Examples 18-1 and 18-2.

EX. 18-1 Invention No. 1 by Johann Sebastian Bach (1685–1750)

EX. 18-2 Invention No. 7 by Johann Sebastian Bach

Questions for Discussion

1. The C Major invention is based on a single thematic idea. Since thematic contrast cannot be used to delineate the structure of the piece, what musical elements serve this purpose? Is this true in the case of the E Minor invention?

2. How is the thematic material presented?

3. After the thematic material has been presented, how is it subsequently developed in each of the examples? What technique is employed in Invention No. 1, mm. 11–13 compared to mm. 3–5?

4. How does Bach sustain our interest in spite of the fact that both pieces present a steady flow of sixteenth notes from beginning to end?

5. Discuss the harmonic rhythm in each piece. How is it related to the structure?

6. How does the lower part differ from the bass parts in Examples 13-2, 16-1, and 17-3?

7. What techniques does Bach use to give the final cadences added weight?

Observations

Imitative genres such as Bach's inventions, canons, and fugues do not adhere to any predictable form or structure; they do, however, exhibit predictable procedures for composition. Bach gives us a variety of structures in his inventions; some appear to have three sections, others two, and still others are virtually seamless (such as No. 2, which is canonic). The inventions, like most Baroque genres, are *monothematic*— based on a single musical idea. We perceive the structure in terms of the tonal plan, the alternation of tonal stability and modulation, and the alternation of thematic "presentations" and "episodes" where development takes place. At the points of alternation we can expect to find strong cadences. Both of the inventions above exemplify these principles.

We will call the musical idea presented at the beginning of an invention its "theme," rather than "motive," which denotes a basic musical fragment, or "subject," which will be reserved for the fugue. In both examples the theme is presented in the upper voice, then imitated in the lower voice at the octave. Following this the theme is presented in the dominant and imitated an octave lower. Example 18-3 shows the *expositions* of the two inventions. If the counterpoint to the theme ("t") is used consistently, it can be designated as the *countertheme* ("ct").

EX. 18-3 Expositions from Invention No. 1 and No. 7

If the theme of an invention is longer than a measure or so it may be given one statement and response before moving into an episode. Although most of the inventions begin with responses in the tonic, a few have the response in the dominant, as in Inventions No. 10 and No. 15. In all cases the exposition establishes the tonic key.

Following the exposition in each example is an episode which develops the theme in sequence which modulates, ending with a perfect authentic cadence (PAC). In Invention No. 1, the episode begins with sequential treatment of the theme in inversion (mm. 3 and 4) followed by a statement in the lower part on D and another in inversion in the upper part (m. 5) with extension (the "y" motive) leading to the cadence in the dominant (m. 7). The episode in mm. 3–7 of Invention No. 7 is similar except that the sequence involves alternation of the theme in the upper and lower parts which modulates (by circle of fifths) to the relative major. It is a common procedure in Baroque music for the first modulation to cadence in the dominant when the tonic is major and in the relative major when the tonic is minor.

Sequence and imitation are the tools most often used by Baroque composers to develop their ideas. Repetition and alteration are also very useful techniques. Another important technique to be found in these inventions is invertible counterpoint, or double counterpoint. (See Ch. 6, p. 56 for a discussion of double counterpoint). Example 18-4 illustrates double counterpoint in Baroque style.

EX. 18-4 Double counterpoint in Baroque style

a) at the octave

b) at the twelfth

In Ex. 18-1, the music of mm. 3–5 reappears with the parts interchanged at mm. 11–13, providing us with a fine example of double counterpoint at the octave, transposed to D minor.

Both inventions sustain constant sixteenth-note motion by a judicious distribution of movement between the parts. The texture is varied by first alternating the motion, then letting one part move for a longer passage while the other rests or moves slower, then giving the motion to both parts. In the first example the roles of the two parts are exchanged in the second section compared to the first. This is a feature common to most of the inventions (Nos. 1, 4, 6, 8, 10, 11, 13, 14, and 15).

Harmonic rhythm in these examples is quite stable. It is slower (one harmony to the measure) in the exposition, and faster (two per measure) during the episodes. A noticeable quickening of the harmonic rhythm occurs at the cadences. Each of the three sections of Invention No. 1 begins with a single harmony per measure.

The upper and lower parts are designed as equal partners in the polyphony. In compositions with continuo, the bass plays a different role: to provide a harmonic support for the upper parts. You will notice, however, that at cadences, the lower part in the inventions serves this function as well.

Bach often avoids the first opportunity to bring the final cadence in order to give it more weight when it finally arrives. He uses a number of techniques to do this. In Ex. 18-1, m. 21, the bass is given an E rather than a C, making an inconclusive cadence. The subsequent harmonic move towards the subdominant prepares us for the final authentic cadence. In Ex. 18-2, m. 22, a deceptive cadence promises us more to come, and strengthens the final authentic cadence when it does come. In both examples the melody is given a chance to descend to the lower octave for the close.

Writing a Two-Part Invention With Bach's C Major Invention As a Model

Refer to Ex. 18-5 below and Ex. 18-1 as you work through these steps.

1) Construct your theme. Make sure that it: (a) is limited to just one or two well defined motives; (b) lends itself well to sequence (and possibly also inversion); and (c) has unambiguous harmonic implications. Write it in the upper part in the opening measure(s).

2) Answer the theme with a response in the tonic. (Give the theme to the lower part down an octave immediately following its appearance in the upper part).

3) Write a counterpoint above the theme's first appearance in the lower part. This counterpoint will serve as the countertheme. Theme and countertheme should be composed in double counterpoint at the octave.

4) Continue the upper part with the theme on the dominant (up a perfect fifth or down a perfect fourth).

5) Continue the lower part with a counterpoint which bears some resemblance to the countertheme, then answer the theme with a response on the dominant.

6) Make a harmonic plan for a set of sequences and a modulation to V, if your tonic is major, or III if your tonic is minor.

7) Express your harmonic plan in basic pitches in both parts. These pitches should indicate your sequences and serve as a skeleton for your work.

8) Begin the sequence with quotations of the theme in the upper part, then allow the theme to appear in the lower part. As you approach the cadence the theme may be fragmented with sequential treatment of single motives.

9) Write counterpoint against the theme quotations. Use motives from the countertheme. As you approach the cadence you may wish to have both parts move together in the shorter note values of the theme.

10) A cadence figure should be used which provides some motivic contrast to the theme. This cadence completes the first section.

EX. 18-5 Steps in writing the first section of an invention

As we have observed above, the second section begins with a new exposition of the theme in the new key (V or III) with the parts interchanged: the theme is given to the lower part first, then to the upper part. A similar process is used in writing the second section with the modulation culminating in a new related key (vi, ii, iii, or IV when the tonic is major, v, VI, or iv when the tonic is minor).

The third section usually begins immediately with sequences, the theme in alternation between the parts. The final cadence in the tonic is often delayed by a deceptive move (once the dominant has been reached).

Exercises

EXERCISE 18-1. Complete this invention exposition.

EXERCISE 18-2. Write expositions on these invention themes.

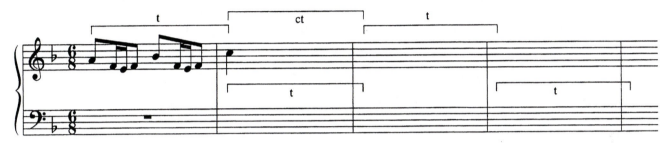

EXERCISE 18-3. Complete as an example of double counterpoint at the octave.

*EXERCISE 18-4. Complete the first section of an invention using this beginning. Make a cadence in B♭. (Total length of the section: about 12–18 measures.)

*EXERCISE 18-5. Write an invention in B minor using the following plan:

SECTION I

	Exposition				Episode	Cadence
Upper part	t	ct	t	ct	Development of t motives	
Lower part	—	t	(ct)	t	″	
B minor:	i	i	V	V	modulating to	D major

SECTION II

	Exposition			Episode	Cadence
Upper part	—	t	(ct)	Development of 1/t motives	
Lower part	t	(ct)	1/t*	″	
D major:	I	V	I	modulating to	F♯ minor

SECTION III

	Episode	Deceptive Cadence	Codetta
	Development of t and 1/t motives		
F♯ minor	modulating to	B minor VI	B minor

* 1/t = theme inverted

Sources for Further Study

Scores:

Bach: Fifteen Two-part Inventions
Telemann: Keyboard Fantasias

Readings:

Gauldin—18th c.: pp. 122–130
Kennan: pp. 125–143

CHAPTER

19

Three-Part Counterpoint

Bach's Sinfonias

The composition shown in Ex. 19-1 is a superb example of three-part writing which does not involve a continuo. It also shows Bach's skill in triple counterpoint and use of chromatic harmony. Notation of the piece is in three staves to show the parts more clearly.

EX. 19-1 Sinfonia No. 9 by Johann Sebastian Bach (1685–1750)

Questions for Discussion

1. How many distinct thematic ideas are developed in this piece? How do they differ as to character?

2. Describe how these ideas are distributed among the parts.

3. What is the key scheme of the piece? Where are the cadences? Where are the modulatory passages? How are the themes used during these modulatory episodes?

4. Can you give a definition of triple counterpoint? When composing and combining themes in triple counterpoint, what principles must you keep in mind?

5. What kinds of chromatic harmonies do you find in this piece?

6. How does the texture of this sinfonia differ from that of the trio sonata with continuo?

7. The pieces from which this example is taken are called "sinfonias" by Bach. They have also been called "three-part inventions." What reasons can you give for this alternative title?

Observations

Three themes are developed in the sinfonia illustrated in Ex. 19-2. Theme A is characterized by a downward–moving chromatic scale in quarter notes from the tonic to the dominant (a) followed by a cadencing figure (a'). Theme B is characterized by a "sighing" motive (b) beginning and ending "off the beat," then treated to a sequential repetition up a step, followed by a falling diatonic scale motive (b'). Theme C begins after beat two with a quick rhythmic figure (c) involving a chromatically altered double neighbor (resulting in a diminished third between upper and lower neighbor tones), then repeated a fourth higher and slightly altered, ending in a cadencing figure (c') which is treated freely throughout the piece. It is interesting to note that motive (c) is a decorated version of motive (b), a fourth higher.

EX. **19-2 Themes from Sinfonia No. 9**

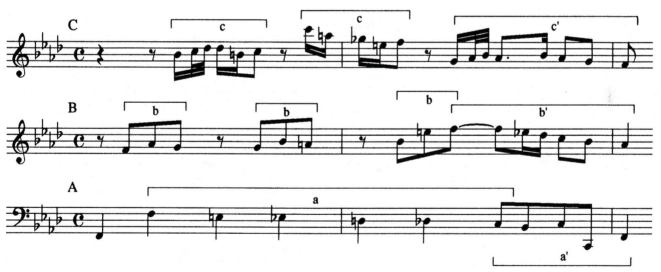

Table 19-1 shows how the three themes are distributed and developed as the piece unfolds. Upper case letters indicate theme statements; lower case letters indicate motives developed in episodes. The key scheme (in Roman numerals showing "regions") is given on the bottom line. Notice that when the statements come in pairs, they are related by falling fourth (F-C in mm. 1–4, A♭-E♭ in mm. 11–14; and D♭-A♭ in mm. 24–27). The statements end in authentic cadences, and the keys they represent are all closedly related to F minor—that is, keys which are at most only one flat removed from the tonic key.

TABLE 19-1

DISTRIBUTION OF THEMES IN EX. 19-1

1 2 3 4 5 6 7 8 9 10 11 12 13 14 15 16 17 18 19 20 21 22 23 24 25 26 27 28 29 30 31 32 33 34

—	B	b,c	A	b′a	C	B	b a	A	b′a b	b′a b	A	B	a b	B	C
B A		b,c	C	b	B	A	a b	B	ab′ ab′	b′b′ ab′	C	A	b a	A	B
A C		—	B	ab′	A	C	b b	C	b	b′a b	b′a	B	C	b b	C	A
i	v	mod	i	mod.	III	VII	mod.	v	mod.		VI	III	mod.	i	i

All of the modulatory episodes except the first one develop motives of themes A and B. The bridge-like episode in mm. 5-6 develops the "c" motive primarily, but it does not use the thirty-second notes which we find in theme C. In fact, it is the absence of these quick notes which sets the episodes apart rhythmically from the statements.

A quick look at the table above shows that themes A, B, and C appear in several vertical arrangements. If three contrapuntal parts reappear in a piece with their vertical positions exchanged, they are said to be in *triple counterpoint.* Satisfactory musical results must be obtained whichever part is given the lowest position. The most important consideration is the inversion of triads. Root position and first inversion can be exchanged in most contexts, but the second inversion ($^6_4$ position) must be carefully used: (a) in a cadential pattern; (b) as the result of arpeggio motion in the bass; or (c) as the result of decorative pitches (passing tones, neighbor tones, appoggiaturas, etc.) in the upper parts. Since the interval of a fifth inverts to a fourth, a root–position triad will appear in second inversion in another configuration in triple counterpoint. Parallel chords in first inversion should be avoided since they will appear as parallel root–position chords in another configuration, resulting in parallel fifths. Good triple counterpoint often employs triads with the fifth omitted, implied seventh chords, a good deal of contrary motion, and a lighter texture punctuated with rests.

Bach's F Minor Sinfonia is rich in chromatic harmony. Example 19-3 is a chordal reduction of mm. 33–35 where all three themes are together in the tonic. The same progression appears at all statements of the themes but in triple counterpoint—that is, employing inversions and appearing in various keys.

EX. 19-3 Basic progression for theme statements

Reduction:

f: i   ii°$_2^4$ V$_6$ vii°$_3^4$/IV   IV$_6$ ii°$_3^4$ i $_4^6$ V$_7$ i

Note the use of seventh chords, secondary dominant, and mutated IV chord. The modulating episodes make use of secondary dominants as well, especially of the diminished seventh type. The first episode also hints at the Neapolitan sixth in the use of G♭s (mm. 5–6).

The sinfonias of Bach (with the possible exception of No. 5) treat all parts with equal contrapuntal importance. This is in contrast to trio textures employing continuo, where the bass part more often provides harmonic support. The fact that all parts share in the thematic development in the sinfonias accounts for the alternative title "three-part inventions."

Exercises

EXERCISE 19-1. Rewrite this passage twice, once with theme B in the bass and again with theme C in the bass.

EXERCISE 19-2. Rewrite the passage above in the key of G.

EXERCISE 19-3. Add "divisions" (decorations or diminutions) to this sequence of harmonies to make a three-part contrapuntal texture. Try to use some imitation.

*EXERCISE 19-4. Write a sinfonia or three-part invention using this plan.

1	2	3	4	5	6	7	8	9	10	11	12	13	14	15	16	17	18	19	20	21	22*
A			C		Episode No. 1 using motives from A,B				B		Episode No. 2 using motives from B,C			A		Episode No. 3 like Episode No. 1			B		C
B			A						C					C					A		B
C			B						A					B					C		A
i			v		mod. to				III		mod. to			VI		mod. to			iv		i

* optional measure

Sources for Further Study

Scores:

Bach: Sinfonias (Three-part Inventions)

Readings:

Gauldin—18th c.: pp. 157–193
Kennan: pp. 144–191

CHAPTER

20

Canon

Two-Part Canon; Accompanied Canon; Canonic Chorale Prelude

The canon is a species of composition in which composers can display their highest degree of contrapuntal skill. Examples 20-1–20-3 show a simple two-part canon at the unison, a canon at the sixth with accompanying bass, and a chorale prelude with canon between the outer voices.

EX. 20-1 Sonata I, Third movement from *Sechs Sonaten oder Kanons für zwei Querflöten oder violinen* by Georg Philipp Telemann (1681–1767)

EX. 20-2 Variation 18 from *Goldberg Variations* by Johann Sebastian Bach (1685–1750)

EX. 20-3 "Erschienen ist der herrliche Tag" from *Orgelbüchlein* by Johann Sebastian Bach

Questions for Discussion

1. A canon at the unison presents special problems for the composer. What are some of these problems, and how has Telemann solved them?

2. Telemann's canon has the comes only two scant quarters behind the dux. What special problems does this pose?

3. How should one proceed when composing a canon?

4. What is the formal structure and tonal plan of Ex. 20-1?

5. Bach's *Goldberg Variations* consists of an aria with thirty variations based on the same harmonic progression and tonal plan. What is the tonal plan of this variation?

6. Variation 18 is one of the nine canons in the set which includes canons at various intervals. What special problems did Bach have to solve in writing canons at different intervals all following the same succession of harmonies?

7. In the *Orgelbüchlein* there are several canonic chorale preludes of which Ex. 20-3 is one. In these preludes the chorale itself appears in canon. Since the melodies were not originally conceived as canons, some adjustments must be allowed. What liberties has Bach taken with this chorale?

8. How should one proceed in writing this type of chorale prelude?

Observations

Two-Part Canon at the Unison

Telemann wrote six sonatas in canon for two treble instruments, each with three movements. Example 19-1 has been transposed so that it can be played by two alto recorders. Writing canons in unison presents certain difficulties: In order for the parts to be heard independently, they must either move together in one direction or cross each other. In mm. 3–4, Telemann has allowed one voice to descend by step while the other leaps over it; in m. 6 the voices come to a unison before recrossing; and in m. 30 the leader crosses over the follower which is sustaining on a quarter note. Telemann carefully avoids part-crossing when both parts rise or fall in the same rhythm. When the comes is as close behind the dux as it is in this example, it is difficult to make interesting harmonic progressions. Telemann's solution is to give us a harmonic rhythm of quarter notes, allowing for two harmonies between dux and comes. He also provides variety by register shifts and modulation.

At this point it would be useful to review the guidelines for writing a two-voice canon given in Chapter 5, p. 47. Here is a brief summary of those guidelines: When writing a canon it is best to compose only as much of the dux as the distance between it and the comes. The resulting notes of the comes should be filled in immediately. Next, the dux is given a suitable counterpoint to the notes just transcribed in the comes. This counterpoint is then transferred to the comes, etc. Example 20-4 illustrates the process with music in Baroque style.

EX. 20-4 Review of the steps in writing a two-voice canon

The formal plan of the canon by Telemann, Ex. 20-1, is a simple rondo—A B A C A. Measures 1–20 comprise the rondo theme, a period with extension beginning in B♭ major and ending with an authentic cadence in the tonic. The B section, mm. 21–38, begins in the tonic with a new idea but quickly modulates to the dominant with a transposition of the antecedent phrase of the rondo theme. Next is a verbatim repetition of the A section. At m. 59 we find ourselves in the relative minor for the beginning of the C section, but a quick modulation takes us to the mediant key (D minor) from m. 64 to m. 79, and again the material is taken from the closing measures of the rondo theme. A single measure is used to provide a link which returns us to the tonic for the final A.

Accompanied Canon

Bach's "Aria mit dreißig Veränderungen," the proper title for the *Goldberg Variations,* has a unique overall structural plan. The thirty variations are divided into ten groups of three, each group consisting of a character piece (fughetta, aria, overture, etc.), a toccata-like piece, and a canon (except for No. 30, which is a *quodlibet,* a piece where snatches of familiar tunes are combined). The canons proceed from the unison through the ninth. If you divide the number of the variation by three, the result is the interval distance between the canonic voices. Variation 6 is a canon at the second; Variation 21 is a canon at the seventh, for example. With the exception of the canon at the ninth, these are accompanied canons, the two upper voices are in canon and are accompanied by an independent bass part. The canons at the fourth and the fifth are special since they are canons at the inversion. Example 20-5 shows the basic harmonic plan for each variation. Since all of the variations follow this harmonic scheme, the beginning pitches and the distance between leader and follower are severely limited. Variation 18 is the canon at the sixth (18÷3=6). Bach decided to allow only a half measure between the canonic voices so that a harmonic rhythm of one to the measure could be used. In the canon at the unison he gives two measures between dux and comes so that the follower would harmonize with the E–minor chord; in the canon at the second, the comes could begin in m. 2, etc.

EX. 20-5 Harmonic plan for the *Goldberg Variations*

(a) In the major mode

(b) In the minor mode

In Variation 18 the lively bass provides a fine support for the syncopations and suspensions in the canonic voices. Note that the canon is allowed to start fresh after each cadence. Note also that the final eight measures are a repetition of mm. 9–16 a fourth higher.

Canonic Chorale Prelude

The canonic chorale prelude is a special genre in which at least two of the voices are in canon. The canonic preludes in the *Orgelbüchlein* present the chorale itself in canon. Few chorale melodies will support canonic treatment, but some are close enough that a few minor adjustments will allow their use as canons. In Ex. 20-3, the chorale tune was altered in the pedal part in m. 8 to avoid an unpleasant seventh, and in mm. 10–12 to avoid direct octaves and an unresolved second inversion chord. Other than these small alterations, the chorale melody is intact throughout. When a composer wished to write this type of chorale prelude, the first requirement was to find a chorale tune which was suitable to canonic treatment, allowing for slight modifications such as we have discussed above. Once the chorale canon was sketched in, a basic harmonization would be planned. Finally a figure would be chosen for the accompanying voices.

Bach wrote another type of canonic piece based on the chorale. In it the chorale melody was presented as a cantus firmus with a canon in the accompanying voices. A fine example of this is the first in his set of variations on the chorale "Von Himmel hoch," shown in Ex. 20-6.

EX. 20-6 Opening of *Canonic variations on Von Himmel Hoch* by Bach

Exercises

EXERCISE 20-1. Continue this canon for two violins. Make a cadence in B♭ major in mm. 10–12.

EXERCISE 20-2. Continue this canon at the fifth. Make a cadence in D minor in mm. 8–10.

EXERCISE 20-3. Use this as a skeleton for an accompanied canon at the third based on the harmonic plan of the *Goldberg Variations,* first 16 measures.

EXERCISE 20-4. Provide a bass for this canon at the seventh based on the minor version of the *Goldberg Variations* harmonic plan, first 16 measures.

*EXERCISE 20-5. Using your solution for the previous question as the first half of a variation with canon at the seventh, compose the second half.

*EXERCISE 20-6. Complete this canonic chorale prelude on the tune "Puer nobis."

Sources for Further Study

Scores:

It is useful in the study of Baroque canons to examine a few canonic works from the Renaissance. The following are suggested:

> Anonymous: *Non nobis, Domine,* attributed to William Byrd
> Josquin: Chanson "Bassiez moi"
> Palestrina: *Missa ad fugam*
> Zarlino: Canons from *Le Istitutioni harmonice*

Canonic music from the Baroque:

> Bach: Canons from *Das musicalische Opfer, Goldberg Variations,* Invention No.
>   2, Canonic variations on *Von Himmel hoch;* and canons from *Art of Fugue*
> Telemann: *Sonaten im Kanon* for two flutes
> Kirnberger: Modulating canon (quoted in Horsley, pp. 28–29)

Readings:

> Gauldin—18th c.: pp. 117–122; 202–208
> Jeppesen: pp. 234–240
> Kennan: pp. 90–113; 255
> Mann: pp. 227–282
> Morley: pp. 150; 177–187

CHAPTER

21

Fugue I

Overview; Subject and Response; Countersubject

Fugue represents the highest and noblest in the art of polyphonic composition. It combines the techniques of imitation and canon with those of variation and development. Fugues can be long or short, fast or slow, sombre or gay, and they come in a variety of structural forms. First we will try to discover some generalities about fugue, and then we will focus on the subject, its answer, and its deployment in the exposition.

Examine the fugues shown in Ex. 21-1–21-3 and the pieces we considered in Chapter 14 as you discuss the questions below.

EX. 21-1 Fugue in C by Johann Pachelbel (1653–1706)

EX. 21-2 Fugue in G by Johann Kaspar Fischer (1662–1746)

EX. 21-3 Fugue II from *The Well-Tempered Clavier*, Book I by Johann Sebastian Bach (1685–1750)

Questions for Discussion

1. What will you find in all fugues, including these examples?
2. How does a fugue differ from a two-part invention? A three-part invention?
3. What generalizations can you make about the tonal plan of a fugue?
4. How would you describe a good fugue subject—its character, rhythm, shape, motivic content, and tonal implications? What scale degrees do you expect to find as the first note of a fugue subject? Why would a period make a poor subject?
5. In Chapter 14 we discussed real and tonal responses. In the examples above, which have real responses and which have tonal responses? Which type of response would you expect if the subject begins on the fifth degree of the scale or if the tonic triad is prominent in the "head motive"? How many of the fugues in Bach's *Well-Tempered Clavier* have real responses? Can fugue subjects modulate? Can they be chromatic?
6. After the subject has been presented by the first voice in a fugue, that voice continues with counterpoint against the entrance of the subject in the second voice. Has this counterpoint played an important part in any of the above examples or those in Chapter 14?

Observations

What Is a Fugue?

When we hear a Baroque piece of music which begins with a strong musical idea presented in solo or in unison (without accompanying voices), it is very likely that we are hearing a fugue. If the piece continues by adding two or more voices in succession, all of which in turn present the opening musical idea while those ahead of them continue in counterpoint, we are even more certain that the piece is a fugue. If the musical idea is subsequently developed until the end of the piece, it is without doubt a fugue. All fugues begin with a subject presented in exposition, then continue with development of that subject. Some special fugues may have more than one subject, but the exposition and subsequent development are the only "formal" requirements for a fugue. This is obviously congruent with the often quoted statement that "fugue is a process of composition, not a form."

Inventions are quite similar to fugues except that their themes are usually shorter, and the second voice usually imitates the leader at the octave. Bach's Sinfonia in F Minor, Ex. 19-1, might be considered a "triple fugue" since it has three "subjects" which are exposed and then developed until the end of the piece.

Fugues normally begin with subjects which emphasize the tonic. The response normally emphasizes the dominant (or dominant minor when the subject is in minor). The entrance of the third voice re–establishes the tonic, and a fourth voice, when there is one, reintroduces the dominant. This tonic-dominant pairing of voices is normal for Baroque fugues. After the exposition the tonal plan may involve modulations to closely related keys. In Ex. 21-1 there is a modulation to the relative minor before the tonic returns at the end. In Ex. 21-2 all of the subject statements are on G or D, but in m. 15–16, the tenor statement on G is treated as if it were in E minor. In Ex. 21-3, after establishing C minor in the exposition, Bach takes us to the relative major for a statement beginning in m. 11. The final statements are in the tonic. Tonal variety is generated in the episodes, which employ modulating sequences. Longer fugues may stray farther afield from the tonic key, but for the most part, Baroque composers including Bach, rarely move outside of the closely–related keys.

What Makes a Good Subject?

As we have seen, subjects come in various lengths, moods, and styles. An examination of the best subjects, however, reveals some general characteristics which they share. A good subject exhibits the following attributes:

1) It has a "high profile": a strong enough character to be easily identified in the midst of the polyphony.
2) It is expected to establish the tonic, if not in its head motive, at least in a strong concluding cadence.
3) It has a small enough range so that it can be managed in the polyphony in any of the voices—usually an octave or less.
4) It has a pleasing melodic shape (not one which is skewed suddenly in one direction, wavers up and down undecidedly, or overemphasizes a few pitches).
5) It is limited to just a few easily recognized motives.
6) It usually begins on the tonic or dominant scale degree and often ends on the third scale degree.

The subject may begin boldly with longer notes, then move off with quicker notes in a "tail" preparing the way for the responding voice. On the other hand, it may begin with quick figures, ending with slower notes for a cadence. It prepares the way for its response or answer in the dominant. A melody which is in the form of a period is likely to make a poor subject since it "answers" itself, pre–empting the responding voice.

Fugue subjects (with their responses) covering a span of a hundred years are quoted in Ex. 21-4. See how many of these desirable characteristics can be found in each of the subjects.

EX. 21-4 Examples of fugue subjects and their responses

(a)   Allesandro Scarlatti (1660-1725): Sonata a quattro in G minor

(b)   François Couperin (1668-1733): Messe pour les Paroisses

(c)   Bach: Fugue V, WTC II

(d)   Handel: Trio Sonata in F

(e)   W. A. Mozart (1756-1791): Fantasy and Fugue in C, K394

Real and Tonal Responses

The little fugue by Fischer, Ex. 21-2, has a real response to the subject. Remember that a real response is an exact transposition a fifth higher or a fourth lower. The others have tonal responses. In Pachelbel's miniature fugue the Cs in the subject become Gs in the response, and the Gs in the subject become Cs in the response. Thus, the subject begins with a rising fourth and the response with a rising fifth. The same is true with Bach's C Minor fugue, Ex. 21-3. Here, the falling fourth is answered by the falling fifth.

Example 21-5 shows the beginning motives of several types of subjects which require tonal responses. In the examples, scale degree 1 in the head motive is answered by scale degree 5 in the response and vice versa. As soon as this adjustment is made, the response proceeds as if it were a real one.

EX. 21-5 Types of fugue subjects requiring tonal responses

Type (a) includes subjects which begin with scale degrees 1 to 5 (and vice versa); type (b), subjects with triadic figures in the head motive; type (c), subjects which begin on the dominant note; and type (d), subjects with the leading tone in a prominent position in the head motive. Note that the leading tone is answered by the third degree. Subjects which modulate also require tonal responses.

Modulating Subjects

Some subjects modulate to the dominant (but not to any other region). Such subjects require responses which are adjusted in order to return to the tonic, as shown in Ex. 21-6.

EX. 21-6 Modulating fugue subjects

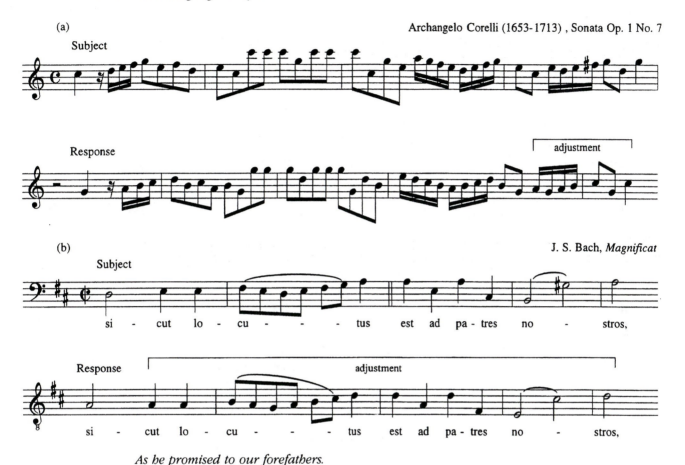

(a)

Archangelo Corelli (1653-1713) , Sonata Op. 1 No. 7

As he promised to our forefathers.

If these modulating subjects were given real responses, they would end in V of V (D major in example (a) and E major in example (b). Note that the adjustment in example (a) involves only the last few notes. The adjustment is made immediately in example (b) to preserve the character of the subject. Some examples of modulating subjects may be found in the *Well-Tempered Clavier* (WTC): Fugue 7, Book I and Fugue 15, Book II.

It is no surprise that a majority of Baroque fugues have tonal responses. The majority is not substantial, however, in the forty-eight fugues in the WTC, Books I and II by Bach; twenty-seven have tonal responses and twenty-one have real responses.

Chromatic Subjects

Chromatic subjects are quite common in the seventeenth and eighteenth centuries, especially those involving segments of the rising or falling chromatic scale. They are encountered far more often in fugues in minor keys than in major keys. When the head motive is strongly chromatic, the key is not established until the end of the subject. Subjects of this type often require real responses (Ex. 21-7).

EX. 21-7 Chromatic fugue subjects

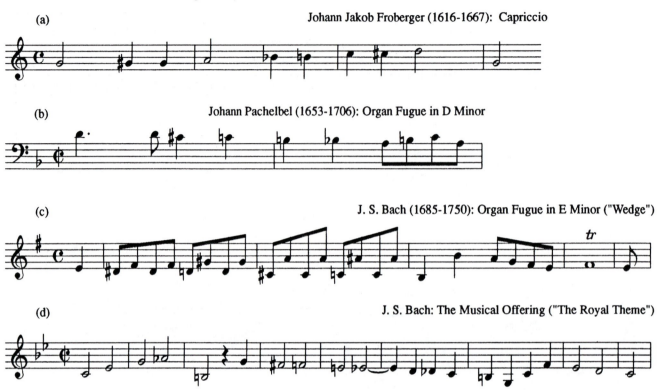

(a)   Johann Jakob Froberger (1616-1667): Capriccio

(b)   Johann Pachelbel (1653-1706): Organ Fugue in D Minor

(c)   J. S. Bach (1685-1750): Organ Fugue in E Minor ("Wedge")

(d)   J. S. Bach: The Musical Offering ("The Royal Theme")

The Countersubject

If the counterpoint to the subject or the response is used consistently in the fugue, it is referred to as the countersubject (CS). The first appearance of a countersubject is normally found in the opening voice immediately following the subject. Occasionally, however, the countersubject appears after the exposition, and some fugues make use of two different countersubjects. A countersubject should be easy to recognize, but it should not compete in character with the subject itself. It should be capable of producing double counterpoint so that the subject or response may appear above it or below it with equal success. The countersubject can be treated with more freedom than the subject as long as its character is retained.

We have a clear example of a countersubject in Bach's C Minor fugue. The descending scale in sixteenth notes and then in eighths not only appears with subsequent subject entries but it is featured in the episodes. In the Pachelbel fugue the parallel thirds are used rather consistently against the subject and may be considered as CS material. In the examples at the beginning of Chapter 14 we find Maschera using a short subject which is presented in stretto at the beginning and elsewhere in the canzona. Here, the second motive of the subject itself serves as counterpoint to the first motive. No clear CS appears in Kerll's ricercar. In Purcell's fantasia there is a hint of a CS in the top part, mm. 4–6, which reappears somewhat altered in mm. 7–9. In the Schütz chorus, the descending half notes following the subject might be regarded as CS material. Bach uses a CS in many of his three-part fugues. Example 21-8 is typical.

EX. 21-8 Exposition of Fugue XIII from the WTC I by Bach

Exercises

EXERCISE 21-1. Compose ten fugue subjects. Use a variety of lengths, keys (major and minor), meters, registers, tempi; begin some on the tonic note, others on the fifth degree; include a few chromatic subjects and one which modulates to the dominant; include some which will require tonal and some which require real responses.

EXERCISE **21-2.** Indicate weaknesses in these subjects.

EXERCISE **21-3.** Write responses for five of the subjects you wrote for Exercise 21-1.

EXERCISE **21-4.** Write tonal responses for these subjects.

EXERCISE 21-5. Write countersubjects for the five responses you wrote for Exercise 21-3.

*EXERCISE 21-6. Write subject, response, and countersubject based on the first phrase of the chorale "Aus tiefer Not schrei ich zu dir."

Sources for Further Study

Scores:

Subjects and countersubjects of fugues in the WTC, Books I and II, and *The Art of Fugue* by Bach; *Ariadne Musica* by Fischer; and *Magnificat Fugues* by Pachelbel

Readings:

Benjamin: pp. 218–234
Gauldin—18th c.: pp. 209–214
Horsley: pp. 65–154
Kennan: pp. 173–184; 201–207
Mann: pp. 31–52; 80–103; 161–175

CHAPTER

22

Fugue II

The Exposition in Three and Four Parts

Examples 22-1–22-3 show three expositions from fugues by Bach which serve as excellent models.

EX. 22-1 Exposition of Fugue XV from the *Well-Tempered Clavier*, Book I

EX. 22-2 Exposition of Fugue I from *The Art of Fugue*

EX. 22-3 Exposition of Kyrie II from *Mass in B Minor*

Questions for Discussion

1. What qualities do these subjects possess which make them excellent fugue subjects?
2. Which of these subjects take real responses and which take tonal responses?
3. Do any of these expositions make use of a countersubject?
4. What is the order of voice entries? Does it agree with the principles we discussed in Chapter 14?
5. What is the tonal plan of the expositions? Are there any differences in treatment when the tonic is minor as opposed to major?
6. The entrances in Ex. 22-2 are evenly spaced in time; each entry begins four measures after the preceding entry. This is not true of the other examples. How do you explain the difference?
7. How do we know when we have reached the end of the exposition?

Observations

The subjects of these three expositions by Bach possess attributes of good fugue subjects. They have a strong musical character, they establish the tonic, they have a limited range, a pleasing melodic shape, and a limited number of motives. Example 22-1 has a playful character. The tonic is emphasized at the very outset as G major. Its range is a ninth. It contains just two motives, one consisting of a tone with a decorative turn around it, the other a descending scale and a seventh leap. Example 22-2 begins with a bold presentation of the D–minor triad, then turns on the leading tone and ends with a "tail" of descending eighth notes. Its range is only a sixth. Its shape resembles a wave with damped oscillations. The four notes that begin the subject of Ex. 22-3 form a "musical cross" about the tonic. The immediate move from tonic to Neapolitan sixth is very striking and leaves the tonic for a moment in doubt, but the end of the subject provides the strong cadence which establishes the tonic.

The subject from *The Art of Fugue* begins with a rising fifth from first to fifth degree of the scale, which requires a tonal response of a rising fourth from the fifth degree up to first degree. In Ex. 22-1, the fifth degree comes too late in the subject to necessitate a tonal response. The Kyrie subject never reaches the fifth degree of the scale, and so it has a real response. In regard to the use of countersubject, we find that the counterpoint provided by the soprano in mm. 6–8 in Ex. 22-1 is used again by the alto in mm. 13–15 as a counterpoint to the subject entrance of the tenor. The counterpoint to the response provided by the alto in mm. 6–8 reappears in the bass in mm. 14–15, and the syncopated motive of m. 7 is used by the soprano in mm. 10–11. The clearest example of countersubject is provided by Ex. 22-3 where bass, tenor, and alto provide the same counterpoint to the entrance which follows them. The order of voice entries in the three examples are S-A-T, A-S-B-T, and B-T-A-S, all in full agreement with the principles we discussed earlier in Chapter 14. The principle could be restated as follows: High voices (S or T) are answered by low voices (A or B) and vice versa. A notable exception is Fugue I from WTC, Book I, whose entries are in the order of A-S-T-B, subject, response, response, subject. Other unusual features of this fugue are the fact that it is virtually without episodes, and its development is concerned mainly with stretto.

In our examples, subjects in the tonic are answered by responses in the dominant. In minor keys, however, the responses are in the *dominant minor.* It is a simple thing to return to the tonic from the dominant in major keys, but the return from the dominant minor often requires more maneuvering; and if the subject itself modulates to the dominant, as some do, extra time is needed to return from the end of the response (V of V) to the tonic for the third entry. This explains the bridge or link which is found in most fugues between the end of the first response and the beginning of the next subject entry. Sometimes this bridge is very brief as in Ex. 14-2, m. 5, Ex. 14-3, m. 7, and Ex. 21-2, m. 7. At other times the bridge becomes a longer episode, often with sequences, as in Ex. 21-3, mm. 5–6, Ex. 22-1, mm. 9–10, and Ex. 22-3, mm. 6–8. Some fugues use no bridge, and their entries are equidistant, as in Ex. 21-1 and Ex. 22-2.

The exposition is that part of a fugue which encompasses the first entries of all voices. Usually it ends with the final note of the subject in the last voice to enter, but it may be extended to include a "tail" attached to the subject. Occasionally there will be a cadence which marks the end of an exposition, but most fugues proceed immediately with development.

In some fugues, the exposition is immediately followed by a *counter exposition,* where the music of the exposition is restated in the same tonic-dominant relationships. The order of entries in the counter exposition, however, is usually different from the original exposition, and free contrapuntal music is given to the voices before their second entry.

Exercises

EXERCISE 22-1. Circle the sequences of voice entry in an exposition which are likely to be awkward.

T-A-B-S   S-B-A-T   A-T-S-B   S-T-A-B   S-A-T-B   A-S-B-T

EXERCISE 22-2. Complete this short three-part exposition.

EXERCISE 22-3. Write a three-part exposition on this subject and countersubject.

EXERCISE 22-4. Write a four-part exposition using this subject.

EXERCISE 22-5. Write the exposition of a choral fugato on this subject.

Be - ne - di - ca - mus Do - mi - no

Sources for Further Study

Scores:

Expositions of fugues in the WTC, Books I and II and *The Art of Fugue* by Bach; *Ariadne Musica* by Fischer; and *Magnificat Fugues* by Pachelbel

Readings:

Benjamin: pp. 233–242
Gauldin—18th c.: pp. 211–217
Horsley: pp. 155–178
Kennan: pp. 205–217
Mann: pp. 176–179

CHAPTER

23

Fugue III

Development; Episodes; Contrapuntal Techniques and Devices; Stretto; Concluding Techniques

While the order of events in the exposition of a fugue is relatively predictable, what happens in the remainder of the fugue depends upon the nature of the subject, the general character of the fugue, and the composer's skill and imagination. Study and perform Examples 23-1 and 23-2 and those at the beginning of Chapter 20 as you discuss the questions which follow.

EX. 23-1 "Fuguing by Doing" by the author

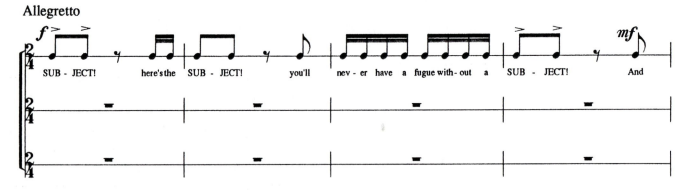

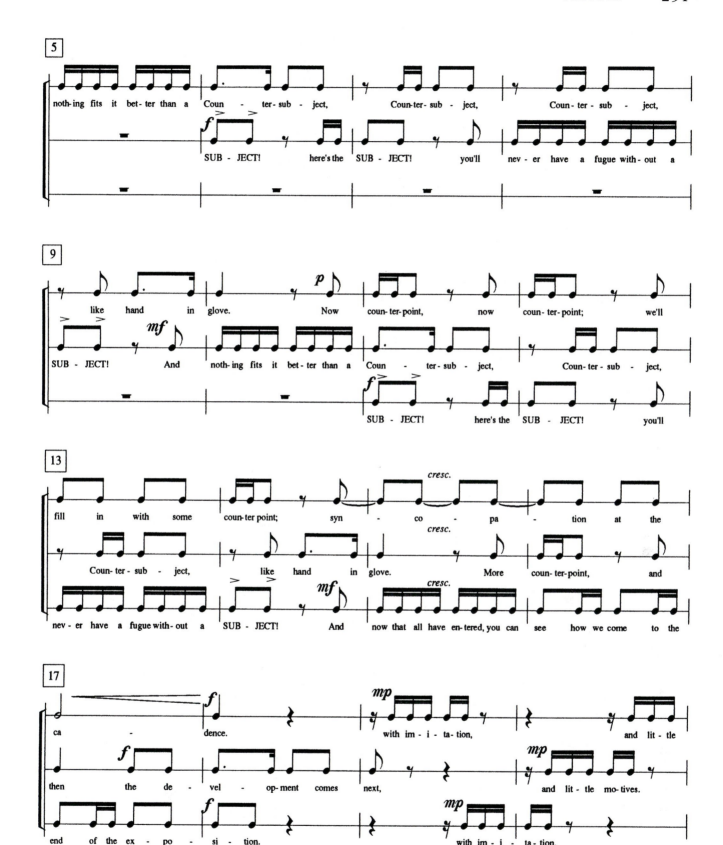

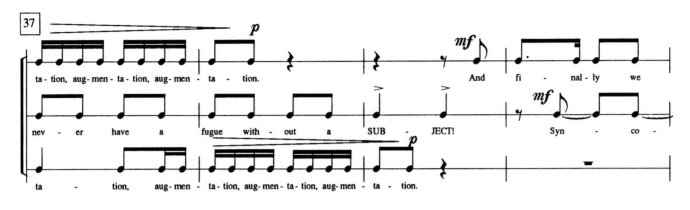

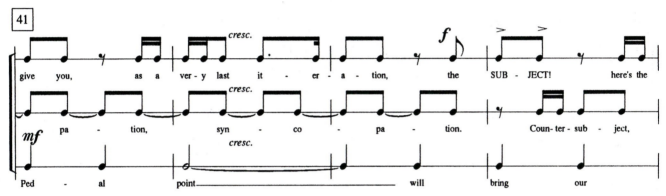

EX. 23-2 Fugue VI from *The Well-Tempered Clavier*, Book I by J. S. Bach

Questions for Discussion

1. Is the text of Ex. 23-1 an accurate description of the events in a fugue? What techniques are to be found in the development? What other techniques might have been used in a fugue without pitches? What techniques *depend* upon pitches, and for that reason could not be included in this spoken fugue?

2. In Ex. 23-2 Bach develops more than just the subject itself. What other musical ideas are consistently developed throughout this fugue?

3. Subject statements after the exposition and before the concluding section of a fugue are called *middle entries*. How do the middle entries in Ex. 23-2 compare to the entries in the exposition?

4. In Chapters 14 and 18 we encountered "episodes." What is an episode? What usually happens in an episode? Can a fugue be written without episodes?

4. How would you describe the episodes in Fugue II from Book I of the WTC, Ex. 21-3?

5. What is diminution? What is a false entry? Can you name other techniques for development in a fugue which have not been mentioned thus far?

6. What signals the concluding section of a fugue? What is the purpose of a pedal point? What other compositional devices are used in the concluding section of a fugue?

Observations

Although the text of Ex. 23-1 is intended to be whimsical, it still gives a generally accurate description of the activities in a fugue. The exposition, mm. 1–18, is quite normal; each part enters with the subject in turn. The countersubject appears in its normal location as the counterpoint to the second and third subject entries in turn. There is no bridge between the second and third entries (since without pitches there is no modulation back to the tonic to consider). A small extension to a "cadence" extends the exposition beyond m. 15.

According to the text, "the development comes next." It begins with a three-measure episode which treats "little motives from the subject" to imitation. The first "middle entry" comes in the middle part, m. 21, and the other parts quote motives from the countersubject. Episode 2 follows in mm. 25–26 "in sequence," the most common trademark of episodes. The next series of middle entries overlap, creating a stretto, mm. 27–32. The middle part has the subject in augmentation, mm. 33–39, with motives from the subject as contrapuntal material in other parts. Episode 3 prepares the way for the closing section. It makes use of a pedal point and a quote of the "syncopation" motive from mm. 14–15. The final entry of the subject (presumably "in the tonic") appears in the upper voice at m. 44, and a three-measure codetta brings the fugue to a close.

Imitation, fragmentation, augmentation, diminution, rhythmic alteration, and stretto are devices that can be used in a fugue without pitches. Tonal responses, sequences, modulation, and inversion are devices that are pitch dependent. Although pedal point serves to "slow down" the motion, its harmonic dimension could not be used in Ex. 23-1.

Ex. 23-2 is a fine model of fugue-writing in three parts. Every motive in the exposition is developed throughout the fugue. These motives are identified in Ex.

23-3. The subject (S) has two distinctive features: a string of rising eighth notes ending in a double neighbor gesture (a) and a set of sixteenth notes moving up a third to a neighbor tone figure followed by a sixth leap, then a falling third with trill (b). A tail (t) consisting of two sets of descending sixteenths acts as a first countersubject, and a sequential turn with repeated pitches (cs) acts as a second, more extended countersubject. All of these motives are subsequently developed.

EX. 23-3 Motives in the exposition of Fugue VI from the WTC, Book I

The subject of this fugue takes a real answer. The exposition follows the normal pattern we discussed in Chapter 21 except that two countersubjects are used. The second (cs) appears in the expected voices at the expected times. The first (t) is used in the bridge, m. 5, in the alto, and again in the soprano, m. 6. Table 23-1 gives a graphic representation of the complete fugue.

TABLE 23-1

FUGUE VI FROM THE WELL-TEMPERED CLAVIER, BOOK I

TIME-LINE GRAPH OF THEMATIC ACTIVITY

Measure No.	1	2	3	4	5	6	7	8	9	10	11	12	13	14	15	16	17	18	19	20
	Exposition							Development-Middle Section											
					bridge					episode		stretto				stretto			
Soprano	S		t	cs	b	t		S		b	b		S		t	t	cs	cs		(b)
Alto	—	—	S		t		cs	(a)	b	b	b	ai		SI		b		S		
Tenor	—	—	—	—	—	S		t	cs	cs	cs	b	t	a	(a)	(a)	S		cs	(a)
Tonal region:	i		v		→		i	(V)					(V)		→		v	i	→	

	21	22	23	24	25	26	27	28	29	30	31	32	33	34	35	36	37	38	39	40	41	42	43-4
	Development-Middle Section (continued)																		Conclusion				
	stretto			episode			stretto				episode					episode			stretto			cadence	
		SI		cs	csi	csi	SI		cs	cs	cs	b	t	a	t	t	t		cs	cs		(t)	
	—	—	—	ai		S				b	b	a	a	ai	ai	ai	ai		S				ai
	S	SI		ai	t		SI		(b)	(b)		S		ai	ai	ai		S		cs	(a)	a	
	v	i			i						→			iv		→			i				pedal

The subject undergoes some interesting transformations in the middle entries. In m. 8 the subject begins on the second degree, then leaps a fourth into m. 9 in order to end on the tonic. The harmonies it creates in m. 9 are N_6-V-I_6. The next entry is in m. 13, beginning on the fifth degree but still in the tonic key. This casts the subject in the dominant, a kind of tonal complement to the original subject in the tonic. Before it ends, the alto enters in stretto with the subject in inversion (SI). A second stretto occurs with an entry in the tenor in m. 17 and another in the alto in m. 18. Note the curious mixture of major and minor: The C♮s and C♯s are reversed in the two entries. A third stretto begins in m. 21 with the "dominant version" in the tenor, an inversion in the soprano, and another inversion again in the tenor. The fourth stretto begins in m. 27 and involves all three voices in descending order, SI on V, S on i, and SI on V with the ending changed to modulate to the subdominant. An entry in the tenor in m. 34 begins on the tonic, but it uses F♯, yielding a V of iv harmony. The final entries are once more in stretto, beginning in m. 39 on the tonic, but F♯s appear again, preparing the way for the Picardy third in the final cadence.

The Episode

Episodes are passages in a fugue in which the complete subject does not appear. An episode may develop motives of the subject, of the countersubject, or it may develop motives that do not belong to the subject or countersubject, although this is quite rare. Episodes almost always contain sequences based on motives from the subject, and they often make use of double or triple counterpoint. It is in episodes that modulations generally take place. It is possible to write a fugue which has no episodes (such as Fugue I from WTC, Book I), but this too is very rare. In some fugues the episodes are just as important and occupy just as much time as the subject entries themselves. A case in point is Fugue II from WTC, Book I, Ex. 21-3. Episode 1, mm. 9–10, develops the head motive of the subject in canon while the tenor has the sixteenth-note scale from the countersubject introduced in m. 3. Episode 2, mm. 13–14, develops the same CS motive in inversion against the eighth-note motive from the CS, m. 3. Episode 3, mm. 17–19, develops the bridge material from mm. 5–6. Finally, Episode 4, mm. 22–26, begins with a transposition of Episode 1 a fifth lower. The episodes in Ex. 23-2 develop the subject motives (a) and (b) and the countersubject motives (t) and (cs) in their original and inverted forms (see Table 23-1).

Inversion

Melodic inversion is accomplished by turning a melody upside down. The original form is called the *rectus* and the mirror image is called the *inversus.* Melodic inversion may be tonal or real. In *tonal inversion* the scale degree pattern is normally as follows:

Scale degree of the rectus: 1 2 3 4 5 6 7 1
in the inversus becomes: 5 4 3 2 1 7 6 5

Notice that both forms share the third degree of the scale. This is called the *axis tone.* The first and fifth degrees are interchanged. This technique allows the inversus to be in the same key and mode as the rectus. In Ex. 23-4 both the original and the tonal inversion have the note C at the same positions in the melody.

Real inversion is created by rendering all melodic intervals exactly in the opposite direction. Real inversion usually results in a mode change. In the real inversion in Ex. 23-4, where the tonic note, A, is used as the axis tone, the mode becomes major. In 23-4b the inversion of the chromatic subject can be both real and tonal since the third degree is not present in either form.

EX. 23-4 Tonal and real inversion

Middle Entries

When the subject of a fugue appears in middle entries (that is, following the exposition) it may appear in the following ways:

1) unaltered, in the tonic or in the dominant (or dominant minor)
2) transposed to closely related keys, requiring mode change in some cases
3) in tonal response form but not necessarily following a subject entry (as in the exposition)
4) with some alteration of intervals to accommodate the harmony (especially in a modulation)
5) in tonal or real inversion
6) in inversion together with the original form producing a mirror (generally limited to the concluding section)

7) in stretto

8) in augmentation, its time values doubled (or occasionally quadrupled)

9) in diminution, its time values halved (a device usually saved for the second half of a fugue)

10) with added tones (often to fill in leaps in the original)

11) with rhythmic alterations (such as a change of the time value of the first note)

12) as a false entry (usually the head motive only)

When you are writing the development of a fugue, consider the items in the list above like tools in a tool kit. You choose the tools which best suit the length and character of the fugue you are writing. As we have seen, some fugues concentrate on stretto, while others have extensive episodes. Some fugues treat the subject to inversion and other alterations of pitch or time values. Some fugues remain very close to the tonic and dominant keys while others seem to be in constant modulation. Even in the latter case, Bach rarely moves beyond the closely related keys.

Stretto

Stretto is the extreme test of a composer's contrapuntal skill. If you plan to use stretto, it is wise to work out the subject in stretto before composing the fugue. A two-part stretto with a small amount of overlap is quite easy to accomplish. Use the same procedure as writing a two-voice canon (described in Chapters 5 and 19). "Close stretto" involving entries just a beat or two apart is more difficult to write, and stretto involving three or four voices is the most challenging. Here are some guidelines to keep in mind while constructing a stretto:

1) The imitating voices are usually at the interval of an octave, a fifth, or a fourth above or below.

2) Successive entries keep the same position of strong and weak beats as the first entry.

3) Short subjects which begin with the leap of a fourth or fifth lend themselves to stretto.

4) If you design a subject so that its tail makes a good counterpoint for its head, it can be used in stretto.

5) When the subject has a tonal response, either form may be used in a stretto, and the two forms may be used together in a stretto.

6) Stretto may involve a combination of rectus and inversus forms of a subject; augmentation or diminution may also be used in a stretto.

7) Composers in the Baroque, including Bach, allowed themselves some freedom to alter the pitch of an occasional note of the subject in multi-voiced strettos. The rhythm, however, is usually not altered.

Example 23-5, a stretto from Fugue I, WTC, Book I, is an eloquent example of multi-voice stretto.

EX. 23-5 Stretto from Fugue I, WTC, Book I by J. S. Bach

S1 presents the subject in its original form and key. S2 is the response form but lacks the tail. S3 is another response, this time complete. S4 is a false entry, being only the head motive. S5 presents S in original form up an octave with S6 as a response one beat later. S7 presents the subject on the dominant of D minor followed closely by the bass with S8 on the tonic of D minor; note the lengthening of the first note. S9, beginning on the dominant of D minor is altered to fit S10, a statement in E minor.

S11 is another false entry. S12, the response in original form, and S13, the response up a third, are deployed over a dominant pedal preparing for the fugue's conclusion.

The Concluding Section

A fugue is expected to conclude in its key of origin. A statement of the subject (and countersubject material) in the tonic key is a sign that we have arrived at the final section. Composers often set this statement of the subject in a different voice from the one which began the fugue for the sake of variety. In fugues which make use of stretto, a final stretto often occurs in the concluding section, as it does in Ex. 23-2. A tonic pedal point is often employed to "slow down" the harmonic rhythm and emphasize the tonic. The texture may be thickened in the final measures by the addition of chords or new voices in fugues for keyboard (see Ex. 23-2, mm. 43–44 and Ex. 21-3, mm. 29–31).

Exercises

EXERCISE 23-1. Make a graph similar to that of Table 23-1 for Ex. 23-1.

EXERCISE 23-2. Write the following subject in the relative major, in inversion, as a tonal response, in augmentation, and in stretto involving two or more voices.

EXERCISE 23-3. Make an analysis of this short fugue.

H.J.O.

*EXERCISE **23-4.** Write out this canonic fugue for four recorders. The tenor answers the bass after two measures. The alto begins in m. 9, followed by the soprano in m. 11.

*EXERCISE **23-5.** Write a three-voice fugue on the subject given in Exercise 23-2. Make use of some of the altered forms requested in that exercise.

*EXERCISE **23-6.** Write a four-voice version of the fugue given in Exercise 23-3.

*EXERCISE **23-7.** Provide Ex. 23-1 with appropriate pitches scored for SAB chorus.

Sources for Further Study

Scores:

THREE-PART FUGUES:

Bach, WTC, Book I. Nos, 7, 8, 11, 13; WTC, Book II, Nos. 3, 6, 15.

FOUR-PART FUGUES:

Bach, *Art of Fugue,* Contrapunctus I; WTC, Book I, Nos. 1, 5, 12, 16; WTC, Book II, Nos. 2, 9, 17

Fischer, *Ariadne Musica,* Nos. 3, 6, 8

Pachelbel, *Magnificat Fugues,* No. 15

Readings:

Benjamin: pp. 243–280

Gauldin—18th c.: pp. 218–228; 260–266

Horsley: pp. 155–185; 303–338

Kennan: pp. 219–236

Mann: pp. 177–190; 199–212

CHAPTER

24

Genres Using Fugal Technique

Gigue; Fugal Sonata Movement; Fugal Chorus

Throughout the seventeenth and eighteenth centuries, composers often applied fugal technique to movements of suites, sonatas, and concertos, motets, anthems, and choruses from cantatas, oratorios, and passion settings. Compare Examples 24-1–24-3 with the fugues we discussed in the previous chapters.

EX. 24-1 Gigue from French Suite IV by Johann Sebastian Bach (1685–1750)

EX. 24-2 Fuga da cappella (Alla breve), Sonata VI from *Il pastor fido* by Antonio Vivaldi (1675–1741)

EX. 24-3 Chorus: "And with His stripes" from *Messiah* by G. F. Handel (1685–1759)

Questions for Discussion

1. What is a gigue, and where does it come from? Where is it to be found in the music of the Baroque period?
2. What are the general characteristics of a gigue—tempo, meter, and structural and harmonic plan? Is Ex. 24-1 typical of gigues in general?
3. How many "voices" are there in this gigue? How does the exposition (mm. 1–7) compare to the fugue expositions we have encountered? How does the exposition at the beginning of the second strain, or reprise, compare to mm. 1–7? Describe the development of the subject and the treatment of cadences in this gigue.
4. Vivaldi calls this sonata movement "Fuga da cappella" (Ex. 24-2). What did he mean by that? Is it a fugue? What is unusual about the exposition? Describe the events in the development.
5. The chorus "And with His stripes are we healed" is a fugue for voices. What technical considerations must be taken into account in writing a fugue for voices as compared to keyboard?
6. What makes the subject of Ex. 24-3 so striking? Can you find fugues with similar subjects?
7. Describe the exposition of Ex. 24-3. What constitutes the countersubject? How is it used in the development? How would you characterize the texture?
8. Some fugal choruses are fughettas and others can be described as containing fugato. What is the distinction between these terms? How would you expect the texture to be handled in a chorus employing fugato?

Observations

The Gigue

The English jig ("jigg," "gigg," or "gigge") is a vigorous dance in fast tempo which originated in the sixteenth century. The French and the Italians developed independent models in the seventeenth century which were used as instrumental pieces. The French version, the *gigue,* featured imitative openings for each strain, a moderate tempo, and a characteristic rhythm with upbeat short note and longer downbeat, as in Ex. 24-1. The meter could be 3/8, 6/8, 9/8, 12/8 or common time with dotted rhythms. The Italian model, the *giga,* was faster, employed running eighths and triadic motion, and was almost always in 12/8 meter. In Germany, the two types were often blended. Both types can be found in Bach's English and French suites and the partitas. The gigue became the normal final movement in the eighteenth–century keyboard suite. It is also found in sonatas and orchestral suites.

Like the other dances in the suite (allemande, courante, and sarabande), the gigue is set in the Baroque binary structure—two strains, or reprises, each repeated. The harmonic plan is: opening in the tonic, closing on the dominant in the first strain; and opening in the dominant, closing on the tonic in the second strain. A balanced effect is often achieved by concluding the second reprise with a transposition of the music which ended the first reprise.

Ex. 24-1 is typical of eighteenth–century gigues which follow the French model with its imitative entries but also employ the running eighths and fast tempo of the

Italian model. Although the expositions involve three parts, most of the development is in two. The coming and going of parts in this manner is very typical of gigues for keyboard. The exposition in the first strain of Ex. 24-1 is a regular three-part exposition with a subject and its tonal response, then the subject again in the lower voice. The subject in a gigue may be very short, as it is here, or longer and more formal (as in Ex. 24-4d). With a subject as brief as this, a bridge between second and third entries is not needed.

Perhaps the most interesting feature of the polyphonic gigue is the way in which the subject is inverted in the second strain. In most cases it is a tonal inversion of the original response (RI) with the fifth degree as the axis tone that begins the second reprise. Example 24-4 a-c illustrates this principle. Since the subject in Ex. 24-4d requires a real response, it uses a real inversion with the third degree of the scale as the axis tone.

EX. 24-4 Gigue subjects and their inversions

(a) From French Suite IV

(b) From English Suite III

(c) From English Suite V

(d) From Partita VI

There is always a strong feeling of "harmonic reciprocity" in the beginning of the second strain. Tonic is answered by dominant and dominant by tonic. The entries are often in the configuration RI-SI-RI, and sometimes RI is answered by another RI transposed so that it leads into the region of the subdominant. Note that the RI in m. 29 leads to IV$_6$ in m. 31 before preparing for the third entry in m. 33.

The motives of this gigue's subject are freely developed, especially through sequences, but there are no complete and unaltered statements in mm. 7–26. In the second strain, only the RI form is used in the exposition, and again in m. 39 where the middle part reappears. The SI appears in a number of places in the lower part: m. 41, m. 44 three times in sequences up a third, and finally in the tonic in m. 54. The cadences are balanced by the use of double counterpoint. The music in mm. 22–26 reappears with the parts exchanged and transposed to the tonic in mm. 56–60. The development in the second reprise of a Baroque gigue may or may not include statements of the original subject as well as the inverted subject. Example 24-1 does not.

The Fugal Sonata Movements

The terms *da cappella* and *da camera* appear often as designations in Baroque music. They refer to music "of the chapel" and "of the chamber" with "sacred-secular" or "formal-informal" connotations. More specifically they were used to designate two instrumental types: the *sonata da chiesa,* usually in three or four movements with a fugal allegro as the first or second movement (such as Corelli's Opp. 1 and 3), and the *sonata da camera,* a set of stylized dance movements (such as Corelli's Opp. 2 and 4). The two types tended to merge in the eighteenth century. Vivaldi wishes to indicate by the phrase "Fuga da cappella" that this movement, Ex. 24-2, is a fugue such as would be found in a sonata da chiesa. Only two parts are given, but these are accompanied by the continuo. The subject is a bold, gestic one in half notes with large leaps, easy to recognize. The countersubject, bass part, mm. 4–9, is equally arresting with its repeated quarter notes and sequence of downward-moving scales. It has enough character, in fact, to rival the subject, and its continued use throughout the fugue attests to this. We are tempted to call it a second subject, rather than a countersubject, which would then qualify the movement as a double fugue. The exposition is unusual in that the bass does not enter with the response but presents a subject of its own. The bass does have the first subject in m. 9, and the recorder has the second subject in m. 12. The exposition of the two subjects is completed with a cadence in D minor in m. 17. The development proceeds with quotations of both subjects in double counterpoint in the tonic until m. 32 where a short episode performs a modulation to the relative major. Middle entries of both subjects now in B♭ major appear in mm. 35, 38, and 43. Another episode in mm. 48–52 modulates to C minor with middle entries in mm. 52 and 56. A sequential episode returns us to the tonic in m. 60 where we have a repeat of the first set of entries in the exposition. A final episode prepares us for the concluding entries in the tonic in m. 86. The movement is very tightly constructed with very little material that is not directly related to one or the other of the subjects.

The Fugal Chorus

Choruses are written in a variety of forms and textures. Fugal choruses are quite common, especially for the expression of a short but important phrase of text such as "Kyrie eleison," "Abraham et semini ejus," or "This is the day which the Lord hath made." Ex. 24-3 contains only the one phrase, "And with His stripes are we healed." It serves for both subject and countersubject, and sub-phrases such as "are we healed" are used as episode and free contrapuntal material. Writing a choral fugue poses some technical problems that an instrumental fugue does not. First and foremost, the stresses in the text must receive proper stresses in the music as discussed in Chapter 6. Proper choral ranges must be considered, the effect of high and low tessituras, adequate provision for breathing, and careful voice leading must be taken into account. Although leaps give character to the music, they must be chosen with singers in mind. Conjunct motion is still more prevalent than disjunct motion. Polyphony can become overly thick when all four voices are involved in imitation with competing text. Long notes in one of the parts, such as a chorale tune, can provide a backdrop for faster moving parts; rests can also help to lighten the texture. A pair of voices answered by another pair can make for clarity, as well as one voice part answered by the others.

The subject in Handel's chorus, Ex. 24-3, is very striking because of the opening leaps, especially the descending diminished seventh. This musical gesture has served composers throughout the Baroque period. Example 24-5 shows a few of these.

EX. 24-5 Fugue subjects featuring the diminished seventh gesture

(a) Chorus: "And with His stripes" from *Messiah* by Handel (1685-1759)

(b) Fuga XIII from Preludes and Fugues for Organ by Buxtehude (1637-1707)

(c) Magnificat Fugue in D Minor by Pachelbel (1653-1706)

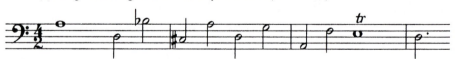

(d) Fuga XX from W.T.C. II by Bach (1685-1750)

(e) Fuga XVI from W.T.C. I by Bach

(f) Kyrie from *Requiem* by Mozart (1756-1791)

The exposition of Ex. 24-3 is straightforward. The soprano enters with S, answered four measures later by the alto with a tonal R in the minor dominant. A three-measure bridge leads back to the tonic for S in the tenor. Another three-measure bridge separates this with the tonal R in the bass. The countersubject in the soprano, mm. 7–9, is used in the alto at m. 14, in the tenor at m. 21, and again in the alto at m. 23. It will be used throughout the remainder of the fugue not only as a counterpoint to the subject but as the material developed in the episodes.

The development unfolds as follows:

Measure	Activity	Region
25	R in soprano, cs in bass	v
31	S in tenor, cs in alto	iv
37	S in tenor and bass (doubled in thirds), cs in soprano	i
41–48	Episode based on cs	modulating
48	S in alto, cs in bass	♭VII
55	S in soprano, cs in tenor	III
59–63	Episode based on cs	modulating
63	S in soprano, cs in tenor	i
67	R in bass, cs in alto	v
71–79	Episode, alto and tenor have cs in imitation and sequence	modulating
79	R in soprano, cs in tenor	v
83	S in bass, cs in alto	i
88–92	Extension to half-cadence in preparation for next chorus	i

The texture of this fugal chorus is quite open due to the frequent use of rests. The voice parts "take turns" with the subject and countersubject. We hear three voices at a time throughout most of the fugue. There are only a few places where all four are used together.

Some choruses are very short but complete fugues. A diminutive fugue is called a *fughetta.* In larger compositions a section may have fugal entries as in an exposition, but the resemblance to fugue stops there. *Fugato* is the term used to describe these sections. Many choruses contain fugato passages which alternate with homophonic textures.

Fugues With More Than One Subject

While we are considering the fugue, let us briefly discuss the topic of compound fugues—fugues with more than one subject. In some fugues the counterpoint to the subject is strong enough to be called a second subject. It often appears together with the first subject at the beginning of the fugue. This is one type of double fugue. Example 24-2 is an example of this type of double fugue as is the Kyrie (and also the "cum sanctis tuis in aeternum") from Mozart's *Requiem.* "Kyrie eleison" is Subject 1 and "Christe eleison" is Subject 2. There is also a second type of double fugue in which the Subject 2 is not introduced until the Subject 1 has been exposed and briefly developed. Subject 2 is given its own exposition after which both subjects are combined in development. Contrapunctus X of *The Art of Fugue* exemplifies this type, and we will see in Ex. 28-1 that the Fugue in A from *Ludus Tonalis* by Hindemith is also of this type. A variant of the second type shortens the procedure by exposing Subject 2 while Subject 1 continues its development. Contrapunctus IX from *The Art of Fugue* is of this type. In fugues with more than two subjects, the order of events is not predictable except to say that each subject is combined in various ways with the others. Example 19-1 could be considered a triple fugue since it has three subjects developed together. Contrapunctus VIII from *The Art of Fugue* is a triple fugue. The final fugue from that monumental work was to be a quadruple fugue, but it was left unfinished at Bach's death.

Exercises

EXERCISE 24-1. Write a three-part gigue exposition on this subject, then write the exposition for the beginning of the second strain.

*EXERCISE 24-2. Here is the first strain of a gigue. Make an analysis of it, and compose its companion strain using a proper inversion of the subject.

EXERCISE 24-3. Write a short fughetta on this subject for solo with continuo (about 24 measures).

*EXERCISE 24-4. Write out a realization for the continuo part of Ex. 24-2 and try to incorporate in it some entries of Subject 1 or 2 or both.

EXERCISE 24-5. Write a short choral setting of the text "Enter into his courts with thanksgiving" for SAB. chorus which contains a fugato section.

*EXERCISE 24-6. Write a fugal chorus for SATB using the "Benedicamus Domino" subject of Exercise 22-5.

Sources for Further Study

Scores:

BACH:

Gigues (final movements) from French and English suites and partitas
Fugal sonata movements from Sonatas for Violin and Harpsichord
Fugal choruses from the passions, motets, and larger cantatas

HANDEL:

Gigues from keyboard suites; fugal choruses from oratorios

MARCELLO:

Fugal movements from solo sonatas

MOZART:

Gigue for piano, K 273, fugal choruses from Masses and the *Requiem*

TELEMANN:

Fugal movements from solo sonatas

VIVALDI:

Fugal movements from solo sonatas

Readings:

The gigue is not discussed at length in the scources we have suggested in previous chapters. We recommend the article on gigue in the *New Grove's Dictionary.*

PART FIVE

Polyphony in the Classical and Romantic Eras (1750–1900)

CHAPTER

25

Polyphony in the Classical Era

Counterpoint in Haydn, Mozart, and Beethoven

In the middle of the eighteenth century musical tastes moved away from polyphony toward homophony dominated by melody in the topmost voice. The Baroque binary was enlarged to become the sonata form, and the ritornello with digressions used in the Baroque concerto gave way to longer rondo forms. Contrast in keys, themes, and textures supplanted the Fortspinnung technique of the Baroque. Nonetheless, Haydn, Mozart, and Beethoven were masters of counterpoint, as shown in Examples 25-1–25-3.

EX. 25-1 Finale from Trio No. 40 for Baryton, Viola, and Cello by Haydn (1732–1809)

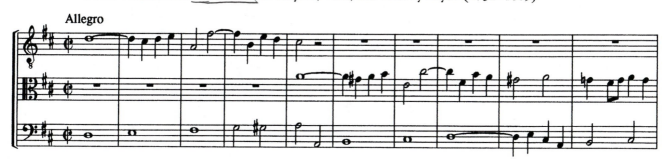

EX. 25-2 Minuet and Trio from Serenade in C Minor, K. 388, by Mozart (1756–1791)

Menuetto da capo.

EX. 25-3 First movement from String Quartet in C♯ Minor Op. 131, by Beethoven (1770–1827)

Adagio, ma non troppo e molto espressivo

Questions for Discussion

1. How would you describe Classical style in a few general statements?
2. Where are you most likely to find counterpoint in the music of the Classical period?
3. What contrapuntal techniques are used in the Haydn example? What similarities to baroque polyphony do you find? How does the polyphonic writing differ from Baroque practice?
4. Describe the harmony in Ex. 25-1. What is the harmonic rhythm? Where are the major cadences? What regions are explored?
5. What contrapuntal techniques do you find in the Mozart example? Without using a dictionary, what do you think the words "al rovescio" mean?
6. Describe the texture in Ex. 25-2. Which instruments are involved in the canons? Where does Mozart abandon the canonic writing? How would you interpret the indication "mezza voce" in the Trio?
7. What is the key scheme of this minuet and trio? What is the formal structure? Compare the harmony of this example with that of the Haydn example. Describe the cadences.
8. What is Baroque about the Beethoven example? What is Classical? What is Romantic?
9. Compare Ex. 25-3 with Fugue VI from the WTC, Book I, Ex. 23-2. Does it do what you expect a fugue to do?
10. Describe the texture and the harmony in Beethoven's fugue.

Observations

Classical Style

A complete and detailed description of Classical style as represented by the music of Haydn, Mozart, and early Beethoven would fill many pages, but a few generalizations will serve our needs here. The following list describes some of the more important stylistic trends after 1750:

1) Homophony with the melody in the top voice becomes the predominant texture.
2) Harmonic rhythm is generally slower than in Baroque style; the primary triads are given priority.
3) Authentic cadences stress the $^6_4$–$^5_3$ configuration.
4) The key scheme becomes a decisive factor in the articulation of form; tonal centers are more firmly established before and after modulations.
5) Periodic phrase structure with symmetrical phrase lengths becomes the norm for the presentation of melody.
6) Melody is infused with graceful ornaments and rhythmical detail; the appoggiatura becomes a common feature and is often found in cadences.
7) Between the melody and the bass, inner parts often assume a subservient role and provide the harmonic support formerly supplied by the continuo.
8) While Baroque movements tend to be "made of one cloth," classical movements often use dramatic contrasts in themes, textures, and dynamics.

While homophonic textures are favored, polyphony is still important to the composers of the latter eighteenth century. Contrapuntal textures provide contrast and relief, especially in transitions and development sections. Music for the church has always tended to be more formal and conservative, and it is no surprise that the sacred works of Haydn, Mozart, and Beethoven contain some of their best contrapuntal writing. All three of these composers admired Bach's contrapuntal skill, and it would be safe to say that their polyphonic music tends to take on a Baroque feeling, especially in their church music.

The epoch-making treatise by Johann Josef Fux, *Gradus ad Parnassum,* which appeared in 1725 (see Chapter 4), became the Classical manual of composition and had a profound influence on the works of the Viennese masters. His method of composing counterpoints in the five species against a cantus firmus can be seen in many passages in Haydn, Mozart, and Beethoven. In Ex. 25-3, especially mm. 27–33, there are several instances where all four parts move in first species. An example of second species occurs in Ex. 25-1, mm. 60–64, between the outer parts; third species is operating in mm. 20–28 and 67–73. Beethoven shows his skill with suspensions, fourth species, in Ex. 25-3, mm. 102–112. A rather "pure" example of fifth species, a judicious mixture of first through fourth species, is used in the opening measures of the Haydn movement: m. 1 is first, m. 2 is third, m. 3 is second, and m. 4 begins with fourth.

Haydn

Haydn's patron, Prince Nicolas Esterházy, played the baryton, a bowed string instrument similar to the viola da gamba with the addition of sympathetic strings. Haydn composed 126 trios for the baryton with viola and cello. This instrumental combination lent itself very easily to three-part polyphony. Several of the trios end with fugues or fugato movements such as the one in Ex. 25-1. It is similar to a double fugue where the subject appears together with its countersubject at the beginning. The piece makes use of sequence, imitation, and fugal entries in various keys. For the most part, the counterpoint resembles Baroque style, but when the upper parts move together against the bass, the style becomes more Classical. The cadential passages such as the one in mm. 30–35 seem to abandon the polyphonic texture altogether. The structure, however, is the Baroque binary, like that of the gigue. The dominant pedal point and subsequent statement of the subject in mm. 76–89 recall the usual events which close a Baroque fugue.

The harmonic rhythm is very stable: one harmony per measure with few exceptions. Cadences are unambiguous: authentic cadences to the dominant in the first section and tonic in the second. The only region explored other than the dominant is an excursion to the relative minor in mm. 50–60.

Mozart

Mozart indicates that the minuet and trio, Ex. 25-2, is "in Canone." The canon in the minuet is between the oboes and bassoons in the first strain. The clarinets continue the canon at the beginning of the second strain until m. 22 where it is interrupted by a diminished seventh chord. The canon resumes in m. 29 with *vorimitation* or "anticipating what is to come" in the clarinets in m. 28. The trio is of particular interest because it is a double canon *at the inversion,* hence the indication "al rovescio." We encountered a similar canon in Ex. 1-2g. Oboe II is dux 1, with Oboe I as comes 1 in inversion. Dux 2 is Bassoon I, answered in inversion by comes 2 played by Bassoon II. Again the canon is suspended in order to make the cadence which ends the strain. The instruments continue their canonic roles in the second strain but now with dux 1 and 2 preceding comes 1 and 2. A varied repetition of the opening of the trio occurs in m. 21, and the canon continues right up to the cadence in mm. 31–32.

In spite of the canon, the minuet is basically homophonic with the harmony attached to the bass line. The trio, with all four instruments involved in the canon, is more polyphonic. Only the cadence measures relax the counterpoint. The indication "mezza voce" ("medium voice") is equivalent to a dynamic level of *mf*. It appears in all four parts, indicating they are of equal importance.

Mozart adheres to the customary key scheme for a minuet in a minor key: beginning in the tonic, then modulating to the relative major in the first strain; beginning in the relative major, then modulating back to the tonic in the second strain. The trio, cast in the tonic major, modulates to the dominant in the first strain, then back to the tonic in the second strain. The structure in the minuet is A-A' ‖B-A'. The trio is the same except that a six-measure development of A replaces the B. Mozart's harmony is somewhat more adventuresome than Haydn's. The minor key and the increased number of voices allows for richer harmonies such as the dominant ninth chord in m. 1, diminished seventh chords in mm. 22, 24, and 26, the augmented sixth chord in m. 42, and several secondary dominants. The canon accounts for several deceptive cadential moves such as we find in mm. 36, 38, and 40, but the cadences which end each of the strains are perfect authentic cadences.

Beethoven

The opening movement of Beethoven's String Quartet Op. 131 is Baroque in that it is a fugue. It has an exposition, episodes, middle entries in closely related keys, a concluding section with the customary subject statement in the tonic, and a tonic pedal point in the closing measures. Like many extended Baroque fugues, it develops momentum by compounding the rhythmic motion with the use of eighth notes in the development.

The subject is four measures in length, and the entries are each four measures apart. This symmetrical arrangement is a classical trait. Also Classical is the careful disposition of areas with strong tonal focus, alternating with transitional modulating passages. The contrast afforded by the high tessitura and thinner texture in mm. 63–82 might also be considered a Classical feature. The use of sequence as a developmental technique is both Baroque and Classical.

Romantic traits in this fugue include the use of multiple suspensions and syncopations which tend to weaken the normal measure accent, the fluctuating harmonic rhythm, the extended instrumental ranges, the chromaticism which weakens the tonal focus in many places, the sudden accents on weak beats, and the thickness of the sonorities in the final measures.

This fugue possesses many of the familiar Baroque fugal techniques, but as it unfolds we discover some unusual features:

1) The subject is given a real response in spite of the fact that it begins on the fifth scale degree. This causes the response to be in the subdominant instead of the expected minor dominant.

2) There are very few complete subject entries after the exposition in spite of the length of the fugue, and each of these entries contains some altered tones or rhythms.

3) There is no discernible countersubject; however, the tail motive often is used like a countersubject against the head motive.

4) The head and tail motives are extensively developed in imitation and sequence in the episodes; both motives are subjected to alteration and fragmentation. Every note in the movement seems to be related to these motives in one way or another.

5) The closing section of the fugue incorporates stretto, although the subject is freely altered. In mm. 92–96, the viola enters with the subject followed a measure later by the second violin with a strongly altered version of the tail motive. In m. 98, the first violin enters with the subject beginning in the subdominant but quickly turning to the tonic as the cello enters in m. 99 with the subject in stretto and augmentation. This entry begins on F♯, rather than G♯ to accommodate the violin.

The overall texture of this fugue is rather thick because of the large amount of four-part writing, the quick and shifting harmonic rhythm, the chromaticism, and the prevalent note-against-note counterpoint. Only the two-voice textures in mm. 67–79 and the three-part passage in mm. 91–99 provide a textural contrast. The harmony is rich with secondary dominants and diminished seventh chords and other chromatic harmonies. Cross relations are common, especially in the exposition and first episode. Example 25-4 shows several of these traits.

EX. 25-4 Excerpt from String Quartet Op. 131 by Beethoven, mm. 17–24

The example begins after the cello entry in the exposition which is in the subdominant region. The tail motive, mm. 15–16, is sequenced in mm. 17–18, touching on the key of B minor. Circled notes in Ex. 25-4 are decorative pitches: neighboring tones (m. 20) creating a transitory augmented sixth chord, appoggiaturas (mm. 22–23) creating cross-relations, and accented passing tones (m. 24). Note that the "+" marks are associated with the head motive of the subject. These marks indicate a dissonance caused by the delayed resolutions on the third beat in mm. 21–24. These delayed resolutions put the motive "out of sync" with the moving parts, thus setting them apart from the other voices. In m. 24, we expect a D♯ for the cello on the downbeat, which would be consistent with the circle-of-fifths sequential progression. However, the cello has a D♮ rather than a D♯. Perhaps the natural is a scribe's error.

Exercises

EXERCISE 25-1. Write variations in Classical style on this familiar tune following the directions given.

(a) Use mostly eighth notes in the treble and quarters in the bass.

(b) Continue the appoggiaturas in the treble and the pattern in the bass.

(c) Continue with free imitation.

EXERCISE 25-2. Complete this phrase for string trio.

*EXERCISE 25-3. Complete the final section of the *Gloria in excelsis* from the Mass using this beginning.

Sources for Further Study

Scores:

HAYDN:

Sacred works, especially oratorios and Masses, particularly the final chorus of *The Creation*

several of the finales of the Baryton Trios (such as Ex. 25-1)

String quartets: finales of Op. 20, Nos. 2, 5, and 6 (a double fugue); Op. 76, No. 2, III (canon); Op. 55, No. 1, IV (fugato in mm. 61–69)

Symphony No. 101, Rondo (mm. 189–218)

MOZART:

Fugato sections in the late symphonies, especially No. 38, I (mm. 143–181), No. 40, IV (mm. 161–175), No. 41, IV throughout (especially the fugato, mm. 36–115 and quintuple counterpoint, mm. 387–402)

Fugue for Piano in G Minor, K. 401

Fugue for Two Pianos in C Minor, K. 426 (particularly good example of stretto and inversion)

Gigue for piano, K. 574.

Sacred works, especially the masses, *Requiem* (Kyrie and Cum sanctis tuis), and *Vesperae Solemnes* (Laudate pueri)

String quartets: finales of K. 168, 173, and 387

BEETHOVEN:

Finale of Cello Sonata Op. 102, No. 2.

Finales of piano sonatas: Op. 101 and 106 and of the *Diabelli Variations*

Fugue in D Op. 137 for string quintet

Missa Solemnis (especially the conclusion of the Gloria)

String quartets: Op. 18, No. 4, II, Op. 59 No. 2, III (cantus firmus variations in mm. 52–135)

Symphonies: No. 3, II (mm. 114–145) and IV (mm. 117–163 and 277–314), and No. 7, II (mm. 183–210)

Readings:

Crocker: pp. 355–430

Gauldin—eighteenth c.: pp. 289–309

Kirkendale: *Fugue and Fugato in Rococo and Classical Music*

Mann: pp. 53–61; 213–314

Salzer and Schacter: pp. 117–143; 210–225; 367–373; 438–444

CHAPTER

26

Polyphony in the Romantic Era

Counterpoint in Mendelssohn, Brahms, Franck, and Others

The nineteenth century saw sweeping stylistic changes, especially in harmony, tonality, and form. Although homophony remains the predominate texture for music in the romantic era, the major composers were nonetheless skilled in counterpoint and produced masterpieces of polyphony. Contrapuntal texture served very well as a medium for the new chromaticism which would eventually lead to the end of absolute sovereignty of the major-minor tonal system. Examples 26-1–26-4 by Mendelssohn, Brahms, Schumann and Franck exhibit many of the qualities of nineteenth-century counterpoint. Examine also Ex. 1-2g and Ex. 2-1d as you consider the questions below. Space does not permit the inclusion of equally fine examples by such masters as Schubert, Wagner, Liszt, Bruckner, Mahler, Fauré, and Tchaikovsky.

EX. 26-1 Responsory for Evensong: "Lord, have mercy" by Felix Mendelssohn (1809–1847)

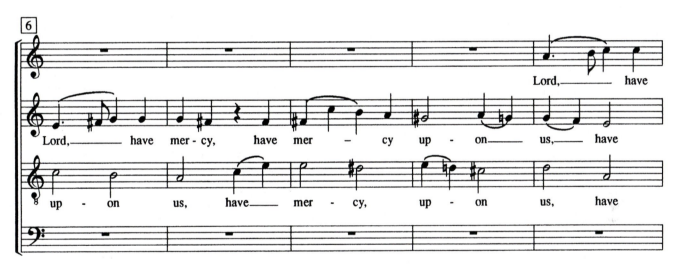

EX. 26-2 Chorale Prelude: ''Es ist ein Ros' entsprungen'' for organ by Johannes Brahms (1833–1897)

EX. 26-3 Exposition of the Fugue from *Prelude, Chorale, and Fugue* by César Franck (1822–1890)

Questions for Discussion

1. "The shadow of Bach stretches across all polyphony from his time to the present." Is this a fair statement? Is it supported by these examples?
2. Briefly describe Romantic style in terms of melody, harmony, texture, and temporal considerations.
3. How are these traits applied to polyphonic texture in these examples?
4. How are the musical ideas developed in the Mendelssohn motet?
5. Brahms has given us a fanciful rendition of the tune "Lo how a rose e're blooming." How has the melody been decorated? Describe the cadences.
6. Trace the tonality in the Franck fugue exposition. How and where is the tonality established; how and where is it in doubt?
7. How is the canon by Brahms, Ex. 1-2g, constructed?

Observations

The Influence of Bach on Nineteenth–Century Polyphony

During his own time, Bach was considered to be the greatest master of counterpoint. Haydn, Mozart, and Beethoven based their technique upon a dual foundation: the study of Fux's *Gradus ad Parnassum* and Bach's fugues. It is true that Bach's works were neglected after his death for some seventy-five years, but students of counterpoint were still introduced to his polyphonic music. In 1829, Mendelssohn staged a performance of the *St. Matthew Passion* which sparked a Bach revival, and Bach's music has been performed and revered ever since. The name B-A-C-H has been used as a musical motive by many composers, among them Bach himself, Schumann, and Liszt. In German notation, B is equivalent to B♭ and H is equivalent to B♮. The chromatic nature of this motive was exploited by these composers. Example 26-4 is the opening of the first of six organ fugues on B-A-C-H by Schumann. Note that the tonality is constantly in doubt. The authentic cadence at the end of the example is quite weak. Only at the very end of the piece is the tonic finally affirmed as B♭ major.

EX. 26-4 Exposition of Fugue No. 1 from Six Fugues on B-A-C-H, Op. 20, by Robert Schumann (1810–1856)

Example 26-1 is a fine example of a choral fugue in the Baroque tradition. The contrapuntal writing is Bach-like except for some details of melody and harmony which will be discussed below.

Example 26-2 is in the tradition of chorale preludes that dates back to the seventeenth century. It is an example of the ornamented melody type (see Ex. 17-4). Like Bach's settings in this genre, it also embellishes the harmonies.

Example 26-3 is the final section of a larger work for piano. The cadence at the beginning serves to close the second section and establish B as the tonal center for the beginning of the fugue. The first twelve measures of this piece were discussed in Chapter 2 in a comparison of style among several examples of two-part polyphony. It is a fugue exposition which adheres to the Bach models in terms of order of entries and key relationships. The entries follow the pattern T-A-S-B, cadencing in tonic, dominant, tonic, and dominant, as expected. Real responses are used. A definite departure from Bach's fugues may be seen in the harmonic progressions, which sometimes give focus to the tonality and sometimes make it ambiguous.

Counterpoint in the nineteenth century takes Bach as its foundation and adds to it the expansion of harmony, melody, rhythm and treatment of tonality developed by the major composers of the period. Following is a list of some of the major characteristics of music of the Romantic era.

Major Characteristics of Romantic Style

Melody

1) The melody is most commonly found in the upper voice.
2) Active tones are given great prominence. The melody often contains chord seventh, ninth, eleventh, or thirteenth; and appoggiaturas are often strengthened by being prolonged, chromatically altered, anticipated or approached by large leaps.
3) Phrases are often longer than four measures; periods are often asymmetrical.
4) Chromaticism is common in the form of chromatic passing or neighbor tones, appoggiaturas, mutated chord members, and modulatory sequences.
5) Melismatic decoration is common.

Harmony

1) Chord mutation, or "borrowing" of chords from the parallel key, is often encountered.
2) Root motion by step and by third (third relation) is more frequently encountered than in previous periods.
3) Extended dominants, nondominant seventh chord types (m-m7, M-M7, m-M7, Aug-M7) are common.
4) Deceptive cadences and irregular resolutions of dominant chords are common.
5) Chromatic chords, especially the augmented sixth chords, the Neapolitan sixth, and secondary diminished seventh chords, are favored sonorities.
6) Modulation to remote keys, often employing enharmonic spellings, becomes commonplace in the nineteenth century.

7) The tonality is weakened or suspended through the use of deceptive resolutions, chords without apparent root, or modulating sequences.

8) The augmented triad, especially in V+ to I progressions, is often used.

Texture

1) The texture is most often top-dominated and homophonic—melody and accompaniment.

2) Figural accompaniment patterns such as broken chords (with or without decorative pitches) are often used.

3) Quasi-polyphonic textures are frequently encountered where one voice is predominant and other non-imitative voices are subordinate, where a countermelody is used, or where voice leading involves chromatic passing tones.

4) The number of voices may expand and contract freely.

5) Expanded ranges and extremes of tessitura are often employed.

6) Virtuosic writing for instruments and voices is common.

Temporal Considerations

1) Rhythms within a single piece may make use of a large range of time values including subdivisions and "tuplets" of various sizes.

2) Tempo may be subject to rubato (especially in slower music) or sudden changes—stringendo, stretto, accelerando, allargando, etc.

3) Rhythms involving 2 against 3 are relatively common, especially in the music of Brahms.

4) Syncopations, suspensions, and rests may be used to weaken the normal measure accent.

Romantic Traits in the Examples

Of the three examples at the beginning of this chapter, the Mendelssohn is the least romantic, but some details of the writing do suggest nineteenth-century style. The untied suspensions on the word "mercy" and the expressive tritone leap give a feeling of penitence to the whole motet. The chromatic countersubject, which appears first in the alto in mm. 24–27, gives rise to some richness in the harmony. The dominant seventh chord in m. 17 and the i $^6_4$ in m. 27 are given unexpected resolutions. A dramatic moment comes at the end of the E pedal point in the bass, m. 39; the bass leaps a seventh as the soprano leaps a tritone. At the same time, the alto is ascending with the chromatic countersubject. The resulting harmony is a dominant ninth chord which cadences to the tonic, but the chromatic countersubject appearing now in contrary motion in soprano and tenor in m. 40 leads to a French augmented sixth chord in m. 41, the climax of the tension, quickly relaxed by the final cadence.

The outstanding romantic trait in the Brahms chorale prelude is the incessant use of accented dissonances—appoggiaturas, accented passing and neighboring tones —many of which are chromatically altered. Other traits are the deceptive resolution of the dominant in mm. 2, 6, 12, and 18, and from G7 to A minor in m. 16. The A♭ passing tone in the alto part, m. 16, results in a mutated chord (minor iv in C major), a favorite of Brahms. Also typical of Brahms is the de-emphasis of the downbeat in the melody caused by the eighth-note motion across the bar line and the tying of the final note of each phrase into the next beat.

As we have mentioned above, Franck's harmony is very different from Bach's. The authentic cadence at the beginning establishes B as the tonal center. The chromatic head motive of the subject gives us both D♯ and D♮, which leaves the mode in doubt. The end of the subject in m. 4, however, establishes the mode as minor. The subject begins on E, the fourth degree, quite unusual for a subject. When the response (a real one) begins on B, it reinforces the tonic. But as it descends chromatically, the tonality is again unclear until the end of the response establishes the expected key of the minor dominant, F♯ minor, in m. 8. This is followed by a sequentially modulating bridge which prepares for the third entry. Although he gives us a V^6_5 on the downbeat of m. 13, Franck immediately sidesteps the normal resolution by harmonizing the D♯ on the second beat with an incomplete diminished seventh chord. The harmonies which follow render the tonality ambiguous. The continuity of the progression depends upon the smoothness of the voice leading and the use of sequence rather than on tonal harmonic function. There is a brief moment of tonal focus again as the subject ends in the tonic and the last entry is made in the bass. Tonal ambiguity is created again in mm. 17–19 by the modulating sequence and the lack of strong functional harmonies. This type of progression is common also in Richard Wagner's music, as Ex. 26-5 shows. Note the root movement by step and third and the voice leading involving chromatic steps and enharmonic equivalents.

EX. 26-5 Excerpt from Act II of *Tristan und Isolde* by Wagner (1813–1883)

(etc.)

Franck's counterpoint is quite dissonant throughout this exposition. Note the chromatic countersubject which is related to the tail motive. The untied suspensions create fourths in mm. 5-7. In the bridge, mm. 10-12, we find the same type of chromatically altered decorative pitches as Brahms has used in Ex. 26-2. Here we see a new approach to first, second, and third species counterpoint which allows the stronger dissonances (appoggiaturas, accented passing and neighboring tones) to be used against the cantus firmus.

Structural Organization in the Examples

Example 26-1 is a very regular small fugue following the introductory chords. The tenor has the first entry which is given a real answer in the alto, m. 3. The tenor continues with a countersubject. Measure 9 is all that is needed as an extension of the tail to return to the tonic. The S appears in the soprano as expected, and the cs is in the alto. The bass has the final entry in m. 14 with the cs in the soprano. The development opens with an episode, mm. 17–23, that employs sequences and seems to modulate to the relative major, but a middle entry in the soprano returns us to the tonic. A new countersubject appears in the alto, mm. 25–27, consisting of a rising chromatic scale. This second cs is developed along with the S from this point to the end except for the declamatory episode in homophonic texture, mm. 30–34. A quasistretto begins in m. 35 with the final entry in the soprano over a dominant pedal in the bass, followed by the climactic final appearance of the second cs described earlier.

The Brahms chorale prelude is organized by the structure of the original chorale melody itself, Ex. 26-6, which is AABA.

EX. 26-6 Chorale: **Es ist ein Ros' entsprungen** by Johannes Brahms (1833–1897)

Text: anonymous   Melody: Cöllnisches Gesangbuch, 1599

The last two phrases are repeated with slight variations in the Brahms setting, resulting in the scheme AABAB′A′. Brahms uses double neighbor tones, cambiatas (normal and inverted), and appoggiaturas to decorate the melody. Since most of the decorative pitches come on the beat, most of the tones of the original melody come between beats. All of the phrases begin with upbeats, giving the music a steady forward flowing motion. The phrases end in authentic cadences, but cadential extensions at the ends of the "A" phrases add on a plagal cadence. Brahms has made two subphrases out of the "A" phrase, and he uses a deceptive cadence at the end of the first of these. The Eb in the tenor in the final cadence recalls the Mixolydian mode and sounds to our ears curiously like a "blue note."

As we have observed earlier, the Franck example does not deviate from the structural plan for the exposition of a four-part fugue. The points of tonal focus occur at the ends of each subject entry. The tonality is obscured as each part enters with the head motive. This alternating pattern of tonal stability and instability helps to underscore the structure of the exposition.

Brahms, Master of the Canon

Brahms was exceptionally skilled at writing intricate canons: double canons, inverted canons, and *perpetual canons. A perpetual canon* is one which, once started, continues indefinitely. The last measure of notation contains a repeat sign, and no final ending is provided. Example 1-2g is a fine example of this type of canon. It is also a double canon: Soprano II is the comes for Soprano I, and Alto II is the comes for Alto I. At the same time it is a canon at the inversion since Soprano I is the inversion of Alto I, and Soprano II is the inversion of Alto II. All parts are derived from the opening voice, Alto I.

Exercises

EXERCISE 26-1. Create a contrapuntal variation on this modulating sequence by adding decorative pitches. Try to include chromatic passing tones or neighbor tones, appoggiaturas, suspensions, or syncopations.

EXERCISE 26-2. Write three variations on this passacaglia bass. Score the first variation for two parts, the second for three parts, and the third for four parts.

EXERCISE 26-3. Write a four-part round on the text below using the given progression.

The Macedon youth left behind him this truth:
    That nothing was done with much thinking;
He drank and he fought, and he got what he sought,
    And the world was his own by fair drinking.
He wash'd his great soul in a plentiful bowl,
    He cast away trouble and sorrow;
His mind did not run, of what was to be done,
    For he thought of today, not tomorrow.

                                            —*Anonymous*

*EXERCISE 26-4. Write a four-part fugue exposition on this subject.

*EXERCISE 26-5. Extend this double canon to 8–16 measures. It may be given a free ending, or it may be designed as a perpetual canon.

Sources for Further Study

Scores:

BRAHMS:

Choral music: anthems, canons, and motets (especially "Lass dich nur nichts nicht dauren," an accompanied double canon), Symphony No. 4 (Finale is a type of passacaglia)

Haydn Variations (the final variation is a passacaglia)

Organ works: Prelude and Fugue in A minor and G minor, Fugue in A-flat minor, 11 chorale preludes

FRANCK:

Choral music, especially two masses

Organ music (many figural variations)

Prelude, Aria, and Finale for piano

Prelude, Chorale and Fugue for piano

Symphonic Variations (piano and orchestra);

Violin Sonata (accompanied canon in the Finale)

Piano trios and piano quintet

MENDELSSOHN:

Cantatas

Chamber music: octet for strings

Fugues for piano
Oratorios: *Elijah* and *St. Paul*
Piano trios, Organ: preludes and fugues, 6 sonatas

Readings:

Crocker: pp. 437–451; 456–473
Horsley: pp. 264–299
Jeppesen: pp. 48–53
Kennan: pp. 103–104; 110–111
Mann: pp. 63–71; 263–268

PART SIX

Polyphony in the First Half of the Twentieth Century

CHAPTER

27

Serial and Atonal Counterpoint

Wagner's *Tristan und Isolde* had a profound effect on the musical world in the latter half of the nineteenth century. It shook the foundations of the major and minor tonal system, and composers were polarized for and against its implications. Pervasive modulation, unorthodox chord resolutions, root movement by third and by step, and melodic and harmonic chromaticism were portents of the eventual breakdown of the tonal system. After Wagner, the trend was intensified in Germany by Reger, Mahler, Richard Strauss and the young Schoenberg, Berg, and Webern. By the early 1920s Schoenberg's music had dispensed with tonality, and in the last piece of his *Five Piano Pieces* Op. 23, we see his first systematic use of what he called his "method of composition with the twelve tones." Examples 27-1 and 27-2 show an atonal composition on the threshold of twelve-tone serialism and a work which shows a mature and elegant application of the system.

EX. 27-1 No. 4 from *Five Piano Pieces* Op. 23, by Arnold Schoenberg (1874–1951). Copyright 1923 by Wilhelm Hansen, Copenhagen. Reproduced with kind permission of Edition Wilhelm Hansen AS, Copenhagen.

EX. 27-2 *Variations for Piano* Op. 27, Movement II, by Anton Webern (1883–1945).
Copyright 1937 by Universal Edition. Copyright renewed. Used by permission of European
American Distributors Corporation, sole U.S. and Canadian Agent for Universal Edition.

Questions for Discussion

1. Describe the texture of Ex. 27-1. How does it differ from all other textures we have studied thus far and yet qualifies as polyphony?

2. This piece by Schoenberg does not depend upon tonal harmony or any recognizable scale or mode for its pitch organization. How, then, does it maintain cohesiveness?

3. The use of consonance and dissonance has been of primary concern to the composers we have studied to this point. What can you say about consonance and dissonance in this music? What observations can you make about melodic and harmonic intervals and chords?

4. What observations can you make about the temporal elements, rhythm, pulse, and meter?

5. Example 27-2 was written only about a dozen years after Ex. 27-1, but the twelve-tone system was well established by that time. What are the basic principles of the twelve-tone system? What qualities should prevail in serial counterpoint, and what should be avoided?

6. The Webern variation is based on a twelve-tone pitch set or row which accounts for the sequence of pitch classes. How are the pitches organized with regard to their octave location?

7. The piece is a strict canon. Can you explain how it works?

Observations

The texture in Schoenberg's *Five Piano Pieces* Op. 23 is in constant change with regard to the number of tones sounding at one time. This is especially true of the fourth piece in the set, Ex. 27-1, from one in m. 1 to as many as seven in m. 16; there is no set "number of voices." Melody is fragmented and often moves from one hand to the other. In the textures we have examined from the sixteenth through the nineteenth centuries there was always a clear distinction and integrity maintained among the strands of the polyphony. In Schoenberg's piece, strands of melody come and go in all registers without warning. The fabric consists of independent melodic gestures, however, and so it is unquestionably polyphonic.

Although this piece is not written in the twelve-tone technique, its pitch content is based on tone sets, or perhaps more accurately, interval sets. Example 27-3 shows one of these pitch sets as it appears in several places in the piece. The set consists of pitch classes D♯ (E♭), B♮, B♭, D♮, E♮, and G♮ indicated by Xs.

EX. 27-3 Pitch set from Schoenberg's Op. 23, No. 4

A harmonic continuity is maintained through the use of minor or major thirds and minor or major sixths in close juxtaposition. These melodic and harmonic intervals are found in the first measure and continue to be featured throughout the remainder of the piece. It could be said that the piece is a continuous development of the intervallic relationships found in the first measure.

Further continuity is created by sequence and imitation. As examples of this you will note that in m. 3 a sequence appears in the sixteenth-note figure in the inner part; the three-note figure beginning with the last note in the left hand in m. 7 is imitated immediately in the right hand in m. 8; and sequence and imitation are combined in the cascading passage in mm. 19–20. Similar examples can be found elsewhere in the piece.

Outside of a tonal context the concept of consonance and dissonance is relatively meaningless. All tones are treated equally, and hence all intervals tend to be treated the same—with the exception of those intervals that tend to establish a tonal focus. A quick examination of Ex. 27-1 reveals that the interval of the octave is conspicuously absent. The perfect fifth is rare. Of the remaining intervals, the minor second and major seventh are to be found in every measure. As we have noted, the thirds and sixths are a special feature of the piece and give it a special flavor. Note, however, that when triads appear they are accompanied by tones which negate their tonal implications.

The composer indicates that the piece is to be played vigorously and in a moderately quick tempo, but there is no strong feeling of pulse. This is due to several factors: (1) changing meter; (2) rests and motion through many of the downbeats, (3) lack of repeated rhythmic patterns; (4) frequent ritards and an accelerando; and (5) phrase gestures of unequal length. Rhythmic variety and freedom from strong metric pulse are common features of Schoenberg's music.

As we noted above, No. 5 of Schoenberg's Op. 23 piano pieces is the first composition to use the twelve-tone system throughout. It is based on the pitch set ("row" or "series") shown in Ex. 27-4. The set is deployed as shown in Ex. 27-5 in the opening measures of the piece.

EX. 27-4 Twelve-tone set for Schoenberg's Op. 23, No. 5

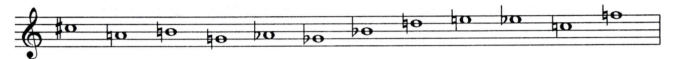

EX. 27-5 Opening of Op. 23, No. 5 by Schoenberg. Copyright 1923 by Wilhelm Hansen, Copenhagen. Reproduced with kind permission of Edition Wilhelm Hansen AS, Copenhagen.

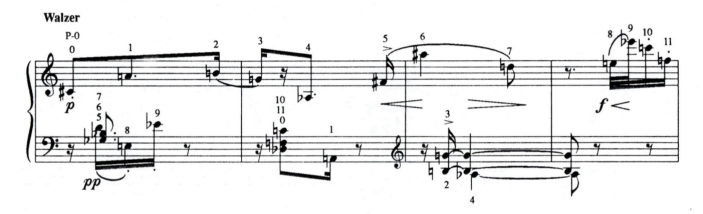

At this point it will be useful to state briefly the basic principles of twelve-tone or "dodecaphonic" music. In our discussion, the term "pitch class" refers to the name of a degree of the chromatic scale and its enharmonic equivalent regardless of its octave location. For example, the pitch class E♭ denotes any E♭ or D♯ in any octave. In counting the tone order and the number of semitones involved in a transposition we will use numbers 0, 1, 2, 3, . . . 11. For example, "RI-9" indicates a retrograde inversion beginning nine semitones (equivalent to a Major sixth) above the initial note of the prime set.

1) All of the melodic and harmonic tone relationships in a piece are derived from a set or series determined by the composer in advance.

2) The set is made up of all twelve pitch classes of the chromatic scale arranged in a fixed sequence.

3) No pitch class may appear more than once in a set (except as noted in No. 8 below)

4) The set may be presented in its original form (Prime), in inversion, in retrograde, or in retrograde inversion.

5) These four set forms may appear on any degree of the chromatic scale (the set may be transposed).

6) The set (or any permutation of the set) may be deployed sequentially (one tone after another) or simultaneously (two or more tones sounding together)

7) Each pitch class may be presented in any octave (or register).

8) Any tone may be repeated before the next tone of the series is introduced; trills or tremolo figures are allowed between consecutive tones of a set.

9) Melodic or harmonic relationships that suggest tonality should be avoided.

In melodic writing, the final note of phrases or themes does not need to coincide with the final note of the set. Ostinato figures may be limited to a segment of the set.

In contrapuntal textures, a single set form may be divided among the parts (provided the set order is retained), a single set form may be used as a counterpoint to itself, or two or more set forms may be used simultaneously. Two parts may occasionally come together in a unison, but the interval of an octave should be avoided between two independent parts. A single tone may represent a member of two different set forms used simultaneously, or the final tone of one set form and the initial tone of a different set form.

Webern's *Variations for Piano* Op. 27 are based upon the pitch set shown in Ex. 27-6. In Ex. 27-2, Webern uses the prime set transposed up four semitones (P-4) beginning in the left hand, and the inversion set transposed up six semitones (I-6) beginning in the right hand. Notice in Ex. 27-7, m. 4, that after the first nine notes have been presented in each hand, the sets are continued in the opposite hand.

EX. 27-6 Prime set for Webern's Op. 27. Copyright 1937 by Universal Edition. Copyright renewed. Used by permission of European American Distributors Corporation, sole U. S. and Canadian Agent for Universal Edition.

Similar exchanges occur in mm. 8, 17, and 18. Webern has chosen set forms which allow him to assign pitch class A to the A above middle C. All pitches above this central tone are exactly mirrored below it. This produces a "mirror canon" where the leader is the part which initiates movement after rests. The follower is in the opposite hand, always an eighth note later.

The piece is organized not only in terms of pitch but in terms of rhythm, dynamics, and articulation. Only five motives are used: (a) a slurred set of eighths, played forte (except in m. 10); (b) a staccato set, played piano (except in m. 12); (c) a set of overlapping quarters with tenuto marks, always played forte; (d) a set of eighths, each with a grace note, played piano (except in m. 6); and (e) two accented eighth-note chords, containing notes 5-6-7 of the current set form and played fortissimo (except in mm. 3–4). Variety is achieved in this piece by the changing order of these motives and whether they are separated by rests.

These piano pieces by Schoenberg and Webern show a marked contrast in style between the two composers. Whereas the Schoenberg example seems to be an extension of late Romanticism with a proliferation of ideas and a relatively rich and complex texture, the movement by Webern seems to represent a Classical control, transparent texture and economy of means.

EX. 27-7 Webern's Op. 27, Movement II, mm. 1–7. Copyright 1937 by Universal Edition. Copyright renewed. Used by permission of European American Distributors Corporation, sole U. S. and Canadian Agent for Universal Edition.

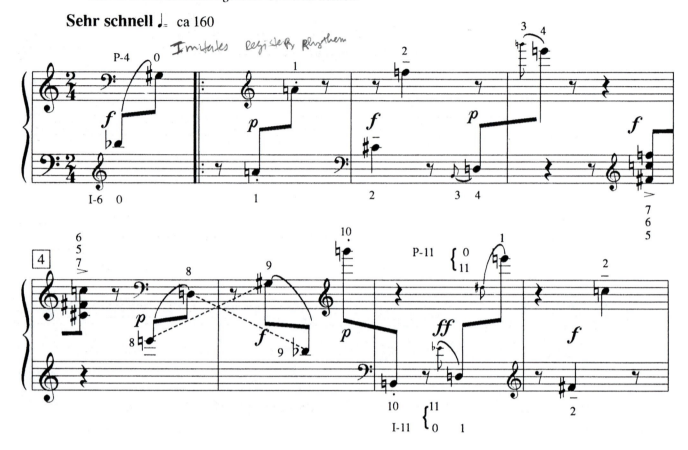

Exercises

EXERCISE 27-1. Continue the lower part in canon at the inversion.

EXERCISE 27-2. Write a contrapuntal part for bassoon using any form of the set used in the flute part.

EXERCISE 27-3. Write a short passage (6 to 10 measures) for violin and cello first using free atonal counterpoint, then using the set given in Exercise 27–1. Use a few double stops in each part and provide articulations (bowing) and dynamics.

*EXERCISE 27-4. Write a three-part fugue exposition for two pianos on this subject.

*EXERCISE 27-5. Write a short passacaglia for string quartet on a set of your own devising.

Sources for Further Study

Scores:

BERG:

Operas: *Lulu* and *Wozzeck* and *Lyric Suite*
Violin Concerto

KRENEK:

Suite for Violoncello Solo Op. 84
Twelve Short Piano Pieces Op. 83

SCHOENBERG:

Five Pieces for Piano Op. 23 (No. 5), Piano Concerto Op. 42
Fourth String Quartet Op. 37
Violin Concerto Op. 36

WEBERN:

Concerto for Nine Instruments Op. 24
Kantata II Op. 31
Symphony Op. 21
Variations for Piano Op. 27

Readings:

Dallin: pp. 180–194
Krenek: *Studies in Counterpoint Based on the Twelve-Tone Technique*
Leibowitz: *Schoenberg and His School*
Marquis: pp. 185–218
Middleton: pp. 141–151
Perle: *Serial Composition and Atonality*
Searle: pp. 71–117

CHAPTER

28

Counterpoint in Hindemith, Bartók, and Stravinsky

While Schoenberg and his followers were concerned with an alternative to the tonal system, Hindemith, Bartók, and Stravinsky pursued the extension of the tonal system, each in his own way. All three were masters of counterpoint. Along with the emancipation of dissonance and rhythm, the first half of the twentieth century saw a renewed interest in contrapuntal writing. As you study Examples 28-1–28-3, review also Ex. 1-2f and Ex. 2-1e.

EX. 28-1 Fuga quarta in A from *Ludus Tonalis* by Paul Hindemith (1895–1963). Copyright © Schott & Co., Ltd., London, 1943. Copyright renewed. All rights reserved. Used by permission of European American Music Distributors Corporation, sole U.S. and Canadian agent for Schott & Co., Ltd., London.

With energy (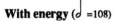 =108)

EX. 28-2 "Theme and Inversion" from *Mikrokosmos*, Book IV, by Béla Bartók (1881–1945).
Copyright © 1940 by Hawkes & Son (London) Ltd.; Copyright Renewed. Reprinted by
permission of Boosey & Hawkes, Inc.

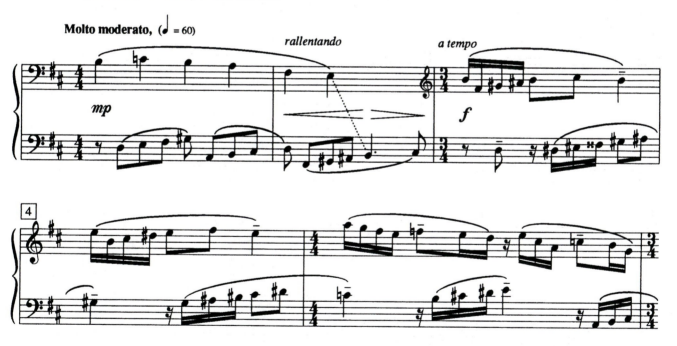

EX. 28-3 "Great Chorale" from *L'Histoire du Soldat* by Igor Stravinsky (1882–1971). Copyright © 1924 by J & W Chester Ltd. (London). All rights for the U.S. and Canada assigned to G. Schirmer, Inc. (New York). International copyright secured. Used by permission.

Questions for Discussion

Hindemith

1. Compare the melodic style of Hindemith's fugue with that of Schoenberg's piano piece, Ex. 27-1. Consider conjunct vs. disjunct motion, diatonicism vs. chromaticism, continuous vs. varied rhythm. When Hindemith employs disjunct motion, what intervals tend to be favored?

2. What observations can you make concerning harmonic intervals used in Ex. 28-1 when the counterpoint is note-against-note (first species counterpoint)? Schoenberg and Webern avoided the octave as a harmonic interval. What do you find in this example?

3. How would you describe the vertical sonorities, the cadences, and the treatment of the major triad? What is the significance of the title "Fugue in A"? What is the overall tonal plan?

4. Describe the temporal aspects in Hindemith's fugue and compare them with those of the Schoenberg and Webern examples in Chapter 27.

5. How does this fugue compare structurally to the fugues we have studied? What is the significance of the three sections? What contrapuntal techniques and devices are used in the fugue?

Bartók

1. Why has Bartók used two sharps in the signature? What appears to be the tonal center of the piece? How did you determine the tonal center? Are there places in the piece where the tonal center shifts or seems to disappear altogether? Can you detect any scale or mode in operation?

2. Describe the melody in this example as you did for the Hindemith example.
3. What intervals are used in places where the parts move note-against-note? How are the cadences articulated?
4. Explain the significance of the title "Theme and Inversion."
5. How are the parts related and yet maintain their independence?
6. How is the structure of the piece related to the rhythmic treatment? What other factors contribute to the articulation of the form?
7. Compare this piece to the "Chromatic Invention," Ex. 2-1e.

Stravinsky

1. In what ways does the "Great Chorale" resemble a Bach chorale? How is it different?
2. In what key is this chorale? What other regions are visited? Describe the cadences.
3. There is liberal use of chromaticism, and yet the voice leading is overwhelmingly diatonic. How do you explain this?
4. Stravinsky makes considerable use of triads in the harmony. What would be considered unorthodox in his voice leading, spacing, and doubling in the light of eighteenth- and nineteenth-century practice?
5. Several terms have been applied to the music of Stravinsky. What is your understanding of: (a) pandiatonicism; (b) octave displacement; (c) displaced accent; (d) polyharmony; (e) polyrhythm?

Observations

There are as many approaches to counterpoint in the twentieth century as there are composers. Hindemith, Bartók, and Stravinsky, however, were important figures in the renewed interest in counterpoint and its application to their own styles of expanded tonality. We will use the examples to explore a few of their major contributions.

Hindemith

The melodic style in Schoenberg's piano pieces Op. 23 is disjunct, chromatic, and constantly varied in rhythm. Hindemith's melody is in sharp contrast on all counts. It is primarily conjunct, diatonic, and consistent in its rhythmic unity. When there are leaps in the melody, they tend to be within the octave. Disjunct melodic motion favors the perfect fourth and fifth, minor and major thirds and sixths, minor sevenths, and octaves. Major sevenths, minor ninths, and tritones are used more sparingly.

The same favored intervals (and their expanded equivalents: major ninth, minor tenth, perfect eleventh, etc.) prevail in the harmony. First species examples bear this out: In m. 4, beat two, we find minor seventh to major ninth; in m. 10, beat two, a minor third (equals a minor tenth) is followed by a perfect fifth (equals a perfect twelfth) the upper parts in mm. 13–14 move in perfect fourths, minor sevenths, and major seconds. The octave is used especially at cadences, but it is not excluded elsewhere.

When the intervals with the strongest dissonant quality (minor second, major seventh, and tritone) are removed from melody and harmony the result is pentatonic. If we remove F and B from a C–major scale, we have a C–pentatonic scale—C, D, E, G, and A. Example 28-4 shows several sonorities which can be derived from a single pentatonic pitch collection.

EX. 28-4 Sonorities derived from a pentatonic set

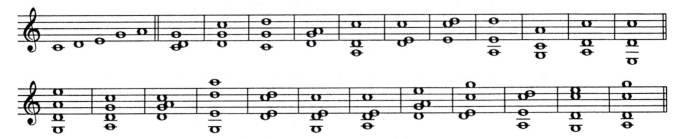

Hindemith considered the perfect fourth and the perfect fifth as acoustic consonances, and he used sonorities featuring these intervals rather than using the triad as the basis for harmony. Consequently, his music abounds in the types of sonorities illustrated in Ex. 17-4. When harmonies are based on perfect fourths, perfect fifths, major seconds, and minor sevenths more often than on thirds and sixths, we apply the term *quartal harmony.* Hindemith uses triads freely but less often. They are usually to be found at strong cadences. It is an idiosyncrasy of Hindemith, however, to conclude movements and sections with a major chord. In general, Hindemithian cadences consist of chords of higher dissonant quality moving to chords of higher consonant quality. Some typical cadences from Ex. 28-1 are shown in Ex. 28-5.

EX. 28-5 Typical cadences from Fuga quarta, *Ludus Tonalis*

Notice the use of perfect octave and perfect fifth in the final chord with the root in the lowest part doubled in an upper part. These cadences are similar to the Phrygian cadence in the Renaissance, where the leading tone motion is downward by half step from second to first degree of the scale.

In his theoretical treatise *Craft of Musical Composition,* Hindemith arranges the intervals in a series which represents their "relative harmonic value." Beginning with the perfect octave as "of highest value" or "most pure" (most consonant), he continues with intervals of diminishing purity (increasingly dissonant), ending with the tritone (Ex. 28-6).

EX. 28-6 "Series 2" from Hindemith's *Craft of Musical Composition*, p. 81

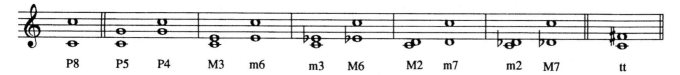

P8   P5   P4   M3   m6   m3   M6   M2   m7   m2   M7   tt

The head motive of the subject in Ex. 28-1 seems to suggest F as tonic, but the tail concludes with A and is reinforced by the E, a perfect fifth higher in the responding voice. Section 1 ends on E, the dominant. The tonal center at the opening of Section 2 is either G♯ or C♯, with evidence for both tones, and the section ends with the tonality in doubt. Section 3 begins like Section 1 seemingly in F, but A is established by m. 48. The final cadence of the third section firmly asserts A as tonic with a Mixolydian cadence, culminating with the usual major triad.

In the fugue, the metrical pulse is strong and regular. The rhythm is conservative, not much different from rhythm in Baroque counterpoint. A definite pulse is lacking in the Schoenberg piano piece, and the rhythms are gestic and constantly varied. The Webern variation stands between these extremes with a limited number of rhythmic figures and a pulse generated more by the gestures of sound and silence than meter.

Fuga quarta is a double fugue. The first section fits the description of a normal Baroque fugue with exposition (mm. 1–8) followed by extended development. There is a counter-exposition in mm. 9–14 on the inversion of the subject. The tail of the subject is treated to sequences in an episode, mm. 15–17, after which the subject and its inversion appear in stretto, mm. 18–23. The closing entries are stated in mirror in mm. 24–25, with a short extension to the closing cadence in E. Section 2 exposes a second subject in mm. 28–43. A short episode leads to a set of middle entries and a closing episode. Section 3 exposes the subjects of sections 1 and 2 together, and the remainder of the piece develops Subject 2 with Subject 1 and its inversion in various combinations. The final section again features Subject 1 in mirror, now with the tail of Subject 2. A coda on the tail of Subject 1 ends the piece.

A quick look at Ex. 1-2f, Fuga secunda from *Ludus Tonalis* reveals the same characteristics of style but in a lighter mood.

Bartók

Example 28-2 is an elegant example of Bartók's melodic writing and two-part counterpoint. The tonal center is B, and the two sharps in the signature seem to proclaim that B minor is the key, or at least the nearest approximation to a key in the major-minor system. Some of the clues are: (a) the first phrase begins and ends on B; (b) there is a cadential move to B in the rising tetrachord, F♯-G♯-A♯-B in the left-hand part, m. 2; (c) the second phrase ends on B, m. 6; and (d) the piece ends on B much like the first phrase. A shift to D as tonal center takes place at m. 11, but modulatory sequences lose the tonal focus until it returns at the end to B. Although B and F♯ seem to function as tonic and dominant, there are mixed clues as to the establishment of any single scale or mode. The second degree is sometimes C♮, sometimes C♯. The third degree appears as D at times and D♯ at others. E and E♯ vie for consideration as the fourth degree. The sixth and seventh degrees likewise can be "raised" or "lowered." This technique can be described as *pan-modality,* "all modes in one." Looking at the right hand part, the opening phrase seems to be B–Phrygian, m. 3 looks like B major, m. 6 qualifies as B–Mixolydian, and m. 7 has G and G♯ and D and D♯ in contest for the sixth and third scale degrees. Bartók mixes modes freely by raising or lowering scale degrees. A logical term for this practice is *degree inflection.*

The melody in Ex. 28-2, like that of Hindemith, is diatonic and predominantly stepwise. It is more chromatic than Hindemith's melody, and the rhythm is a little more adventuresome, especially the sixteenth-note motion interrupted by a rest (mm. 5, 13, and 16). No intervals appear to be favored in disjunct motion, and as for harmonic intervals, thirds and sixths are more numerous than fourths and fifths. Some of the more dissonant intervals appear in harmonic context such as tritone and minor ninth in m. 3, cross-relations in m. 5, augmented second, augmented third, and tritone in measure 8. The melody is a stronger indicator of cadence in this piece than the harmony.

Bartók gave us his *Mikrokosmos* with a twofold purpose: first, it serves as a progressive method for piano technique, and second, it is a lexicon of contemporary compositional techniques. The title "Theme and Inversion" indicates to us that inversion will play an important role in the counterpoint. The piece is a binary structure, A-A', where the A' section is concerned with the inversion of the materials of the A section. Example 28-7 shows this relationship.

EX. **28-7 Inversion of materials in Ex. 28-2**

Inversion also takes place on the motivic level. The rising tetrachord, which appears in the left hand in m. 1 becomes the basic motive. It appears in every measure of the piece either in its original or inverted form. Note that at the climax this motive is set against itself in inversion, as shown in Ex. 28-8.

EX. 28-8 Motivic inversion in Ex. 28-2

The sharing of this motive by the two parts is similar to the kind of motivic development we found in the two-part invention. With the parts so closely related, Bartók is free to exploit their independence. He accomplishes this through the use of bitonality. The lower part imitates the upper at a minor tenth in m. 3, which sets it in the key of G♯ minor in opposition to B minor in the upper part. The tetrachord motive carries its own strong tonal focus; wherever it is used it has the potential of creating bitonality. In the A′ section the right hand suggests F minor while the left hand suggests D minor. In m. 14 all feeling of tonality is lost because the motive has been altered and subjected to modulating sequence (see Ex. 28-8). At the end the two parts are allowed to agree on B as the ultimate tonal center.

Rhythmic treatment plays a key role in the articulation of the form. The opening gesture, mm. 1–2, acts as an introduction and presents the primary musical material in augmented form. It appears again as a transition to the second section in mm. 9–10 and again at the end beginning in m. 17. The striking aural effect of moving from eighth-note motion to sixteenth-note motion makes the structure clear to the listener. Other factors contribute to this effect. Changes in dynamics and tempo accompany the rhythmic shifts, and the quarter rest which interrupts the motion in m. 10 prepares for the shift of roles between the parts in the A′ section.

This piece has a number of features in common with the "Chromatic Invention," Ex. 2-1e. Both pieces use canonic imitation, inversion, and development of a small primary motive through sequence. Where they differ is in the manipulation of tonality. "Theme and Inversion" has a melody which is strongly tonal accompanied by counterpoint which creates bitonality. In "Chromatic Invention" the parts are of equal importance, and the melodic writing is so chromatic that there is little or no tonal focus.

Stravinsky

The "Great Chorale" from Stravinsky's *L'Histoire du Soldat* is a caricature of a Bach chorale. It is in four parts (although orchestrated for sextet), has the same quasi-polyphonic texture, and has a hymn-like melody in the top voice, which is divided into several short phrases, each with fermata at its end. The tonality moves from the tonic to various closely related keys before returning to the tonic, and the voice leading is primarily diatonic and stepwise. It is in the harmony that the chief difference lies. Secondary differences are the phrase lengths, the meter change, and the exaggerated duration of the final chords of principal phrases.

The chorale is in G major. Temporary modulations are to the regions of V, ii, IV, and II (V of V). The cadences resemble authentic, plagal, and half–cadences but are all unorthodox in some way. The half–cadence in m. 3 is IV-V, but the IV has a ninth added (D in the alto), and the V has the leading tone doubled. In m. 4, the cadence is to V of ii, also with added ninth in the penultimate chord. When ii is reached in m. 6, a B♭ has unexpectedly entered the scene, giving a Phrygian flavor to the cadence. In reaching IV in m. 9, the bass has offered an E♭, causing a cross–relation, and the cadence seems to be Mixolydian. The V chord which ends the phrase in m. 14 comes as a surprise, although it is reached by step in all voices but the alto, which has D as a common tone. The remaining cadences each have some kind of unusual treatment of common practice. This is one of Stravinsky's strongest style traits.

We have observed that the voice leading is diatonic and stepwise. The introduction of altered tones appears to be for the sake of color rather than for harmonic function since the music is free from the stricture of tonal functional harmony. Stravinsky is not bound by the old rules of spacing and doubling in his use of triads. Wide spacings with tones clustered near the bottom of the chord, doubling or trebling of the chord third, addition of unaccountable dissonances, presence of both minor and major third, and unrestricted use of the $^6_4$ position are some of his favorite uses of the triad.

The voice leading seems to be so independent that each voice appears to reach its goal with no regard for the movement of other voices. This is, of course, not true. Stravinsky purposefully juxtaposes tones of the diatonic scale so as to dilute or destroy the normal chordal functions. This explains the D in the C chord on beat four of m. 2, the F♯ in the G chord on beat four of m. 3, the E in the G–minor seventh chord on beat four of m. 5, etc. This is accomplished by shifting a simple diatonic line in one of the parts either in pitch or time. If the alto part in m. 3 were changed to D-G-A-B, something more like eighteenth–century harmony would result. This free use of all the tones of a diatonic scale is called *pandiatonicism*. The practice also led to the expression "wrong note school."

Space does not permit extensive examples which show other important techniques used by Stravinsky, but a few of them can be briefly discussed. Octave displacement, employed in serial composition, is used by Stravinsky in a tonal environment, as shown in Ex. 28-9. If all the pitches were within the same octave, much of the character would be lost.

EX. 28-9 (a) Opening of the second movement, *Symphony of Psalms* by Stravinsky. (b) The same rendered without octave displacement. Copyright © 1931 by Edition Russe de Musique; Copyright Renewed. Copyright and Renewal assigned to Boosey & Hawkes, Inc. Revised edition copyright © 1948 by Boosey & Hawkes, Inc., Copyright Renewed. Reprinted by permission.

(a) Original

(b) Without octave displacement

Stravinsky uses octave displacement in many other works including his orchestral arrangement of "Happy Birthday" (Ex. 28-10). Stravinsky also likes to displace the accent, especially in ostinato passages and those employing motoric rhythm (Ex. 28-11).

EX. 28-10 Stravinsky's version of "Happy birthday to you"

EX. 28-11 Displaced accent

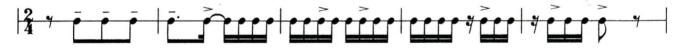

Ravel and others discovered the efficacy of adding one harmony with another to produce polychords and polyharmony. Stravinsky makes liberal use of this technique in many pieces, especially *Le Sacre du Printemps.* When independent rhythms are superimposed, the result is polyrhythm, another device used extensively by Stravinsky.

By the middle of this century all of these techniques had become commonplace tools in the hands of composers born after 1900. After 1950, several trends have affected the place of polyphony in the world of music: Post-Webern serialism led to the total serialization of Babbit and others where counterpoint tended to lose its freedom. The avant-garde composers, including Cage, sought to overthrow any and all restrictions, including the discipline of counterpoint. The focus on texture for its own sake developed in the 1970s and led to the popular place of minimalism in the 1980s. Counterpoint became relegated to the overlays of ostinato in the music of Reich, Glass, Adams, and others. At the same time a "neo-romanticism" led to a renewed reverence for nineteenth-century musical ideals in the music of Rochberg,

Del Tredici, and others. However, the mainstream of composers whose style is eclectic in its most positive sense have continued the long and illustrious history of polyphonic music, which has been part of our heritage for more than a thousand years.

Exercises

EXERCISE 28-1. Complete the inner part to produce quartal harmony (Hindemith style).

(Instruments are at concert pitch)

*EXERCISE 28-5. Write a two-part invention using the following opening measures:

*EXERCISE 28-6. Write a passacaglia on this theme:

*EXERCISE 28-7. Write a fugal chorus on this subject:

Rage, _____ rage _____ a - gainst — the dy - - - - ing of the light.
...... *Dylan Thomas*

Sources for Further Study

Scores:

BARTÓK:

Concerto for Orchestra

Forty-four violin duets

Mikrokosmos, especially Books III through VI

Music for Strings, Percussion and Celesta, especially the first movement

Sonata for Two Pianos and Percussion, especially the fugue in the first
    movement and the imitative passages in the finale

String Quartets, especially No. 1, first movement, No. 5, finale, and No. 6, finale

HINDEMITH:

Concerto for Orchestra, especially the second movement (passacaglia)

Kleine Kammermusik; Symphony, *Mathis der Maler*

Ludus Tonalis

Sonata for Two Pianos, especially the Finale (fugue)

String Quartets, especially No. 3

STRAVINSKY:

Canticum Sacrum (final section is a retrograde of the first)
Concerto for Two Solo Pianos, especially the finale (fugue)
In Memoriam Dylan Thomas, especially the Dirge-Canons
L'Histoire du Soldat
Piano sonata
Symphony of Psalms, especially the second movement

Readings:

Dallin: pp. 33–159; 170–179; 210–211
Hindemith: *Craft of Musical Composition*
Marquis: pp. 1–184; 219–253
Middleton: pp. 11–69; 91–113; 125–140
Searle: pp. 7–70

APPENDIX

A

Identification of Examples in Chapter 1

Examples 1-2 a through g were not identified in Chapter 1 so that students in a classroom discussion or class assignment could describe them and make intelligent guesses as to composer and period. The examples are as follows:

a. Benedictus from *Mass for three voyces* by William Byrd. Period: late Renaissance. Composition date: c. 1593.

b. Prelude in C Minor from 24 Preludes by Frederick Chopin. Period: Romantic. Composition date: 1838.

c. Excerpt from "Charlie Rutledge," song by Charles Ives. Period: twentieth century. Composition date: 1920/21. Copyright © 1939 Arrow Music, Inc. Assigned 1957 to Associated Music Publishers, Inc., a division of Music Sales Corporation. Copyright renewed. International copyright secured. Used by permission.

d. Chorale setting by Johann Sebastian Bach from Cantata 140, *Wachet auf ruft uns die Stimme.* Period: late Baroque. Composition date: 1731.

e. Opening of the final movement of Clarinet Quintet in A, K. 581, by Wolfgang Amadeus Mozart. Period: Classical. Composition date: 1789.

f. Opening of *Fuga secunda in G* from *Ludus Tonalis* by Paul Hindemith. Period: twentieth century. Composition date: 1943. Copyright © Schott & Co., Ltd., London, 1943. Copyright renewed. All rights reserved. Used by permission of European American Music Distributors Corporation, sole U.S. and Canadian agent for Schott & Co., Ltd., London.

g. Double canon for four-part woman's chorus, "O wie sanft die Quelle," by Johannes Brahms. Period: late Romantic. Composition date: c. 1860.

APPENDIX

B

The Ecclesiastical Modes and the Hexacord System

The system of ecclesiastical modes which governed Gregorian Chant was the basis for the tonal organization of the sacred music of the Renaissance (Ex. B-1). A piece that used a chant as cantus firmus took for its mode the mode of that particular chant. The names of the modes were borrowed from Greek antiquity by medieval theorists in order to classify the chants in use in the liturgy.

The mode of a chant can most often be determined by (a) its final note or *finalis,* (b) the overall range of the melody, and (c) the tone that is used for many syllables in longer texts, called the *reciting tone.*

The finalis is generally on D, E, F, or G, as can be seen in Ex. B-1. If the last note is a D, the mode is likely Dorian or Hypodorian (mode I or II). When E is the final note, the mode is Phrygian or Hypophrigian (Mode III or IV). A finalis of F indicates Lydian or Hypolydian (Modes V or VI), and G indicates Mixolydian or Hypomixolydian (Modes VII or VIII).

The approximate range of the chant melody, together with the finalis, determines whether the species of the mode is authentic or plagal. As can be seen from Ex. B-1, the authentic modes (on the left) are the odd-numbered modes. The plagal modes (on the right) are the even-numbered modes. They begin with the prefix "Hypo," and they are a perfect fourth lower than the authentic forms. A melody that has a range from d to d' and ends on d is in the Dorian mode or Mode I. If that melody ended on g, it would be Hypomixolydian, Mode VIII.

EX. B-1 The ecclesiastical modes

The reciting tone is most easily identified in the chants used for singing the Psalms. It is the tone which carries many syllables in the middle of each line of the psalm text. It is also used at important cadences in the melody other than the final cadence. You will notice that the reciting tone is a perfect fifth above the finalis for the authentic modes, with the exception of the Phrygian. Note that it is a sixth or seventh above the finalis for the plagal modes.

B Natural and B Flat

Gregorian chant uses all of the natural pitches (white keys on the piano) and B♭. B♮ was indicated with a square B or *quadratum,* and B♭ was indicated with a round B or *rotundum.* The square B eventually became our natural sign and the round B became our flat sign. B♭ is used in chant to avoid the tritone between F and B. Chants in Mode V (Lydian) often use B♭ liberally throughout the chant, which makes them sound as if they were in major. When B♭ is used in the Dorian, it becomes Aeolian or what we now call natural minor.

The Aeolian and Ionian Modes

In his *Dodecachordon,* 1547, Glareanus recognized a twelve-mode system, adding the four modes shown in Ex. B-2. These modes are the closest to the major and minor, which eventually replaced the modal system by the beginning of the eighteenth century.

EX. B-2 Modes added by Glareanus

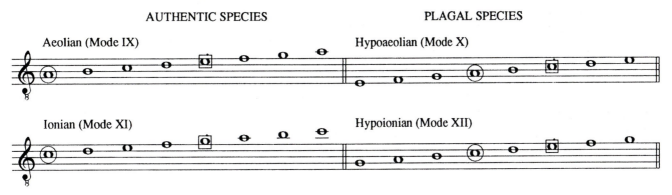

The Hexachord System

A solmization system was devised in the Middle Ages to facilitate the singing of chant by dividing the range of notes in ordinary use into seven overlapping scales of six notes or *hexachords.* These are illustrated in Ex. B-3. The degrees of each hexachord were given the syllables *ut, re, mi, fa, sol,* and *la.* The pitch names are those we use now, that is, A, B, C, D, E, F, and G. Three kinds of hexachords were distinguished:

a) *Hexachordum durum,* "hard" hexachords containing B♮ ; B took the syllable mi.

b) *Hexacordum molle,* "soft" hexachords containing B♭; B♭ took the syllable fa.

c) *Hexacordum naturale,* "natural" hexachords containing neither B nor B♭.

EX. B-3 The hexachord system

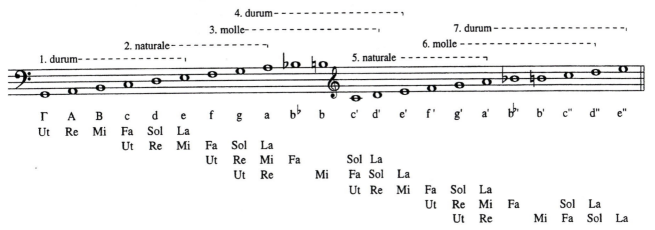

The sequence of whole and half steps was the same in all hexachords: whole, whole, half, whole, whole (tone, tone, semitone, tone, tone). The only half step is between mi and fa.

Specific pitches were identified by letter name and all of the syllable names that could be applied to that pitch. The lowest pitch in the system was called Γ-ut (Gamma-ut, low G in bass clef and incidentally the source of the word "gamut"). It occurs in one hexachord only. Low C is fa in the lowest hexachord and ut in the next, and so it was designated C-fa-ut. Our middle C was called C-sol-fa-ut since it belongs to three hexachords.

APPENDIX

C

A Guide to the Interpretation of Figured Bass Symbols

Figured bass symbols were used in the Baroque period as a kind of short hand notation system to tell the continuo player (at the harpsichord, organ, lute, guitar, etc.) what harmonies to play. It consisted of the written-out bass part with numbers and other symbols that specified such things as: (a) whether the bass note was the root of the harmony or some other member of the chord; (b) whether the harmony was a triad, seventh chord, or some other harmonic construction; (c) whether there were any tones to be played which were not accounted for by the signature (that is, altered tones); and (d) whether there were important dissonances to be accounted for, such as suspensions or appoggiaturas. Like any short hand system, the figures did not give all the details, and the performer was counted on to fill in any missing information.

Since the figured bass communicates only the chord members and certain dissonances, it was up to the continuo player to make the best arrangement of the required tones to suit the occasion. The performer was expected to decide on voicing, doubling, and voice leading on the spot. This is analogous to the keyboardist in a stage band reading from "lead-sheet" chord symbols.

The performer needs to have a sense of when chords are expected. If the bass moves slowly there may be more than one chord for each bass note. If it moves quickly with passing tones, neighbor tones, and arpeggios, a single chord might suffice for several bass notes. In the Baroque period, continuo players were sometimes expected to deduce the harmonies from a bass line with no figures at all, or at most only a few that would indicate unexpected harmonic events. Whenever figures appear, however, they always indicate specific tones to be played. Here are some general guidelines for continuo realization:

In All Cases

1) Numbers indicate interval distance above the bass tone, with or without intervening octaves (3 indicates third, tenth, seventeenth, etc.)

2) A sharp, flat, or natural by itself or on the bottom of a column of figures always applies to the third (tenth, seventeenth, etc.) above the bass note.

3) Any number which is slashed indicates that the tone it refers to is to be raised a half step.

4) A dash after a number indicates that the upper voices are to be held while the bass moves.

5) When two or more numbers are written in succession under a single bass note, voice motion in an upper part is indicated.

6) A flat or natural (and sometimes a sharp) immediately before or after a number shows the alteration of the tone the number indicates.

7) A seemingly incomprehensible stack of figures such as 7-4-2 or 7-5-2 usually indicates that the bass tone is a nonharmonic tone. When the bass moves down a step the first group becomes 8-5-3, a root–position triad; the second group becomes 8-6-3, a first inversion triad.

Triads in Root Position

1) If you sense a chord is needed and the bass note has no figures, play a triad with the bass as the root. The other members of the chord must be consistent with the signature (that is, no alterations).

2) If a 5, a 3, or both 5 and 3 appear below a bass note, a root–position triad is indicated.

3) When a 4 appears below the bass tone, a suspension or appoggiatura a fourth (or eleventh) above the bass tone is indicated. The figure following the 4 designates the resolution. A 3 shows an unaltered resolution to the chord third. A sharp, natural, or flat, shows that the third is to be altered accordingly. Similarly, 9 8 indicates a suspension or appoggiatura a ninth above the bass resolving to the octave.

EX. C-1 Figures indicating root position triads

Inverted Triads

1) A 6 below a bass tone indicates a first inversion triad. The 6 implies a sixth and a third above the bass. Occasionally both figures are given: $^6_3$.

2) 7 6 indicates a suspension or appoggiatura, usually in a treble voice, which then resolves to the chord root while the bass note is sustained.

3) $^6_4$ indicates a second inversion triad.

EX. C-2 Figures indicating inverted triads

Seventh Chords

1) The figures 7, $^6_5$, $^4_3$, and $^4_2$ indicate seventh chords in root position, first, second, and third inversion respectively. Third inversion is sometimes indicated by the figure 2 alone.

2) Occasionally the full set of figures will be used for the seventh chords (7-5-3, 6-5-3, 6-4-3, and 6-4-2).

EX. C-3 Figures indicating seventh chords

Glossary

Accented passing tone. A dissonant tone sounded on a strong beat which connects two consonant pitches a third or a whole step apart by stepwise motion. See Ex. 15-4.

Acciaccatura. A keyboard ornament of the seventeenth and eighteenth centuries involving a sharply dissonant pitch struck together with the chord which it ornaments; usually accented and of very short duration.

Answer. See *response*.

Anticipation. A dissonant tone which is sounded before the chord of which it is a member. It is most commonly found in the highest voice at a cadence point.

Antiphon. A phrase of sacred text in plainsong which precedes and follows a psalm or canticle. In some cases the antiphon is repeated between verses as well.

Antiphonal. Musical call and response between two or more choral or instrumental ensembles or between solo and ensemble.

Applied dominant. See *secondary dominant*.

Appoggiatura. A dissonant tone sounded on a strong beat which is normally approached by leap and resolved downward by step. See Ex. 15-4.

Atonality. The absence of tonality or tonal center.

Augmentation. Lengthening a motive, subject, or other melodic unit by multiplying its note values by a factor of two or more.

Authentic modes. Ecclesiastical modes in which the finalis is the lowest tone. See Appendix B.

Auxiliary tone. See *neighboring tone*.

Axis tone. In melodic inversion, the scale degree which is common to both the rectus and inversus forms.

Ballata. A verse form of the fourteenth century in which the refrain occurs at the beginning and end of the stanza.

Balletto. A dance-song, especially one which answers each rhymed couplet with "Fa, la, la." This is considered by some to be a type of madrigal.

Baryton. An eighteenth-century stringed instrument similar to the viola d'amore, but larger, with six bowed strings and a set of sympathetic strings behind the fingerboard that can be plucked with the thumb. The fingerboard is fretted and the neck is very broad and hollowed out at the rear to accommodate the sympathetic strings. Haydn composed 126 baryton trios for his patron, Prince Nikolaus Esterházy, who played the instrument.

Basso continuo. The bass line and chordal accompaniment in Baroque music, usually provided by a keyboard instrument (harpsichord, organ, etc.) and a bass instrument (cello, bassoon, viola da gamba, etc.). The notation of the continuo may or may not include figures to indicate the harmonies. See Appendix C.

Basso ostinato. A repeated pattern of tones in the bass over which variations are constructed.

Bicinia. Short compositions for two voices, usually contrapuntal in texture.

Bitonal. Music that makes simultaneous use of two tonalities or keys.

Bridge. In the fugue, a short passage following the response or answer in the exposition which modulates to the tonic in preparation for the next entrance.

Cambiata. Abbreviation of *nota cambiata,* a three- or four-note figure used mainly in fifteenth- and early sixteenth-century polyphony in which the second note is dissonant but is followed by the downward leap of a third. The interval sequence with the bass in the three-note figure is usually 8-7-5; in the four-note figure the sequence is usually 5-4-2-3 or 8-7-5-6. See Ex. 15-4.

Canon.   Strict imitation which is sustained throughout a work or a section of a work.

Cantus firmus.   A pre-existing melody to which counterpoint may be added; often presented in longer time values. Chant and chorale melodies are the most common cantus firmi.

Canzona.   An instrumental piece of the sixteenth to eighteenth centuries modelled on the form of the chanson. The early chanson began with a repeated note figure in long-short-short note values which becomes the usual opening for the canzona.

Canzonet, canzonetta.   A short vocal piece with secular text for two or more voices.

Chaconne, ciaccona.   A dance in triple meter with either a repeated bass line or harmonic progression upon which a set of variations is constructed; most often indistinguishable from the passacaglia.

Changing note group.   See *cambiata*.

Chanson.   "Song" in French, generally applied to sixteenth–century French secular polyphonic vocal pieces of three to six parts.

Chorale.   German protestant hymn; generally refers to both the tune and its associated text.

Chorale prelude.   A composition based on a chorale, which can serve as an introduction to the singing of the chorale. In the most common type, the chorale melody serves as cantus firmus and is accompanied by polyphonic figuration in the other parts. In another type, the chorale melody is highly embellished and the accompaniment is slower moving.

Chorale variations.   A composition for keyboard in which a chorale melody serves as the basis for a set of variations.

Chromatic.   Music that makes liberal use of notes foreign to the prevailing mode or key.

Comes.   Follower in a canon or point of imitation. Also called the *consequente*.

Compound melody.   A melody composed in such a way as to give the impression of two or more melodic parts through the use of leaps and register changes.

Conjunct.   Stepwise melodic motion.

Consequente.   See *comes*.

Consonant fourths (and tritones).   Perfect fourths or tritones between two parts, which are treated as consonances.

Continuo.   See *basso continuo*.

Continuous variations.   A set of variations with no pauses between individual variations. Included in this genre are all types of basso ostinato variations.

Contrary motion.   Melodic motion in which voices move in the opposite direction.

Cori spezzati.   Multiple choirs, usually in spatial separation.

Counterexposition.   In some fugues, a second exposition which follows the original exposition using a different order of entries. Voices may continue with counterpoint after the original exposition until their entrances in the counterexposition.

Countersubject.   A melodic idea used as a counterpoint to the subject in a fugue, which appears often enough to have thematic significance. A countersubject should be capable of invertible counterpoint with the subject.

Cross-relation.   The dissonance caused by the close proximity in two different voices of a diatonic Pitch and an altered form of that pitch such as C and C♯ or B and B♭.

Degree inflection.   Free alteration up or down of the degrees of a scale or mode, especially in melodic writing.

Diapason.   Greek name for the interval of an octave.

Diapente.   Greek name for the interval of a fifth.

Diatessaron.   Greek name for the interval of a fourth.

Diatonic.   Music constructed from the tones of a major, minor, or modal scale; diatonic music contains few, if any, chromatically altered pitches.

Diminution.   Making use of smaller time values: (1) varying a melody by interpolating pitches between the original notes; (2) presenting a subject or a motive with time values reduced, usually by half.

Direct fifths, direct octaves.   The approach to a fifth or an octave by two voices in similar motion; to be avoided when the upper voice moves by leap.

Disjunct.   Melodic motion involving a leap of a third or more.

Divisions.   A technique of ornamentation in which notes are interpolated between the notes of a given melody. Synonymous with *diminutions* (1).

Dodecaphonic.   Serial music written in the twelve-tone technique.

Double.   In dance suites, a variation of the dance movement it immediately follows, usually characterized by running passages.

Double counterpoint.   See *invertible counterpoint*.

Double fugue (and triple fugue).   A fugue with two (or three) distinct subjects. Several possibilities exist for the exposition and development of the subjects: (a) they are presented together at the beginning, each being the countersubject of the other; (b) the first subject is presented in exposition and continues in development as the next subject enters in exposition; and (c) each subject is given an exposition and some development after which they are combined in further development.

Double neighbor.   A four-note melodic figure in which

the second and third notes are upper and lower neighbors to the first and fourth, which are identical in pitch. Since either upper or lower neighbor may make dissonances with other voices, the figure allows for the leap of a third in conjunction with these dissonances. See Ex. 15-4.

Dux.   The leading voice in canon or a point of imitation. Also called the *guida*.

Ecclesiastical modes.   Sets of tones, also called *church modes,* that define and categorize the formal resources of music, especially that of the Middle Ages and Renaissance. Their names are borrowed from the Greek modal system, and they are often referred to by number. See Appendix B.

Échappée.   See *escape tone.*

Embellished resolution.   In a suspension, when tones are interpolated between the suspended note and its resolution.

Episode.   A passage in a fugue that does not contain a complete entry of the subject.

Escape tone.   A dissonant pitch that is a step above the consonant pitch which precedes it and a third above the consonant pitch which follows it. For example: if the treble has D-E above a V chord in C major and then proceeds to C above a I chord, the E is an escape tone. See Ex. 15-4.

Exposition.   The statement of the musical material upon which a piece is based. (1) In a fugue it encompasses the first presentation of the subject in all parts. (2) In a movement in sonata form it consists of the first presentation of all of the principal thematic material.

Extended dominant chords.   Chords of a dominant function that include one or more higher dissonant tones—ninth, eleventh, and thirteenth.

False entry.   In fugues, an incomplete subject entry, usually consisting only of the head motive.

Familiar style.   Passages in vocal part music which are basically homophonic or homorhythmic in texture.

Fantasia.   In general, an instrumental piece characterized by imaginative and spontaneous music. In the late Renaissance, however, the fantasia was an imitative composition similar to the canzona and ricercar.

Fauxbourdon.   (1) Parallel motion of triads in first inversion. (2) Music in the fifteenth century in which a third voice is added between the treble and bass, which moves in parallel fourths with the treble. (3) A type of four-part English chant of the sixteenth and early seventeenth centuries in which the cantus firmus (usually a psalm tone), is set in the tenor voice.

Ficta.   See *musica ficta.*

Figured bass.   See *basso continuo.*

Finalis.   The final note of a melody in one of the ecclesiastical modes. It is the first or lowest note in each of the authentic modes and the fourth note in the plagal modes. See Appendix B.

Florid counterpoint.   Fifth species counterpoint, or free counterpoint, which may make use of a variety of time values, suspensions, and syncopations.

Frottola.   A strophic part song of the late fifteenth and early sixteenth centuries, which was one of the forerunners of the madrigal.

Fuga.   Fugue. In the Renaissance fuga referred to canon: *ad fugam* = in canon.

Fugato.   Fugue-like.

Fughetta.   A short fugue.

Gigue.   A quick dance movement in Baroque binary form which became the customary final movement in the Baroque suite and in many Baroque sonatas. It is most often found in compound duple meter with fugal entries at the beginning of both strains. Gigues in German keyboard suites often presented the opening subject in an inverted form in the second strain.

Ground.   A repeating bass line over which variations are constructed. See *basso ostinato.*

Guida.   See *dux.*

Harmonic rhythm.   The rate of harmonic change, usually expressed in number of harmonic changes per measure.

Hemiola.   3:2 ratio. A musical gesture wherein two measures in triple meter are performed as if they were three measures of duple meter.

Hexachord.   A set of six pitches: (1) six-note scale system used for solmization in Medieval and Renaissance theory—See Appendix B; (2) the six-note segments of a twelve-tone set or row.

Homophony.   Melody and subordinate accompanying parts.

Homorhythmic.   Music characterized by the same or similar rhythm in all parts.

Imitation.   The repetition of a motive, subject, or larger melodic idea of one part by one or more other parts in close succession. Imitation may be at any interval, but the octave, unison, fourth, and fifth are most common.

Incipit.   The first few notes or words of a piece, especially a chant. Occasionally in music of the Middle Ages and Renaissance the text or music is indicated only by incipit.

Internal cadence.   A cadence within a work other than the final cadence.

Intonation.   The opening notes of a psalm tone, canticle, or other type of plainchant that serve the purpose of establishing the pitch of the chant.

Invention.   Like the terms prelude and fantasia, there is no set form for an invention. It is generally associated with the fifteen two-part inventions and the fifteen three-part sinfonias by Bach. Most of these pieces are characterized by the use of invertible counterpoint.

Inversus.   The inverted form (mirror image) of a melody.

Invertible counterpoint.   Counterpoint in which a voice can be successfully placed above or below another voice, thereby inverting the intervals between them. Double counterpoint involves two voices that can be treated in this way, and triple counterpoint involves three voices, each of which can occupy the upper, middle, or lower voice position.

La folia.   A dance song used as the basis for basso ostinato variations in the sixteenth and seventeenth centuries. The harmonic sequence is i V i VII III VII i V which is repeated, but ends with an authentic cadence, i-V i.

Leaning tone.   See *appoggiatura*.

Madrigal.   (1) A fourteenth–century Italian secular song with a fixed verse form, usually for two voices. (2) A sixteenth–century polyphonic setting of a secular verse for unaccompanied voices, usually four to six in number. In the seventeenth century, madrigals with instruments and continuo are to be found.

Madrigalism.   See *word painting*.

Mass.   The principal service of the Roman Rite, and also a musical setting of the texts of the Ordinary: Kyrie, Gloria, Credo, Sanctus, Benedictus, and Agnus Dei.

Melisma.   Several notes sung to a single syllable.

Mensurstriche.   Measure bars which are drawn between staves rather than across them in order to facilitate the transcription of the rhythms of early music without the use of ties.

Middle entries.   In fugal compositions, statements of the subject after the exposition.

Minimalism.   Music constructed of a limited range of musical materials. The term is applied to music that appeared first in the 1970s, which featured static harmony and repeated rhythmic patterns with changes taking place over long time spans. Composers associated with the technique are Philip Glass, Steve Reich, Terry Riley, and John Adams.

Missa brevis.   A short Mass, one whose sections are all brief, or one which includes only Kyrie and Gloria.

Modal.   Music based on the church modes rather than on major or minor scales.

Modes.   See *ecclesiastical modes*.

Monody.   Music for a single voice or instrument.

Motet.   From the Renaissance to the present, the term motet refers to a setting of a sacred text. The text of the Renaissance motet is in Latin but not part of the ordinary of the Mass or the canticles, the medium is unaccompanied voices, and the texture is generally polyphonic. In later periods, however, motets could be scored for solo or chorus with or without instruments, and sacred texts in the vernacular could be used. The term first appeared in the thirteenth century when words ("mots" in French) were added to the upper part of a clausula. Eventually the motet became an independent form, usually in three parts and sometimes with secular texts.

Musica ficta.   Accidentals that were intended but not indicated in the original manuscripts. The altered pitches were performed and eventually appeared in later transcriptions.

Neighboring tone.   A tone that is a step above or below the pitch which precedes and follows it. See Ex. 15-4.

Nota cambiata.   See *cambiata*.

Oblique motion.   Upward or downward movement of one part against another stationary part.

Octave displacement.   Pitches of a melody or a tone set may be altered by presenting them up or down one or more octaves. For example, the beginning of the tune "Three blind mice" might be rendered with the pitches e-d′-c″, e′-d-c′.

Pan-modality.   Free use of all modes which share the same tonic pitch. With this technique, the music is tonal but the mode is variable.

Pan-tonality.   Use of all twelve pitches of the chromatic scale without the restrictions of tonal music. Synonymous with *atonality*.

Pandiatonicism.   Free use of the tones in a diatonic scale, not restricted by the principles of traditional harmony. The technique is sometimes referred to as the "white note technique" and is exemplified by the neoclassic music of Stravinsky.

Parallel motion.   Movement of two or more parts in the same direction maintaining a fixed interval distance.

Parody Mass.   A sixteenth–century Mass based on a pre–existing motet, chanson, madrigal, or other polyphonic work.

Passacaglia, passecaille.   A dance in triple meter with a repeated bass line upon which a set of variations is constructed; virtually indistinguishable from the chaconne.

Passamezzo (Pass'e mezzo).   An Italian dance of the sixteenth and seventeenth centuries used as the basis for basso ostinato variations. The harmonic progression for the pass'e mezzo antico is i VII i V III VII i-V i; for the pass'e mezzo moderno it is I IV I V I IV I-V I.

Pavan (pavana, pavane). A slow, stately dance in duple meter that flourished in the sixteenth and early seventeenth centuries.

Period, periodic structure. A musical module, complete in itself, consisting of antecedent and consequent phrases ending with a conclusive cadence. Although most often consisting of two phrases only, periods may be constructed with more than two phrases. The phrases themselves may be made up of shorter subphrases.

Picardy third (tiérce de Picardie). The alteration of the third of the final chord of a cadence changing it from minor to major.

Pitch class. A pitch name representing all octaves in which it may occur. For example: Pitch class E designates all Es regardless of register.

Point. Literally "note." The word came to mean a "point of imitation," a passage in which each voice presents a motive or subject in close succession.

Polychoral. Music for two or more choruses. See *cori spezzati.*

Polychord, polychordal, polyharmony. A sonority made up of two or more simple chords, usually triads. *Polychordal* and *polyharmony* refer to music made up largely of polychords.

Polyphony. Music for two or more voices in a contrapuntal texture.

Polytonality. Simultaneous use of two or more keys.

Psalm tone. A melodic formula for the chanting of psalms, canticles, and other parts of liturgy. There are different formulae for each of the church modes.

Punctum contra punctum. Note against note, the origin of the word counterpoint.

Puzzle canon. A canon that does not specify the starting point of the following voice or voices. The composer sometimes provides a cryptic message as a clue to the solution.

Quartal harmony. In the strict sense, harmony based on the interval of the fourth, rather than the third as in tertian harmony; in a broader sense, music in which the perfect fourth, minor seventh, major second (and ninth) are treated like consonances as in the music of Hindemith.

Real response. In fugal compositions the answer to the subject, which is an exact transposition of it, as opposed to *tonal response* in which pitches are altered. The terms real and tonal are also applied to imitation and sequence.

Realization. (1) The written-out solution of a canon where the dux only is given. (2) A written-out continuo part or figured bass.

Reciting (or recitation) tone. The chanting tone that follows the incipit or intonation in a psalm tone which carries the syllables in the middle of each verse of the psalm, canticle, or other liturgical text. Each psalm tone has a pitch designated as the reciting tone (also referred to as the *tenor* of the chant or the *dominant* of the mode).

Rectus. The original form of a melody, as opposed to *inversus,* its mirror image.

Response. In a fugue, the answer to the subject. In tonal fugues, the response is normally in the dominant key and the same mode as the subject (that is, major when the subject is in major, minor when the subject is in minor). Even-numbered subject entries in the exposition are considered responses. If the response is tonal, it can be distinguished from the subject and may appear in that form in the development of the fugue.

Responsory. A type of liturgical chant in which the choir responds with a refrain after a verse has been sung by soloists or a cantor.

Retrograde. In reverse order. See *twelve-tone music.*

Retrograde inversion. Inverted and in reverse order. See *twelve-tone music.*

Ricercar (ricercare). An instrumental composition of the sixteenth and seventeenth centuries of two types: (1) a rhapsodic type in homophonic texture, and (2) a polyphonic type that uses imitation and various other contrapuntal devices. The second type, along with the canzona and the fantasia are among the major predecessors of the fugue.

Ritornello. A passage in a piece of music that returns after digressions, often with no changes.

Romanesca. In the sixteenth and seventeenth centuries, a sequence of bass tones and associated harmonies upon which variations were made. The progression is usually III VII i V III VII i-V I.

Round. A simple type of vocal perpetual canon at the unison (or octave when men and women sing together) in which each part sings the whole melody an indefinite number of times.

Rovescio. "Reversed" as in inversion or retrograde.

Secondary dominant. A sonority which has a dominant function to a diatonic triad other than the tonic. Example: An E–major triad can serve as V of vi in the key of C. Synonymous with *applied dominant.*

Sequence. (1) The repetition of a melodic unit (motive, phrase, etc.) or a harmonic progression at one or more different pitch levels (usually rising or falling by the same interval when there is more than one repetition). A melodic sequence occurs in a single voice, as opposed to imitation. A sequence may be tonal, in which case it proceeds in a diatonic fashion, or real, in which case it is transposed exactly, effecting a modulation with each repetition. (2) A type of liturgical chant in which each pair of verses is set to a different musical phrase, resulting in the form aa, bb, cc, dd. . . . n. Setting of the text is generally syllabic.

Serial music. Music based upon a set or series of pitch classes including but not restricted to twelve-tone music. Serial technique was extended by some composers to include serialization of rhythm, dynamics, and other musical parameters.

Similar motion. Movement of two or more parts in the same direction but not maintaining a fixed interval distance.

Simultaneity. (1) The sounding together of two or more pitches. (2) A texture created by the sounding together of two or more unrelated musical ideas, exploited by Charles Ives and other composers in the twentieth century.

Sinfonia. (1) The Italian word for symphony. (2) The term is applied to various instrumental works such as canzonas, trio sonatas, and specifically the three-part inventions by Bach. (3) An introductory instrumental movement to a cantata, oratorio, or opera.

Sonata. A piece to be played, as opposed to *cantata*, a piece to be sung, for a solo or small ensemble of instruments. Originally a single–movement piece related to the canzona, the sonata eventually became a sectional piece, and then a multi-movement piece. The Baroque sonata was for solo or a few instruments with continuo, with two types emerging in the works of Corelli. One was similar to the dance suite and the other alternated aria-like movements with fugal movements, the two types merging after 1700. See *sonata da camera* and *sonata da chiesa*. By the latter eighteenth century, it had become almost exclusively a three– or four–movement work for solo or solo with piano accompaniment whose first and sometimes final movement were in sonata form.

Sonata da camera. Baroque "Chamber sonata" consisting of three or more stylized dance movements, occasionally preceded by a slow introductory aria. Examples are contained in Corelli's Opp. 2 and 4.

Sonata da chiesa. Baroque "Church sonata" usually consisting of four movements, slow-fast-slow-fast. The opening movement was aria-like, and the second, fugal. The third, in a related key, was often no more than a transition with a skeletal melody that was highly ornamented in performance, and the fourth, a poly-

phonic gigue. Examples are contained in Corelli's Opp. 1 and 3.

Species counterpoint. A pedagogical method for the teaching of counterpoint formulated by J. J. Fux in 1725. The system proceeds from simple to more complex writing of counterpoints to given cantus firmi. First species is note-against-note counterpoint. Second species involves two (then three) notes in the counterpoint against each note of the cantus firmus. Third species sets four notes to each note of the cantus firmus. Fourth species involves the use of syncopations and suspensions. The four species are combined in fifth species, called florid counterpoint, which allows the occasional use of notes of smaller duration.

Stretto. In a fugue, the overlapping of subject entries.

Subject. In a fugue, the opening theme. It must have a high musical profile or character so that it is easily recognized whenever it appears.

Suite (Baroque). A set of stylized dances for keyboard or instrumental ensemble. Most suites contain an allemande, courante, sarabande, and gigue. Other optional dances might be added such as the bourée, gavotte, and minuet. Many suites open with a free introductory movement such as a prelude, overture, toccata, fantasia, or sinfonia.

Suspension. A musical figure consisting of a note which, when first sounded, makes a consonance, but is then prolonged beyond a strong beat. This causes a dissonance with one or more of the other parts. The note then resolves down by step to create a consonance. See Ex. 15-4.

Syncopation. A rhythmic configuration in which motion has been shifted so that it does not coincide with the prevailing meter or beat. The shift is most easily perceived when other parts, which do not participate in the syncopation, are present. In fourth species counterpoint a chain of syncopations is set up against the cantus firmus. When a dissonance occurs between the cantus firmus and the syncopated counterpoint a suspension is created. See *species counterpoint* and *suspension*.

Tactus. In the Renaissance, tactus is equivalent to the modern word "beat." It was normally considered to be equal to the semibreve, about sixty to seventy per minute, and was indicated by the rising and falling of the hand in performance.

Tessitura. The average range of a musical unit (phrase, section, piece, individual part, etc.).

Thorough bass. See *basso continuo*.

Toccata. A virtuosic piece for keyboard or plucked

string instrument which is quasi improvisatory and features brilliant passagework. The toccatas of the late sixteenth and early seventeenth centuries often alternated running figuration with imitative or fugal sections, especially those of Frescobaldi.

Tonal. (1) Adhering to the tonal system of major and minor as distinct from modal and atonal. (2) Exhibiting a hierarchy of tones in which certain tones are assigned the role of tonic in the music, especially at cadential points. (3) A designation applied to sequence, imitation, and fugal entries implying adjustment to the prevailing tonality as opposed to the term *real*, which implies exact transposition.

Tonal response. In fugal compositions, the answer to the subject in which pitches are altered in order to express the tonality, as opposed to *real response*, which is an exact transposition of the subject.

Tonality. The organized relationships of pitches in which one functions as the center or tonic. In a narrower sense the word is synonymous with the word "key."

Tone row. A set of pitches used as the basis for serial music.

Tonic. The principal or central tone to which other tones are related. In major and minor the tonic is the first degree of the scale.

Trio sonata. A Baroque instrumental piece for two melodic instruments with continuo usually consisting of three or four movements.

Triple counterpoint. See *invertible counterpoint.*

Twelve-tone music. Music based on a series (set, or row) consisting of all twelve pitch classes in the equal tempered scale. The set may be used in any of its four basic configurations—prime, inversion, retrograde, and retrograde inversion, and may be transposed to any degree of the chromatic scale.

Una nota supra la. "A note above 'la'," or A. In medieval and Renaissance music when B is used as an upper neighbor to A, the B is flatted, especially in the Dorian mode. It then becomes *fa* in the hexacordal system. See Appendix B.

Villanella. A form of vocal Italian music usually on a rustic theme for three or more voices in homophonic style popular in aristocratic society in the mid-sixteenth century. The melody is in the top voice and parallel triads in root position are frequently encountered.

Virginal. A small harpsichord popular in England during the Elizabethan period with a single set of strings and jacks.

Vorimitation. Used in a type of chorale prelude where, before a phrase of the chorale melody is stated as a cantus firmus in longer note values, the other voices anticipate it in fugal imitation in shorter note values.

Word painting. Music descriptive of the text either in general mood or with specific reference such as the imitation of bird calls, running scalar passages to suggest flight, falling melodic movement to suggest tears or sighing, etc. Explicit word painting is often called *madrigalism.*

Discography

Most of the examples used in this book are available on recordings. The following is a brief listing of compact disc recordings currently available as of this printing, arranged by century and by genre within each century. The order generally parallels the text. A shorter list of phonograph recordings is also given for works not included in the compact disc listing.

COMPACT DISCS

Sixteenth century

MOTETS

Josquin Desprez: (HARMONIA MUNDI HMC 1243) Herreweghe, Chapelle Royale Chorus.

Palestrina: (NIMBUS 5100) Christ Church Cathedral Choir.

Lasso: (EMI CDC 7 749 210 2) Hiller, Hilliard Ensemble. (also chansons)

Byrd: (CRD 3408) Higginbottom, Choir of New College, Oxford.

MASSES

Josquin Desprez: *L'homme armé.* (GIMELL 019) Tallis Scholars.

Palestrina: *O Rex Gloriae, Viri Galilaei.* (HYPERION CDA 66316) O'Donnell, Westminister Cathedral Choir. (also motets)

————: *Papae Marcelli, Tu es Petrus.* (ARCHIV 415 517-2AH) Preston, Westminister Abbey Choir. (also Allegri: *Miserere*)

Byrd: *Masses for five, four, and three voices.* (GIMELL CDGM 345) Phillips, Tallis Scholars.

Victoria: *Ascendans Christus, O magnum mysterium.* (HYPERION CDA 66190) Hill, Westminister Cathedral Choir. (also motets)

CHANSONS, MADRIGALS, AND CANZONETS

Chanson Collection. (HARMONIA MUNDI 901072) Ensemble Clément Janequin. (works of Janequin, Sermisy, Milano)

Italian Madrigals. (IMP PCD 822 or MCA MCAD-5842) Amaryllis Consort.

Wert: *Seventh Book of Madrigals.* (VIRGIN Classics VC 7 90763-2) Rooley, Kirkby, Consort of Musiche.

English Airs and Duets. (HYPERION 6003) Camerata of London.

Draw on Sweet Night. (EMI Reflexe CDC 7 49187-2) Hiller, Hilliard Ensemble. (includes Gibbons: "The Silver Swan" and works of Morley, Weelkes, Wilbye, Tomkins, and Vautor)

INSTRUMENTAL MUSIC (CANZONAS, FANTASIAS, DANCES, ETC.)

Arbeau: *Orchésographie.* (ARABESQUE Z 6514) Logemann, New York Renaissance Band.

Music from the time of the Spanish Armada. (SAYDISC SDL 373) The Waits of York.

Gabrieli, G: Canzonas. (CBS MK 44931) Canadian Brass, members of the N.Y. Philharmonic and the Boston Symphony Orchestra.

Renaissance Vocal and Instrumental Ensemble Music. (GALLO CD 567) L'Ensemble Terpsichore.

Seventeenth century

VOICE AND CONTINUO

Musiche Veneziane per voce e strumenti. (CLAVES CD 8206) Berganza, soprano; Imamura, theorbo; Ros, viola da gamba; Dahler, harpsichord.

Monteverdi: Solo vocal works. (HYPERION CDA 66106) Kirkby, soprano, Rooley, chitterone.

CHORAL WORKS

Monteverdi: *Vespers.* (EMI CDC8 47077) Andrew Parrott, Taverner Consort, Taverner Choir, Taverner Players.

Schütz: *Symphoniae sacrae* (selections). (ERATO ECD 88150) Saqueboutiers de Toulouse.

————: *Kleine geistliche Konzerte.* (HARMONIA MUNDI HMC 901097) Hennig, treble; Jacobs, countertenor; Christi, organ and ensemble.

INSTRUMENTAL ENSEMBLES: DANCES, CANZONAS, GROUNDS, ETC.

Praetorius: *Terpsichore* (1612) (RICERCAR RIC 001031) Musica Aurea and l'Ensemble Ludi Musici.

Gibbons: Fantasias and In Nomines. (ASTREE AUVIDIS E 7747) Savall, Coin, Casademunt, viola da gamba.

Purcell: Chacony in G minor. (HYPERION CDA 66212) Parley of Instruments.

SOLO AND TRIO SONATAS

Purcell: Sonatas of three parts. (CHANDOS CHAN 8591) Purcell Quartet. (also: Pavans)

Corelli: Sonata Op. 5 No. 12, "La Follia" variations. (TITANIC TiCD 35) Verbruggen, recorder; Gibbons, harpsichord; Mahler, cello.

————: Trio Sonatas Op. 1 and 2, selections. (HYPERION CDA 66226) Purcell Quartet.

————: Trio Sonatas Op. 3. (SMITHSONIAN 035) Smithsonian Chamber Players.

Pachelbel: Canon and Gigue in D. (PHILIPS 416 386-2PH) Mariner, Academy of St. Martin-in-the-Fields.

KEYBOARD

Frescobaldi: Canzonas. (HUNGAROTON HCD-12778-2) Karasszon, organ.

Purcell: "Ground in Gamut" and other pieces. (HUNGAROTON HCD 12666) Sárközy.

Buxtehude: Organ works. (ERATO ECD 75370) Alain, organ.

Eighteenth century, Baroque

KEYBOARD

Bach: *Orgelbüchlein.* (DENON CD 33C37-7809) Rilling, organ.

————: Schübler Chorales. (ERATO ECD 88030) Alain, organ.

————: Canonic Variations on "Von Himmel hoch." (CBC ENTERPRISES SMCO 5043 C.) Isler, Mainly Mozart Orchestra. (transcription)

————: Inventions (2 and 3 part). (DENON C37-7566) Dreyfus, harpsichord.

————: *Goldberg Variations.* (HARMONIA MUNDI HMC 90 1240) Gilbert, harpsichord.

————: *Well-Tempered Clavier I and II.* (HARMONIA MUNDI 901285/88) Moroney, harpsichord.

————: English Suites. (LONDON 421 640-2LH) A. Schiff, piano.

————: French Suites. (L'OISEAU-LYRE 411 811 20H2) Hogwood, harpsichord.

————: Partitas. (DENON 33CO-1153) Dreyfus, harpsichord.

SOLO AND TRIO SONATAS, ENSEMBLES

Vivaldi: Sonatas for flute and continuo, "Il pastor fido." (DENON C37-7572) Larrieu, flute; Veyron-Lacroix, harpsichord.

Bach: Musical Offering. (CAPRICCIO 10023) Leipzig Bach-Collegium.

————:*The Art of Fugue.* (ARCHIV 413 642-2AH3) Goeble, Cologne Musica Antiqua. (also: Musical Offering)

Handel: Trio Sonatas. (ARCHIV 415 497-2AH) Pinnock, The English Concert.

Telemann: Trio Sonatas. (EMI HARMONIA MUNDI CDC 7 47574-2) Camerata Köln.

CHORAL WORKS

Bach: *Mass in B Minor.* (ARCHIV 415 514-2AH2) Monteverdi Choir, Gardiner, English Baroque Soloists.

Handel: *Messiah.* (L'OISEAU-LYRE 411 858-20H3) Hogwood, Academy of Ancient Music.

Eighteenth century, Classical

CHAMBER MUSIC

Haydn: Baryton Trios. (ACADEMY S & V CDGAU 104) Hsu, baryton; Miller, viola; Arica, cello.

————: String Quartets Op. 20. (HUNGAROTON HCD 11332-33-2) Tátrai Quartet.

————: String Quartets Op. 76. (HUNGAROTON HCD 12812-13-2) Tátrai Quartet.

Mozart: Serenade in C Minor, K. 388; Serenade in E-flat Major, K. 375. (MUSICAL HERITAGE MHS 512033A) Scottish National Orchestra Wind Ensemble.

————: Quintet for Clarinet and Strings, K. 581. (AMON RA CD-SAR 17) Hacker, clarinet; Salomon Quartet.

————: Adagio and Fugue. (CBS MK 42124) Kremer, Phillips, violin; Kashkashian, viola; Ma, cello

CHORAL WORKS

Haydn: *Creation.* (ALBANY AR 005-6) Revson, St. Paul Chamber Orchestra; Minnesota Chorale.

Mozart: *Requiem.* (DG 353-2GH) Bernstein, Bavarian Radio Chorus and Symphony.

KEYBOARD

Mozart: Gigue for piano, K. 574. (PHILIPS 412 616-2PH) Uchida.

ORCHESTRA

Haydn: Symphony 101. (PHILIPS 422 240-2PH) Brüggen, Orchestra of the Eighteenth Century.

Mozart: Symphonies No. 40 and 41. (DG 413 547-2GH) Bohm, Vienna Philharmonic Orchestra.

Nineteenth century

CHAMBER MUSIC

Beethoven: String Quartets Op. 18 (EMI CDCC-47126) Berg Quartet.

————: String Quartets Op. 59. 74, 95. (EMI CDCC-47120) Berg Quartet.

————: String Quartet Op. 131. (CALLIOPE CAL 9638) Talich Quartet.

————: Cello Sonatas Op. 69 and Op. 102 No. 2. (CBS-SONY 38DC-23) Tsutsumi, cello; Turini, piano.

Mendelssohn: Octet for Strings. (TELARC CD 80142) Cleveland and Meliora Quartets.

KEYBOARD

Beethoven: *Diabelli Variations.* (PHILIPS 416 295-2PH) Arrau.

————: Variations and Fugue ("Eroica"). (NIMBUS 5133.) Perlemunter.

————: Piano Sonatas Nos. 28-32. (NONESUCH 9 79211-2) Goode.

Mendelssohn: Preludes and Fugues Op 37; Organ Sonatas Op. 65. (ERATO ECO 88112) Alain, organ.

Brahms: Chorale Preludes: Es ist ein Ros', Schmücke dich, O Gott du frommer Gott. (INTERCORD SAPHIR 830.801) Rapf, organ.

————: Variations on a theme by Haydn. (CBS MK 42625) Parahia, Solti, pianos. (also Bartók: Sonata for two pianos and percussion)

Franck, C: Prelude, Chorale, and Fugue. (ACCORD 2-532) Girod. (also: Symphony in D minor, Prelude, Aria, and Finale)

ORCHESTRA

Beethoven: Symphony No. 3. (DG 415 506-2GH) von Karahan, Berlin Philharmonic Orchestra.

————: Symphony No. 7. (EMI CDC 7 49816-2) Norrington, London Classical Players.

Wagner. *Tristan und Isolde.* Preludes to Acts I and III. (ACANTA 45 721) Furtwängler, Berlin State Opera Orchestra.

Brahms: Symphony No. 4 (DG 423 205) von Karahan, Berlin Philharmonic Orchestra.

CHORAL WORKS

Beethoven: *Missa Solemnis.* (TELARC CD-80150) McNair, soprano; Taylor, mezzo-soprano; Aler, tenor; Krause, baritone; Shaw, Atlanta Symphony Chorus and Orchestra.

Mendelssohn: *Elijah.* (PHILIPS 420 106-2PH) Leipzig Radio Chorus; Sawallisch, Gewandhaus Orchestra.

————: Sacred choral works. (ERATO ECO 75489/90) Corboz, Gulbenkian Foundation Chorus and Orchestra of Lisbon.

Brahms: *Requiem.* (TELARC CD-80092) Auger, soprano; Stilwell, baritone; Shaw, Atlanta Symphony Chorus and Orchestra.

Twentieth century

KEYBOARD

Schoenberg: Piano music (including Op. 23) (DENON CD 1060/61) Takahashi, piano. (also Berg: Sonata; Webern: Variations Op. 27)

Webern: Piano Variations Op. 27. (DG 419 202-2GH) Pollini. (see also the previous listing)

Hindemith: Sonatas for organ. (ARGO 417 159-2ZH) Huford.

————: Piano music collection. (KOCH-SCHWANN 310 007 H1) Schenck.

Bartók: *Mikrokosmos.* (HUNGAROTON HCD 31156-56) Szucs and Zempleni, piano.

Stravinsky: Concerto for two pianos. (PHILIPS 420 822-2PH) K. and M. Labeque.

CHAMBER MUSIC

Schoenberg: String Quartets. (DG 419 994-2GH-4) LaSalle Quartet.

Krenek: String Trio. (CALIG 50861) Vienna Trio.

Hindemith: Kleine Kammermusik Op. 42 No. 2 (BIS CD 291) Bergen Wind Quintet.

Bartók: Forty-four duos for two violins. (SOUND 3444) Gertler, Suk.

————: Sonata for two pianos and percussion. (CBS MK 42625) Solti, Perahia, pianos, Corkhill, Glennie, percussion. (also: Brahms Variations on a theme by Haydn)

————: The six string quartets. (DG 423 657-2GH2) Emerson String Quartet.

Stravinsky: *L'histoire du soldat.* (PANGAEA PAND-6233) Redgrave, Sting, McKellen, Nagano, London Sinfonia.

ORCHESTRA

Schoenberg: Violin Concerto. (OLYMPIA OCD 135.) Isakadze, violin; Svetlanov, USSR Academic Symphony Orchestra.

Berg: Violin Concerto. (DG 413 725-2GH) Perlman, violin; Ozawa, Boston Symphony Orchestra.

————: Lyric Suite. (VOX CUM LAUDE MCD 10024) Gielen, Cincinnati Symphony Orchestra.

Webern: Symphony Op. 21, Passacaglia Op. 1; Five canons on Latin texts, Op. 16; Six pieces for orchestra Op. 6 (DG 423 254-2) von Karajan, Berlin Philharmonic Orchestra.

Hindemith: Symphonic metamorphoses on themes of Carl Maria von Weber and Mathis der Mahler Symphony. (LONDON 421 523-2LH) Blomstedt, San Francisco Symphony Orchestra.

Bartók: Concerto for orchestra. (TELARC CD 80174) Previn, Los Angeles Philharmonic Orchestra.

————: Music for strings, percussion and celeste. (PHILIPS 416-831-2PH3) Fischer, Budapest Festival Orchestra.

Stravinsky: Symphony of psalms. (CBS Masterworks 42434) Stravinsky, conductor, CBS Symphony Orchestra.

OPERA

Berg: *Lulu.* (DG 415-2GH3) Stratas (Lulu), Mazura (Dr. Schön, Jack), Riegel (Awa), Minton (Countess Geschwitz), Tear (Painter, Negro), Blankenhem (Schigolch, Professor, Policeman), Nienstedt (Animal-tamer, Rodrigo); Pampuch (Prince, Servant, Marquis); Boulez, Paris Opera Orchestra.

————: *Wozzeck.* (CBS M2K 79251) Berry (Wozzeck), Strauss (Marie); Weikenmeier (Captain); Doench (Doctor) van Vrooman (Andres), Uhi (Drum Major); Boulez, Paris Opera Orchestra.

ALBUMS

Sixteenth century

Morley: Two-part cansonets. (PHILIPS 6500 926) Clarion Consort. ("La Caccia" and "La Sampogna", two-part fantasias are performed on two trumpets.)

Gabrieli, G: Canzonas (including "Sol sol la sol fa mi"). (HMS 998) Kneihs, Collegium Musicum of Radio Vienna.

Seventeenth century

Monteverdi: *Lamento d'Ariana* ("Lasciatemi morire"). Janet Baker Sings Monteverdi and Scarlatti. (EMI HMV SXLP 30280) Baker, soprano.

————: *Scherzi musicali.* (VOX Tournabout TV-S 34388) Cohen, Boston Camerata.

————: Virtuoso madrigals (including "Zefiro torna"). (ARCHIV 2533-087) Rogers, Partridge, tenors; Keyte, Bass; Monteverdi-Chor Hamburg.

Purcell: Fantasias. (GASPARO GS 245) Caldwell, Oberlin Consort of Viols.

Eighteenth century

Telemann: six sonatas in canon. (AMPHION 2144) T. and R. Schultze, recorders.

Twentieth century

Ives: Songs (including "Charlie Rutlege"). American Scenes, American Poets. (COLUMBIA M30229) Laer, soprano; Stewart, baritone; Mandel, piano.

Hindemith: *Ludus Tonalis.* (ORION 75184) Tetley-Kardos, piano.

Selected Bibliography

BENJAMIN, THOMAS. *The Craft of Modal Counterpoint: A Practical Approach*. New York: Schirmer Books, 1979. (Fine text with anthology for sixteenth–century counterpoint. Uses "direct approach.")

———. *Counterpoint in the Style of J. S. Bach*. New York: Schirmer Books, 1986. (Excellent text that instructs students in counterpoint from the perspective of Bach's instrumental music. Makes use of quasi-Shenkerian reductive analyses. Includes extensive anthology.)

BERRY, WALLACE and CHUDACOFF, EDWARD. *Eighteenth-Century Imitative Counterpoint. Music for Analysis*. New York: Appleton-Century-Crofts, 1969. (Excellent anthology with examples from Kerll to Schumann; lists original sources.)

BRANDT, WILLIAM, et al. *The Comprehensive Study of Music*. Four volumes. New York: Harper & Row, 1980. (Comprehensive anthology of music from plainchant through the early twentieth century.)

BURKHART, CHARLES. *Anthology for Musical Analysis*. 4th ed. New York: Holt, Rinehart and Winston, 1986. (One of the most comprehensive anthologies; covers Chant to Crumb and Saylor; appendix contains chorale harmonizations from seventeenth century to Bach.)

CROCKER, RICHARD. *A History of Musical Style*. New York: McGraw-Hill Book Company, 1966. (Traces the development of style from the Middle Ages through the early twentieth century.)

DALLIN, LEON. *Techniques of Twentieth–Century Composition*. Dubuque, IA: Wm. C. Brown Company, 1957. (Summary of twentieth–century techniques to 1950 with suggested assignments.)

DAVIDSON, ARCHIBALD and APEL, WILLI. *Historical Anthology of Music*. Vol. I and II. Cambridge, MA: Harvard University Press, 1959. (One of the first comprehensive historical anthologies. Vol. 1: Chant to Sweelinck; Vol II: Peri to pre-Classical music; notes and translations provided.)

FUX, JOHANN JOSEPH. *The Study of Counterpoint*. Translated and edited from *Gradus ad Parnassum,* 1725 by Alfred Mann. New York: W. W. Norton & Co., Inc., 1965. (A classic text of enormous historical significance.)

GAULDIN, ROBERT. *A Practical Approach to Sixteenth-Century Counterpoint*. Englewood Cliffs, NJ: Prentice-Hall, Inc., 1984. (Excellent comprehensive text on modal counterpoint using a direct approach; species counterpoint is outlined in an appendix; covers two-eight voices; many examples, several complete; focus on use of text.)

———. *A Practical Approach to Eighteenth-Century Counterpoint*. Englewood Cliffs, NJ: Prentice-Hall, Inc., 1988. (Excellent comprehensive text on tonal counterpoint using a direct approach; includes section on polyphony in the Classical period; many examples, charts, exercises; reductive analysis employed.)

HARDY, GORDON, and FISH, ARNOLD. *Music Literature: A Workbook for Analysis. Vol. II: Polyphony*. New York: Dodd, Mead, and Co., 1967. (Anthology covering the mainstream of polyphony from the Middle Ages to Stravinsky; includes translations.)

HINDEMITH, PAUL. *Craft of Musical Composition*. New York: Schott & Co., 1968, reprint of the 1942 edition. (Hindemith's treatise on theory and practice.)

HORSLEY, IMOGENE. *Fugue: History and Practice*. New York: The Free Press, 1966. (Chapters on the history of canon and fugue alternate with those on fugue writing; an accompanying workbook is also available.)

JEPPESEN, KNUD. *Counterpoint: The Polyphonic Vocal Style of the Sixteenth Century.* Translated by Glen Haydon. Englewood Cliffs, NJ: Prentice-Hall, Inc., 1939. (A classic text which presents the study of counterpoint using the species approach; includes a historical summary of the pedagogy of counterpoint.)

KANITZ, ERNEST. *A Counterpoint Manual.* Boston: C. C. Birchard and Company, 1948. (A heroic but limited effort to use a species approach to teach both "strict" —nineteenth–century style—and "free"—contemporary style; no examples from the literature.)

KENNAN, KENT. *Counterpoint Based on Eighteenth-Century Practice.* 3rd ed. Englewood Cliffs, NJ: Prentice-Hall, Inc., 1987. (Very practical text on eighteenth-century style; uses quasi species approach; many examples; workbook is also available.)

KIRKENDALE, WARREN. *Fugue and Fugato in Rococo and Classical Chamber Music,* 2nd ed. Translated by Margaret Bent and the author. Durham, NC: Duke University Press, 1979.

KRENEK, ERNST. *Modal Counterpoint in the Style of the Sixteenth Century.* London: Boosey and Hawkes, 1959. (Manual in strict orientation; examples are all by the author.)

—————. *Studies in Counterpoint Based on the Twelve-Tone Technique.* New York: G. Schirmer, Inc., 1940. (Brief manual on counterpoint using twelve-tone technique; examples are all by the author and are all based on a single pitch set.)

—————. *Tonal Counterpoint in the Style of the Eighteenth-Century.* London: Boosey and Hawkes, 1958. (Manual focuses on two-part writing; examples are all by the author; no exercises.)

MANN, ALFRED. *The Study of Fugue.* New York: W. W. Norton & Company, Inc., 1965. (English translations of significant portions of classic texts by Fux, Marpurg, Albrechtsberger, and Martini with commentary and historical outline.)

MARQUIS, G. WELTON. *Twentieth-Century Music Idioms.* Englewood Cliffs, NJ: Prentice-Hall, Inc., 1964. (A practical compendium of contemporary idioms to 1960; numerous examples; exercises.)

MASON, NEALE. *Essentials of Eighteenth-Century Counterpoint.* Dubuque, IA: Wm. C. Brown Co., 1968. (A manual of Bach-style counterpoint with quasi-species approach.)

MERRITT, ARTHUR T. *Sixteenth–Century Polyphony.* Cambridge, MA: Harvard University Press, 1939. (Analysis of contrapuntal technique and text in modal counterpoint using a direct approach.)

MIDDLETON, ROBERT E. *Harmony in Modern Counterpoint.* Boston: Allyn and Bacon, Inc., 1967. (A systematic approach to the extension of studies in harmony and counterpoint to include compositional techniques of the first half of the twentieth century.)

MORLEY, THOMAS. *A Plain and Easy Introduction to Practical Music.* Edited by R. Alec Harman. New York: W. W. Norton & Company, Inc., 1966. (Classic text presented in dialogue; precepts reflect the English style c. 1600.)

MORRIS, REGINALD O. *Contrapuntal Technique in the Sixteenth Century.* New York: Oxford University Press, 1922. (An English text from the early part of this century; short examples are at end of the book.)

PALISCA, CLAUDE. *Norton Anthology of Western Music.* Volumes I and II. New York: W. W. Norton & Company, Inc., 1980. (Excellent anthology; Vol. 1: medieval through Baroque periods; Vol. II: Classical through early twentieth century; includes translations, lists original sources.)

PARKS, RICHARD. *Eighteenth-Century Counterpoint and Tonal Structure.* Englewood Cliffs, NJ: Prentice-Hall, Inc., 1984. (Species orientation with Shenkerian reductive analyses.)

PERLE, GEORGE. *Serial Composition and Atonality.* Berkeley: University of California Press, 1963. (One of the classic texts on serial music; no exercises.)

PISTON, WALTER. *Counterpoint.* New York: W. W. Norton & Co., Inc., 1947. (Text on eighteenth- nineteenth-century style; non-species approach; companion to his harmony and orchestration texts.)

PROCTOR, LELAND. *Tonal Counterpoint.* Dubuque, IA: Wm. C. Brown Co., 1952. (Teaches tonal counterpoint through Bach style.)

ROBINSON, RAY. *Choral Music. A Norton Historical Anthology.* New York: W. W. Norton & Company, Inc., 1978. (Includes choral music from 1300-1974; translations, glossary, biographical sketches; commentary and source list.)

SALZER, FELIX, and SCHACHTER, CARL. *Counterpoint in Composition.* New York: McGraw-Hill Book Co., 1969. (Species orientation with Schenkerian reductive analyses.)

SCHOENBERG, ARNOLD. *Preliminary Exercises in Counterpoint.* Edited with a foreward by Leonard Stein. London: Faber and Faber, Ltd., 1982. (Reprint of the 1963 edition.)

SEARLE, HUMPHREY. *Twentieth Century Counterpoint: A Guide to Students.* New York: John de Graff Inc., 1954. (Useful summary of contrapuntal techniques of the major composers in the first half of the twentieth century.)

SMITH, CHARLOTTE. *A Manual of Sixteenth-Century Contrapuntal Style*. Newark: University of Delaware Press, 1989. (Direct approach text with a good introductory summary of historical practice; focus on sacred choral style.)

SODERLUND, GUSTAVE F. *Direct Approach to Counterpoint in Sixteenth-Century Style*. Englewood Cliffs, NJ: Prentice-Hall, Inc., 1947. (Text with non-species approach; designed to be used with the author's anthology.)

SODERLUND, GUSTAVE, and SCOTT, SAMUEL. *Examples of Gregorian Chant and Sacred Music of the Sixteenth Century*. Englewood Cliffs, NJ: Prentice-Hall, Inc., 1971. (Companion anthology for Soderlund's text.)

TUREK, RALPH. *Analytical Anthology of Music*. New York: McGraw-Hill Book Co., 1983.

WENNERSTROM, MARY H. *Anthology of Musical Structure and Style*. Englewood Cliffs, NJ: Prentice Hall, Inc., 1983.

WENNERSTROM, MARY H. *Anthology of Twentieth-Century Music*. Englewood Cliffs, NJ: Prentice-Hall, Inc., 1969. (One of a small number of anthologies devoted to twentieth century; Ives to Gaburo, 1906-1967; includes biographical data, notes, study questions.)

List of Musical Examples for Discussion

VICTORIA, TOMÁS LUIS DE (1548-1611)
    Kyrie from *Missa O Magnum Mysterium,* Ex. 9-3

VIVALDI, ANTONIO (1675-1741)
    Fuga da cappella (Alla breve), Sonata VI from *Il pastor fido,* Ex. 24-2

WAGNER, RICHARD (1813-1883)
    Excerpt from Act II, *Tristan und Isolde,* Ex. 26-5

WEBERN, ANTON (1883-1945)
    Variations for Piano Op. 27, Var. 2, Ex. 27-2

WEELKES, THOMAS (1576-1623)
    Canzonet: "The nightingale, the organ of delight," Ex. 8-5

Index

Note: Page numbers in italic indicate pages containing music examples.